LORDS
OF THE
PRESS

GEORGE SELDES

LORDS
OF THE
PRESS

New York
JULIAN MESSNER, Inc.

PUBLISHED BY JULIAN MESSNER, INC.
8 WEST 40TH STREET, NEW YORK

SEVENTH PRINTING, APRIL, 1945

PRINTED IN THE UNITED STATES OF AMERICA
BY MONTAUK BOOKBINDING CORPORATION, NEW YORK

TO

THE AMERICAN NEWSPAPER GUILD
and others interested in a free press

Contents

PART I
LORDS OF THE PRESS

PART II
SERVANTS OF THE LORDS

PART III

BATTLES OF THE LORDS

PART I

LORDS OF THE PRESS

PART I

LORDS OF THE PRESS

CHAPTER 1

The House of Lords

ONCE every year the American Newspaper Publishers Association, the House of Lords of our press, meets in secret. No one cares to spy on it, no newspapermen are present, no photographers interrupt, no representatives of a yellow journal harass or intimidate the members. It would be useless. If a reporter found out what plans are discussed, what plots are made, what schemes proposed, no newspaper would publish the disclosures, sensational as they might be. Nothing is sacred to the American press but itself.

And yet these secret meetings of our organized publishers rank among the most important actions against the general welfare of the American people ever taken (legally) by any small national group in our time. But since the press publishes the news, true or false or half-way, about everything in the world except itself, the American public knows nothing about what the rulers of public opinion annually decide for it.

Only rarely do the millions learn or sense the truth about the activities of this group of leaders. In the repudiation of the press in the 1936 election there was a symptom of the universal suspicion and growing anger of the public, but this awakening was made possible by the fact that millions were already pledged to the party the majority of newspapers attacked, and the radio was used extensively, and there were other means of breaking the press offensive. In social, rather than political, issues there is no means by which the public can defeat the dictation of the press.

The publishers' meetings are secret because their actions cannot bear the light of publicity. Three hundred and sixty days in the year the publishers speak editorially for open covenants openly arrived at, whether in international relations or in the advertising business, but every April they lock the doors and make a hypocritical paradox out of their own ideals.

We know that in the open meetings they approve annually of "freedom of the press as the bulwark of our civilization," and that in the closed meetings they discuss ways and means of fighting labor and their own employees who demand higher wages or perhaps better light or decent toilet arrangements. We do know that in the open meetings they pledge themselves to honesty and truth and the whole bagful of tricks in the ethical code of their profession, and they also discuss the cost of paper, the ways to increase advertising and gain circulation, and other purely materialistic subjects which are necessary if any press, free or kept, is to survive. But it is somewhat of a shock to learn that in the closed sessions they defend the employment of child labor, they take united action against a Congressional measure which would keep drugmakers from poisoning or cheating the American people, and they gloat over their own strike-breaking department which offers scabs not only to members but to anyone who wants to fight the unions.

One of the most recent secret meetings was devoted to nothing but war on the American Newspaper Guild, the association of newspaper workers which offended the publishers when it joined the American Federation of Labor and drove them into hysterics when it later joined the Committee for Industrial Organization. In all American business and industry today there is probably no instance of such bitterness, such conflict, such hatred, such opposition, and such war to the throat as between the newspaper workers and the newspaper owners. The amusing angle to this story is that the publishers still print that cockeyed falsehood about the interests of capital and labor being identical. It certainly isn't in their own line.

What conspiratorial plans are made to fight labor at the secret sessions we can judge best by what happens. We have seen such united action as an attack on Congress when it considered passing the Wagner Labor Act which is regarded as a Magna Carta of the working people of America. We have watched the press of the country condemn it after it passed. And, moreover, we have seen the publishers openly defy the law, declare it unconstitutional, and, when the Guild took the test case to the Supreme Court and the law was declared constitutional, we have seen the publishers inaugurate a movement to repeal or alter or emasculate this law.

We have seen the publishers declare the National Labor Relations Board unconstitutional long before the Supreme Court declared it constitutional. We have seen the publishers unite to fight any and every attempt to increase taxes on the rich and alleviate the burdens of the poor. All sorts of transcendental humanitarian poppycock has been invented by the highly paid editorial writers and rich columnists to hide this fundamental conflict of the Haves and Havenots in America. But the fact is becoming known to the public that the press lords of America are the champions of the former while still flying the pre-war flag of "service to the common people."

There are of course many men of the highest ideals in the membership. But so far as can be learned they have not been able in the past to gain their points even in the most flagrant cases of violation of journalistic ethics.

The La Follette Civil Liberties Investigation Committee has given documentary evidence that four of the biggest newspapers in the country had employed spies or thugs, but no action was taken by the publishers' association.

Some years ago one of its members was found guilty in a Federal court of theft. His news service had stolen the news from another service. But he was not fired from either the publishers' association or the service which he robbed and of which he is still a member.

Another newspaper was found guilty of blackmailing oil companies for a million dollars. And a third of suppressing the scandal for $92,000. There was some talk of taking action.

Twenty or more of the big newspapers of the country were found by a Congressional investigation to be secretly controlled by the power and paper trust. Colonel Robert Ewing, publisher of the *New Orleans States,* president of the Southern Newspaper Publisher Association, a component branch of the A. N. P. A., offered, at the convention of the latter, a resolution condemning the power and paper trust's activities. It was tabled. S. E. Thomason, then of the *Chicago Journal,* went Colonel Ewing one better with a resolution that all the great publishers in America make public all their connections with power and paper trusts, with all the banks, and with all the powerful financial institutions which control the country.

The resolution was defeated with a roar of laughter.

On the other hand, when a speaker for the National Electric Light Association—with its $25,000,000 a year fund for influencing newspapers—said at its convention that "There we are, brothers under the skin, utility and newspaper battling shoulder to shoulder. Our most important contact is . . . the American Newspaper Publishers Association," the latter accepted the remark as a compliment.

In fact every annual convention proves more fully than the last the statement made by William Allen White, now president of the editors' association, that the newspaper business is a business and nothing more. The code of ethics of the journalistic profession is no longer put into practice. But all the anti-social activities of big business have become the program of the A. N. P. A. In fact it is frequently difficult to distinguish its program from that of the National

Association of Manufacturers and the United States Chamber of Commerce.

Heywood Broun, president of the Guild, who attended several open and secret sessions one year, said he was shocked by the smallness "of this collection of very small men so obviously drunk with a smug sense of power and self-righteousness," who "get themselves up as the full and all-sufficient judges of what the public should get in the way of news and of opinion." He listened for days. "The ghost of Thomas Jefferson was sent whirling along the flying trapeze as Bainbridge Colby, exhumed from heaven knows where, uttered dreary tory platitudes about big business and its sacred rights. I was struck by the fact that, with the mild exception of Glenn Frank, all the spokesmen and invited orators of the publishers were old men. And they did not talk of journalism but of the industry. If a man from Mars had happened in, I think he might have spent an hour and still remained puzzled as to whether he had happened in upon a convention of bankers, cotton-mill owners, or the makers of bathroom supplies. ....

"The publishers decided that they would accept no sort of code of fair practice whatsoever. They decided not to disturb carrier boys between the ages of ten and twelve who are already on the job. They condemned the mild Copeland bill on foods and drugs. H. W. Flagg, of the Philadelphia *Public Ledger,* chairman of the Open Shop Committee, unofficially offered the services of his committee to all publishers, members and non-members, for strike-breaking purposes. And so you see once more the publishers have saved the freedom of the press."

When the National Electric Light Association was engaged in buying the good will of the American press, it also maintained a lobby in Washington for the purpose of using Congressmen for its own commercial purposes. This lobby was never exposed or mentioned.

Other lobbies, notably those which are not in any way

affiliated with advertising, have from time to time been the subject of newspaper attacks. They have given the word "lobby" a sinister connotation, associated with such words as "propaganda" and "isms" and other things called "un-American."

But for years there has been a powerful lobby at work in Washington which up to now has been more successful than any except possibly the American Legion lobby. This is the publishers' lobby. It not only is active in making laws, amending laws, and preventing laws, but it has the unique distinction—can it be because of the power of the press?—of recommending that the publishers break the law.

Incidents and illustrations of this group's power are many and important. But before sampling those of New Deal time, I would like to mention an exposure of this lobby which can be found in "62nd Congress, 1st session, Senate Documents, Vol. 6, Reciprocity with Canada Hearings, Vol. 2," because this episode although belonging to another generation nevertheless illuminates not only the means the organization still employs, but also furnishes a clue to subjects of later chapters.

The United States, as many readers may remember, has from time to time been the scene of hefty debate over tariffs on foreign goods. The Republican press has been in favor, the Democratic press has been opposed to them, the industrialist North generally for protection, the agricultural South for free trade, the Republican newspaper propaganda insisting that prosperity and the full dinner pail—what memories these old-fashioned words bring up!—depended entirely upon the tariff wall keeping cheap foreign goods out and the American laborer contented in rich green pastures, the Democrat denying it all at every depression.

At the very time the Republican newspapers were publishing this drivel and propaganda they combined with the owners of Democratic newspapers in lobbying in Washington for the purpose of getting print paper and wood pulp exempt from a proposed severe tariff bill. The matter involved was a mere $5,000,000 per annum for the entire newspaper industry, no awe-inspiring sum in the face of a yearly advertising budget of one and a half to two billions, and the fact that more than one newspaper had net annual earnings of five millions or more. Yet for this sum at least half the entire press of the United States was willing to give up its editorial policies regarding tariff and join with its political enemies in a non-partisan bit of lobbying.

Among those who called on the Secretary of State to demand free wood pulp and free print paper was Frank B. Noyes, of the *Washington Star,* one of the founders of the Associated Press, and its president up to April, 1938. Within a few days after this visit the president of the A. N. P. A., Herman Ridder, sent a letter to every publisher, member or not, which after mentioning a saving of five millions added that the bill, if ratified, would also save our forests and remove "a tax upon knowledge"; therefore "will you promptly communicate with your Senators and representatives in Congress and urge favorable action."

So far the activities of the publishers' lobby had been both legal and ethical. But apparently the matter was not going through unopposed, for in the Congressional investigation there was introduced a copy of a confidential telegram which Ridder also sent, saying that "it is of vital importance to the newspapers that their Washington correspondents be instructed to treat favorably the Canadian reciprocity agreement. . . ." This request was a violation of every code of ethics in the history of journalism.

During the course of the debate it was proved that the "tax upon knowledge" was pure hypocrisy. It was purely a savings for publishers. The claim the reader would be benefited financially was proven false: it would take about thirty-three years for one average copy of a daily to consume a ton, and the duty of $3.75 meant ten cents a year more for each subscriber. And when farmers spoke against the tariff cut the Associated Press men took no notes, whereas those who spoke for it made the headlines. When Melville Stone, head of the A. P., said the press was fair although ninety percent of the publishers were against the tariff, it was proven statistically that the A. P. itself was sending out six times as much pro as anti news, and Mr. Stone was forced to admit that it was due "either to stupidity on the part of the people who were reporting . . . or ordinary weaknesses that attach to human beings."

These human weaknesses eventually rob a nation of a free press as great editors will testify. They are the weaknesses of egotism, of power seeking, of greed for profits, which men in other businesses often admit but which most publishers hide under beautiful words about public service. However, in the actions of the publishers' lobby against all reform legislation in more recent times we can see these motives a little more clearly than in the hypocritical past.

From the earliest days of the so-called New Deal, and immediately following the 1933 pro-Roosevelt parade in which the publishers marched under a friendly banner, their lobby has aimed at getting the press exempt from every law and regulation which affects other businesses and which might also affect their profits. The story is told that Bernard Shaw, leaving an Albert Hall meeting which he had addressed, was stopped by a beggar who held out a tin can. "Press!" said Mr. Shaw, and moved on. Apocryphal as this story may be, it illustrates well the attitude of the American newspaper publishers. In reply to every attempt to apply legislation affecting unionization, child labor, hours, wages, sanitation, working conditions, or other social reforms upon them, they have excused themselves with Mr. Shaw's remark; they have not only whispered, but bellowed "Freedom of the Press!"

The President put them in their place in 1934 when the industrial codes, later outlawed, were hailed as the salvation of the nation. The publishers' lobby favored a code for every business except theirs. But since this could not be, they drew one up which was "the most dishonest, weasel-worded and treacherous document" * ever offered to General Johnson. The publishers' lobby code was so designed that it would permit them to escape all the obligations (for promoting prosperity) which they were urging upon all the rest of the nation.

When General Johnson threw the lobby code aside, the lobby replied by publishing a false statement that it had been accepted. When this intimidation failed, the lobby demanded that Postmaster General Farley put pressure upon Johnson. When this also failed, the attack was continued with other weapons, one tabloid going so far as to publish an untrue story about the General and his party crashing a speakeasy. General Johnson went speaking throughout the country. He was bitter against the publishers, and especially the lobby. "They are few in number, but ruthless in method," he declared. "Some of them control powerful newspapers and they are using these papers to misrepresent every development of NRA. It is no longer possible to get a square deal in truth and accuracy. . . ." But the betting in newspaper offices was ten to one that "the big steamroller, as represented by the American Newspaper Publishers Association, would crush General Johnson, the President himself, and everyone connected with the NRA." This steamroller is still crushing. In several instances, it is sad but true, the President has given in to the publishers; and the latter repaid him by joining—Democrats and Independents with Republicans—in the vast 1936 campaign against his second election.

In 1935 the publishers' lobby won four of its five campaigns in Washington, and barely lost the last, an exemption from the provision of the Wagner Labor Disputes Bill, where the Newspaper Guild was on the side of labor, as opposed to the publishers who represented the employers.

---

* So reported by Washington Correspondent P. Y. Anderson.

During the Senate hearings Elisha Hanson, attorney for the A. N. P. A., attacked the bill as a whole, on the ground that it would infringe freedom to print or fail to print what the publishers wished. In the House, the publishers got Representative William P. Connery (Dem., Mass.) to add a proviso which was nothing more than the old "Freedom of the Press" clause always trotted out when profits are at stake. The Guild spokesman, however, exposed this maneuver, and the amendment was out when the bill passed.

It is now well known that the publishers played the strongest hand in defeating the Tugwell Bill. Nevertheless, when the first Copeland Bill, its mild, emasculated successor, was produced in Congress, the publishers joined the Proprietary Association of Drug Manufacturers in defeating it also. The reason for this sanguinary attack on a bill already weakened to please the drugmakers, was the publishers' insistence on clauses putting all the blame for violations on the manufacturers and dealers, none on the advertising agencies and newspapers.

Along came the Agricultural Adjustment Act, and along came the publishers with amendments, one definitely stating that no marketing order could be issued "prohibiting, regulating or restricting" advertising, and providing that no processing tax can be fixed on material to be made into wood pulp, from which newsprint is manufactured.

The Black Thirty-Hour-Week Bill was kept in Representative Connery's labor committee until it emerged with exemptions for banks, newspapers and magazines.

Finally, there was the Eastman Bus and Truck Bill which was sent to the President for signature. It gives the Interstate Commerce Commission power to regulate motor carriers, but makes four commodity exemptions, the first three being livestock, fish and agricultural products, the last being newspapers.

When this list of 1935 achievements of the publishers' pressure lobby was announced the *Guild Reporter* said it was "overcome with admiration." Of course that provision in the last of the laws which sets maximum hours for truck drivers hauling papers in interstate commerce might well be interpreted as an attack on freedom of the press. Naturally, any attempt by Congress to tax wood pulp is a violation of the constitution which grants liberty to publishers. And of course if Congress insisted that the advertisers of worthless drugs tell the same truth in the newspapers which the 1906 law requires them to tell on the labels, that would curtail sales, curtail advertising, curtail profits for publishers and therefore become the most dastardly attack on the American public's inherent right to a free press which our history has ever known. So you see, the lobby has a lot of work.

It may not. be ethical, or decent, or moral in the higher sense, but it is generally legal. The great publishers of America have never been afraid to defy legality when it was to their own benefit to do so. Openly the House of Lords has always stood for law and order so far as others were concerned. Generally speaking the big press of the nation has always accused labor of favoring and originating violence throughout the long and bloody history of the struggle of the working people for a better life. The exact opposite is true. After the daily newspaper has screamed its charge against the unions, the impartial historian has found, too late to be of any practical use, that in some ninety cases out of a hundred it is the employer or the police or the enemies of labor who are guilty of favoring and initiating violence.

And when it comes to lawbreaking or defiance of the law, actions which are generally charged only to criminals, the publishers have a great advantage when they do so because there can be no "public outcry" against them, no protest, no "vox populi," no "wave of indignation," nor any of the other movements they frequently invent, knowing they themselves are the only channel for such movements.

Here are, for example, two forces which affect the newspapers—and their profits. Despite publishers' opposition the Wagner Act was passed, the National Labor Relations Board came into being. Manufacturers did not like it but they obeyed it. Not so the publishers.

"If," said Elisha Hanson, chief counsel for the A. N. P. A., "the NLRB issues an order in this case, Mr. Hearst will not comply with it."

In October 1936 this same Hanson sent out a general statement to the publishers telling them not to obey the rulings of the same board because, he, Hanson, thought they were unconstitutional. "Publishers from now on," he ordered, "should flatly refuse to have anything to do with the National Labor Relations Board other than to notify it it is without power under the constitution to interfere with their business. . . . In so far as the newspaper business is concerned, I am convinced no order of the Board directed to a publisher requiring him to comply with a decision thereof will, if it is contested, be upheld in the courts."

The order under discussion (the Watson case) was upheld. The NLRB law was upheld.

In other lines of business the government and its laws have also been challenged—but not defied. Government laws and regulations have been obeyed pending the institution of suits to test constitutionality, but in no important instance has there been defiance, as in the case of the publishers. Replying to Hanson's orders to the publishers the *Guild Reporter* called the lawyer an anarchist. Of his opinion it said (October 15, 1936): "All concern for the general welfare, all respect for the right of Congress to establish public policies which it deems to be essential for the country, have been abandoned in this document which its board sponsors. A law that most of the millions of workers of the country believe is needed to protect them in their right to earn a

decent livelihood, treads to some extent on the interests of
1,200 publishers. Out with it! Ignore it!"

From the very first days of the New Deal—under which
incidentally newspaper workers were first enabled to organize—until the present, the American Newspaper Guild has
charged the publishers with violating not only the spirit of
the law but the laws themselves. The publishers' proposed
code was "treacherous and dishonest" but legal; but the
subsequent "dark maneuverings," said the Guild editorially,
proved that "the A. N. P. A. undertakes to set itself above
Congress and the President." The Guild "questioned the
sincerity of the publishers in their sanctimonious espousal
of the freedom of the press. . . . The American Newspaper
Guild has been the only organization in the country with
the courage to bring the lawless spirit of this self-appointed
oligarchy out into the open and denounce it. . . . A truly
free and honest press is of more importance to the members
of the American Newspaper Guild than any immediate
economic interest."

Only one brave publisher agreed with the Guild. J. David
Stern, of the *New York Post, Philadelphia Record, Camden
Courier* and *Camden Post,* withdrew his membership in the
House of Lords.

"We are resigning," he wrote the A. N. P. A., "because
your association, founded to benefit and strengthen the
daily newspapers of this country, has in the past few years so
conducted itself as to lower American newspapers in popular
esteem, to endanger the freedom of the press, and has even
gone so far as to urge its members to breach the law. . . .

"I do not see how a law-abiding newspaper can consistently retain membership. . . .

"Your board recommended to its membership that no
agreement be entered into with any group of employees. As
we understand the Wagner Act it is obligatory upon employers to negotiate with representatives of a majority of
employees. . . .

"Ever since the NRA code, the A. N. P. A. has been using the pretext of protecting the freedom of the press to gain special privilege in purely business obligations.

"That is why I say you are endangering the freedom of the press, and one of the most important essentials of democracy. . . ."

Mr. Stern's *Philadelphia Record* quit the A. N. P. A.; his *New York Post* had never been a member. Within a year from that date no less than twenty-nine charges of violation of the Wagner Act and other laws which not only the Supreme Court but even the publishers' association admit are legal, were made against as many publishers.

There were seventeen instances of intimidation, coercion and actual discharge of employees for utilizing the clauses in the Wagner Act which permit unionization; in six instances the publishers were accused of breaking the law by refusing to bargain with their employees; in two instances the publishers were accused of forming company unions, all these episodes forming a record which the official organ of the newspaper writers called "irresponsible, unscrupulous and contemptible."

Among the newspapers against which charges were filed were (Gannett's) *Knickerbocker Press* and *Albany News, Boston Herald, Boston Traveler,* (McCormick's) *Chicago Tribune, Detroit Times,* (Hearst's) *Los Angeles Examiner,* the Associated Press in New York, (Hearst's) *New York Daily Mirror, Seattle Post-Intelligencer, Seattle Star.*

With the exception of only a handful of liberal newspapers, the press of the country, which first failed to get a clause exempting itself from the Wagner Act, then defied the law, later in many instances violated the law, is today producing bitter and unfair editorials demanding that this measure—and in fact all measures which favor labor rather than capital—should be repealed.

Accused in numerous cases of discharging men for no reason but legal union activity, many publishers have sought to hide their prejudices by posting a "firing code" sent them by the A. N. P. A., and consisting of sixteen "grounds" for discharge, one of which is the failure to return a book to its proper place in the bookshelf before going home. Or leaving the electric bulb turned on over one's desk while going to the toilet. Or scratching the furniture.

The leader in the anti-labor movement of the A. N. P. A. has been its president, James G. Stahlman, publisher of the *Nashville Banner*. He is one of the minor press lords of America, and the story of his battle with the unions, his red-baiting, the sensationalizing of anti-C. I. O. news in his paper and the suppression of news favoring labor, will be found in a later chapter. The man chosen to lead the great publishers of America in their oft-announced fight for the freedom of the press is the same James G. Stahlman who, addressing the members of the Belle Meade Country Club, recently * said:

"If I had my way I would get me six husky policemen, take these labor organizers outside the city limits, and tell them it wouldn't be healthy for them to be seen in the vicinity again."

The foregoing are some of the subjects which the men who do a large part of the thinking, the leading or the misleading of the nation, discuss in their secret meetings. In the open meetings it is of course the welfare of the public, the freedom of the press, with only an occasional word about advertising money.

Strike breaking, the suppression of the labor movement, the maintenance of child labor, the mistakes of its counsel which sought to destroy the NLRB in the Watson case, and all general topics which are not concerned with public wel-

* *Guild Reporter,* August 30, 1937.

fare, but with that of the pocketbook, make up most of the
four days of the secret meetings which occur every year and
the special Chicago meeting which was devoted to nothing
but an attempt to destroy the Newspaper Guild. At that time
an anonymous reporter wrote the "March of the Publishers":

> On to Chicago to fight for our freedom—
> Freedom to hire men, work 'em and bleed 'em—
> Freedom to chisel to heart's content—
> Freedom to make thirty-seven per cent.
> On to Chicago—but don't fail to stress—
> That our battle, of course, is for freedom of the press.

In the following chapters some of the individuals, all but
one or two little known to the people of the country whose
minds they rule, will be discussed at some length, and the
common denominator of their power and their motives suggested. The reader may then judge whether or not the most
powerful anonymous group of men in America can be
classified as the friends or enemies of the American people.

It is the writer's intention to "let the facts speak for themselves," as Euripides suggested, and if there is criticism, expressed or implied, the reader will please remember that
nothing that will be said can equal in severity that which
has already come from within the ranks of the profession,
from the very small minority, it is true, who still upholds the
traditional journalistic liberalism of America. It is William
Allen White, now president of the national editorial association, who first pointed out that the newspapers have
degenerated from a noble profession to an eight percent
investment, and who now states they are dominated by the
"unconscious arrogance of conscious wealth," and it is J.
Roscoe Drummond, executive editor of the *Christian Science
Monitor,* who writes that freedom of the press "is not an
end in itself. . . . A free press in the United States is not, I
believe, in danger from without. It is always in danger from
within. A truly free press requires . . . free men to give it

life. Free men require free minds—minds intellectually honest, intellectually open, and intellectually eager. The press of the United States . . . needs . . . a leadership dedicated to the service of democracy."

The press lords of the United States in one year made this great record:

1. Fought all issues where their profits were involved.
2. Led the attack against a real pure food and drug law.
3. Opposed the Wagner Act, the Magna Carta of labor.
4. Urged amendment of proposed social insurance legislation putting newspapers in a special class.
5. Proposed compulsory arbitration of labor disputes with the outlawing of strikes.
6. Favored child labor.
7. Frowned at the Securities Act.

In its 1935 report which urged members to fight food, drug and cosmetics bills, the Wagner-Connery Law, the Thirty-Hour Bill, Social Insurance and laws "affecting the newspaper business," A. N. P. A. publishers were told to "be constantly alert and vigilant if their properties are not to be destroyed or irreparably injured."

Property, not public welfare, is the program of the A. N. P. A.

Their interests, says Alfred McK. Lee, historian of our present journalism, differ little from that of other industries; the A. N. P. A. "has sometimes been a powerful adjunct in legislative circles to the lobbies of the United States Chamber of Commerce, the National Association of Manufacturers and the trade associations of specific industries."

The press needs free men with free minds intellectually open; but its leadership consists of moral slaves whose minds are paralyzed by the specter of profits. The publishers are not leading the American people forward. They are not facing the social issues. Whether more often they are falsifying the social issues the reader may perhaps judge from the following documentation.

CHAPTER 2

Patterson—Lord of Tabloidia

"Mr. Patterson is a young man who has lately surprised his wealthy friends in Chicago by coming out publicly as a Socialist. He here explains his position."

So READ the editorial note at the head of the article "Confessions of a Drone" which Joseph Medill Patterson, a member of what was then known as "the idle rich class," wrote for the August 30, 1906, issue of *The Independent*. It made a great sensation. It is as interesting an apologia pro sua vita as our generation has produced, and it serves also to explain the numerous seeming paradoxes and exasperating discrepancies which America's first, and now most important tabloid newspaper, presents.

How great a sensation this rich young man caused by becoming a Socialist and renouncing the financial and journalistic system into which he was born, can be judged from the numerous versions of his confessions, which were reprinted throughout a decade and distributed by the tens of thousands, and the comment in the press of the time. When Corliss, the son of Thomas W. Lamont, partner of J. P. Morgan, espoused the cause of Soviet Russia two decades later there was comparative silence. The world was becoming accustomed to sons of wealth defending the enemies of wealth.

"I am talking about myself, the type of the idle, rich young man, not myself the individual. . . . I have an income of between ten and twenty thousand dollars a year. I spend all of it. I produce nothing—am doing no work. I (the type) can keep on doing this all my life unless the present social system is changed." So Patterson begins his confession. "My income doesn't descend upon me like manna from heaven. It can be traced. Some of it comes from the profits of a daily newspaper; some of it comes from Chicago real estate; some from the profits made by the Pennsylvania and other railroads; some from the profits of the United States Steel Corporation; some from the profits of the American Tobacco Company."

Mr. Patterson then judges the Chicago real estate earnings by applying to it the Henry George single tax formula: "The people who came to Chicago to work caused the increase in value—but I get the benefit of it." But the profits from the Pennsylvania Railroad, U. S. Steel and American Tobacco Company he admits are paid him not by fellow capitalists, but by the men who work and ride, the makers and users of steel and tobacco. "The men who run the trains are underpaid for the work they do, and those who ship or travel overpay for the service they get. We capitalists get the margin in between." And Mr. Patterson continues:

"For instance, it takes to support me just about twenty times as much as it takes to support an average workingman or farmer. And the funny thing about it is that these workingmen and farmers work hard all year round, while I don't work at all.

"I have better food, better clothes, and better houses than the workers who supply me with money to spend. I can travel oftener. . . . I have horses to ride and drive, domestic servants . . . the best physicians. . . . My children will never go to work in a cotton mill or a sweatshop.

"In short, I lead a far more highly civilized life than the working people. I have offered me the choice of all the best things that man in his stay upon this earth has discovered, evolved or created. The working people do not have this choice offered them. There are left for them the shoddy things of life— hard work and small reward. I have little or no work and the earth's best for reward.

"The work of the working people, and nothing else, produces the wealth, which, by some hocus-pocus arrangement, is transferred to me, leaving them bare. While they support me in splendid style, what do I do for them? Let the candid upholder of the present order answer, for I am not aware of doing anything for them.

"It is said that I supply a wage fund out of which their wages are paid. Nonsense. If every bond and stock certificate and every real estate abstract were burned today in a huge bonfire, the vacated titles of ownership falling naturally to the community, trains would pull out on schedule time tomorrow. . . .

"That my life is so much completer than the lives of the workers who support me has been excused on the ground that they are less 'cultivated,' and, therefore, less fitted to enjoy things which please me. But that seems a little like begging the question. . . . I don't think it was entirely natural aptitude that marked me out for a university education, since I remember that frequently I had to pay money to tutors to drill into my head information of a remarkably simple character. I was fond of a good time—and that I had. Of course, it took money, which was obligingly supplied, via my family, by the pressmen, the switchmen, the cigarette girls, the rolling-mill men, etc."

When he got out of college Patterson went to work for the *Chicago Tribune*—"I started at the bottom"—at $15 a week, just as his college mates went into their fathers' Wall Street offices. "But," he adds, "I knew it was play-acting all the time, just as they did. I was not living on a $15-a-week basis and they were not living on a $3-a-week basis. I wasn't afraid of losing my job. . . . I got an 'allowance' in addition to the fifteen—and the allowance was by considerable the more substantial figure. The allowance came from the pressmen, switchmen, cigarette girls, the other reporters, etc., via my family. It was just this 'allowance' that makes all the difference." The allowance came from the exploitation of the workers and customers of the corporations whose stocks and bonds the family held. Mr. Patterson concludes:

"If a man produces $2,000 worth of wealth a year, and consumes $10,000 worth a year, he is overpaid. If he is overpaid, some must be underpaid.

"Socialism urges the underpaid to unite and insist on receiving the full amount of the wealth they produce."

This conclusion was not strong enough. In the later reprint for the Pocket Library of Socialism, No. 45, Patterson adds the following paragraphs:

"So it is with all capitalists. Insofar as they receive interest, profit and rent, they are economic idlers, taking toll of the labor of others and returning nothing; insofar as they actively further business, by superintendence or otherwise, they are laborers, worthy in many cases of their hire.

"The wealth appropriated by capital through the agencies of rent, profit and interest is obviously appropriated from the working people, the creators of all wealth. Therefore it is to the working people that Socialism addresses itself, urging them to veto their own further exploitation."

At the time the foregoing confession was written Socialism was still quite a respectable religion, there was little hysterical red-baiting in the press, and one could not really tell the descendant of Joseph Medill to go back to the country he came from if he was dissatisfied with the capitalist system in Chicago. However, young Patterson was attacked in the press, and he retaliated by calling it "the capitalist press" and showing how stupid it was in answering his arguments. He wrote in what I believe was the fourth and last reprint of his "Confessions of a Drone": *

Since the foregoing appeared in the "Independent" many criticisms of it have appeared in the capitalist press. The burden

---

* Students will find the four versions among the bound pamphlets in the New York Public Library: SFC, p. v, 57 and 58; SFC, p. v, 70 and * CX, p. v, 23.

of practically every one of these criticisms has been, "If young Patterson feels that way why doesn't he give away his money to the poor?"

From which it is fair to surmise that the capitalist press cannot explain what useful economic functions young Patterson *and the rest of his class perform.*

The article was written about the whole capitalist class, as explicitly mentioned in the first paragraph. The reason the whole capitalist class doesn't give its money and go to work is *because it doesn't want to.* It is quite satisfied with its present arrangement of luxury, dominion and idleness.

As long as the working class is satisfied with its present arrangement of poverty, obedience and laboriousness, the present arrangement will continue.

But whenever the working class wants to discontinue the present arrangement it can do so. It has the great majority. J. M. P.

Patterson's career as a Socialist reached a considerable height with the publication of his novel, "A Little Brother of the Rich" two years later. In this book the rich are snobs, cads, crooks, and generally wicked people, and the poor are heroic and noble. But there is also an understanding of social issues.

At the very beginning one Paul Potter receives a letter from Sylvia Castle of the Middle West saying, "It seems to me best for your own sake that you should be free." Paul immediately replies "I love you, dearly beloved, with all my heart and soul and strength and mind; and I will marry you because it is ordained." Well, it was ordained for just a few minutes because just as he gets ready to start for the mail box Paul reads of the failure of the Castle bank in Indiana. So he agrees to end the engagement.

Paul's caddishness is surpassed by that of his pal Carl Wilmerding IV, whose father, III, purchases for cash a decision from him to give up the woman he loves, lives with, and with whom he has a child he worships. There is one fine scene in which Wilmerding III lays down the ethics of a capitalist gentleman's relationship with women. He says,

"If a gentleman chooses to indulge himself, he does it like a gentleman. He finds some pretty woman for his left hand, who amuses him for a while, and when he is through, he pays her off and all is done. . . . He doesn't allow children to be born to him and he doesn't keep the thing up for four years with every apparent intention of keeping it up indefinitely. That is not worthy of you, nor of any other gentleman. It shows low tastes of which I am ashamed."

Paul Potter does the dirty work of dissolving the Wilmerding IV liaison and gets a market tip netting $54,000, which his silly high society wife immediately spends in order to join the "old-rich" real aristocracy.

We are then introduced to high society—and to a critic of the era who says of its women: "They can't sing, they can't dance, they can't act, they can't paint, they can't sew, they can't cook, they can't educate. They are inept, unthorough, inconsequential, rudderless, compassless, drifting. They don't know life, because they have never lived life. They are like perpetual typhoid fever patients, supported always on rubber-water mattresses. Helpless, hapless, hopeless, nervous, disappointed, cloyed and cowardly, they exist a few years here, seeking to have all their living done for them by paid dependents. They delegate all their functions in life save one—and even that they don't do well or often."

We meet later the "Great Castleman," the famous American actress who has triumphed in the plays of Ibsen and other giants of the new century, Gorky, Shaw, Sudermann and Hauptmann, and we meet in her the emerging modern young American woman. But to Paul Potter she is more importantly his old sweetheart, Sylvia Castle.

They confess their love, their everlasting love.

Soon enough, while the great Castleman is triumphing in London, Mrs. Potter is most fortunately killed off while philandering with a boy friend in a racing car, and Sylvia, who had but recently offered to live with Paul now expects that the barrier having been removed, he will come across with the conventional offer of marriage. But he frowns. And then Sylvia realizes that it is social position that stands between them and marriage. After all, Paul Potter is a banker and broker, the very epitome of the social-economic-financial system. He cannot marry an actress. But he can "keep" her secretly.

Whereupon the heroine replies:

"You say you fear I might interfere with your social position. Social position!" Her words volleyed forth. "What is it you mean but the chance to go to the garish, vulgar houses of sure-thing gamblers. . . . You are a cheap little tout, Potter, whose business in life is to pull in victims for the operators of gigantic confidence games. . . .

"You live uselessly. The world were better without you. You should be swept away, you and those like you. . . . You add not one jot of knowledge or wisdom or happiness or wealth or health or virtue to the world, and yet, by the skilful, crooked tricks of your vicious trade, you have filched from it ease, emolument, respect, luxury and power. . . .

"To whom does society owe position? . . . to you, who take from it everything you can swindle it out of, and return to it sneers, corruption, evil example, depraved tastes and debased amusement?

"Give Mr. Potter his hat and show him out."

But two years later, when cold and disinterested, Sylvia Castle asks Paul Potter about his forthcoming marriage to Clara Funcke, the only child of the August Funcke St. Louis beer millions, Paul, the capitalist Charlie McCarthy of his time, admits that the system of living he has chosen has been a failure.

"No, Sylvia, it has not been worth while. My whole life is a horrible lie, a poisonous blunder, a soul destroyer. Sometimes

I catch a vision of the truth, but always I turn away from it quickly, or I couldn't keep on.

"... I know it's all rotten and false, but it's too late. ..."

Although the book ended on this tragic note, it was a sensational success. My copy is from the seventh edition; it probably went into many more, it became one of the best sellers of the time, and it caused a great commotion. But not in literary dovecotes and lions' dens.

The general public loved Patterson's novel but the highbrows of the time, the Socialist highbrows too, the very literary circle of which the author in his novel approved of, the novelists and playwrights of the new school, gave this little brother of the rich a rather haughty proletarian shoulder, and left him only the applause of those he did not care anything about.

Thus began the souring-off process in the Socialistic career of young Patterson. I would not be surprised if this snobbery of the literary left lost the radical cause one of the most powerful publishers in America.

There was of course the new responsibility of editing the *Tribune*. James Keeley was doing a great job. Everyone said that the *Tribune* would founder if Keeley ever carried out his threat to quit. Keeley was the pet of Joseph Medill's heirs, Mrs. Patterson and Mrs. McCormick, two old women who refused to let their sons enjoy any power.

But Joe Patterson and R. R. McCormick found a clever way of seizing control. In my *Tribune* days the credit was always given the attorney, McCormick, for planning the coup, but Burton Rascoe gives it to Patterson. At any rate the two discovered that under the Medill will the Medill trust governed the paper, and that their two mothers who owned almost all the stock could only vote two proxies whereas printers and old friends of the founders also owned small blocks of stock each having a proxy. Patterson and McCormick discovered these owners in the Middle West and in Boston. They presented their case. They got the proxies. And one year when Keeley was making a conventional farce of the board meeting, Patterson elected himself president and McCormick chairman. Without a moment to lose Patterson and McCormick moved into Keeley's office and took over editorship and management. They made of the *Tribune* a greater success than Keeley promised.

The World War, acquaintance with the people-haters, Bernhardi and Nietzsche, and the demands of editing and publishing soon completed the change in Patterson's viewpoints on social problems. McCormick never had any.

Patterson's *New York Daily News* is the first tabloid newspaper in America, and claims the largest circulation of any in the world. It employs 2,500 persons, has an annual payroll of six million dollars and is housed in a ten-million-dollar building which is one of the great achievements of modern architecture. The paper is also one of the largest profit-makers in the world.

Tabloids were first successful in England. They are small and full of pictures; in America they are usually sensational, although this can no longer be said of the *Daily News*. (The *New York Evening Post* for a short time experimented with the tabloid form, but remained conservative in type and tenor, and found that there was no consumer demand.) The elements, sex (love), money, and crime, are usually predominant in mass circulation newspapers.

The story goes that Patterson and Lord Northcliffe discussed the press and the public, the latter contending that human nature being pretty much the same the world over, the Americans should take to the tabloid press; but when Patterson countered with the suggestion that human nature being pretty much the same the world over, the British eople should take to the American style of news on the front page, and headlines proportionate to the event, North-cliffe did not accept this thesis. But Lord Beaverbrook did, and his *Express* beat Northcliffe's paper in London circulation.

Patterson's *News*, launched on June 26, 1919, averaged but 57,000 for its first full year. In 1920, it became established with 247,000 copies, and today it has 1,700,000 or more daily, and 3,000,000 Sundays. It has printed a week-day edition of 112 pages and a Sunday edition of 156.

Ignorance, befuddlement and unfairness are apparent in the editorials on the war in Spain. For instance, on January 11, 1938, the thought was expressed that "to those who sympathize with the poor, wretched people of Spain, who will lose and pay for the civil war no matter whether the Reds or the Fascists win, the news of the Fascist garrison's peaceable surrender at Teruel must be welcome news."

Here the word "Reds" is used for the Loyalists, a libelous and misleading appellation which both the United Press and the Associated Press have warned against and which only Hearst and the Catholic hierarchy have repeated. There is no reason except ill will and a desire to spread propaganda (which is the exact opposite of the truth) which can motivate anyone who refers to the popular front in Spain as Communist or Red. In the *Daily News* editorial, moreover, there is the added confusion of lumping Fascists with the democratic Spanish people, "who will lose and pay for the civil war" together. A Fascist victory must mean the exploitation of the Spanish people to pay for the war, because it would mean the restoration of the land and mine owners, the feudal, land-owning, stock-owning church and the exploiters of the agrarian population into power, whereas the victory for the labor unions and other elements chiefly constituting the popular front will mean that the war-makers, the Fascists, the rich, the land owners, mine owners and exploiters will have to pay for the war—not the victorious people. Since the news stories have already reported the mean by which the popular front is already enforcing such a social-revolutionary economic program, there is no excuse for this confusion.

Still more unfair is the January 17, 1938, reference to Spain. After denying the view of ex-Ambassador Dodd that America should do something about preserving democracy which the dictators are destroying, the *Daily News* editorial says:

'Suppose England and the United States should go in together to save Spain. There would be a harsh dispute to begin with among ourselves on whether to save Spain from the Fascists or from the Reds. When Spain was saved, would the Spaniards take democracy, or wouldn't they?"

Again the Hearst, and purely Hearst, falsehood of the conflict in Spain being between Fascism and Communism is accepted, whereas no honest man has ever disputed the fact that the Spanish republic is not Communist or Red, but a coalition which is overwhelmingly democratic. There were about 50,000 who voted the Communist ticket in the 1936 election, and the party in 1938 boasted 250,000—a quarter of a million men and women out of the 12,000,000 population then on the Loyalist side of the front.

Patterson's *Daily News* has been no more liberal or fair toward China than toward Spain. On November 25, 1937, for example, it declared editorially:

"LOOKS AS IF CHINA'S LICKED"

While "we feel gloomy over the impending Chinese defeat," the editorial concluded, "it takes good soldiers to win a war. The Chinese haven't enough good soldiers. . . . And the Chinese seem fated by nature to be a subject people. They always have been kicked around by their rulers, foreign or Chinese. The world is composed of natural-born masters and natural-born servants." (This is the Nietzsche *Sklavenmoral* touch.)

After announcing this social-political philosophy which is at variance with the findings of the greatest thinkers of all time, the *Daily News* turns to the field it knows best: realistic commerce. "If Japan wins," it says, "it will probably build up a powerful mainland empire in China. With that empire we should do business. All the business we can, regardless of our disapproval of the way the land was acquired. . . ."

About a month later the American gunboat *Panay* was sunk. The *Daily News* said editorially "The Chinese are licked," but it also said two other things: it said in plain English that the *Panay* was convoying three Standard Oil Company vessels supplying oil to either Chinese planes or Chinese civilians and it admitted that "we have long backed up our business people and missionaries in China with armed force," recommending that we "scuttle out of China."

Isolationism at any price is the editorial policy of the *Daily News*.

But when it comes to Mexico, there is no longer a question of sincerity, good will, or obscurantism. It is the editorial proof that the fine Socialistic fervor that once coursed in Joe Patterson's humanitarian blood is very, very quiescent. Here again, as in the *Times*, the *Herald Tribune*, the *Sun*, the Hearst press, and Harry Chandler's *Los Angeles Times*, the old battle of human rights versus property is decided in favor of property with all the high-sounding sophistries, euphemisms and propagandist inaccuracies which money can command.

The president of Mexico is continually attacked. "Cardenas Asks For It" is the editorial heading on March 3, 1938, which begins with the story that Italian Bolsheviks seized the factories in 1920 and "Mussolini's March on Rome put an end to that, for better or worse."

I am pretty sick and tired of exploding this myth. I think that every intelligent man and woman in America knows that Mussolini did nothing of the kind and that he wrote in June 1921 that "Bolshevism is dead" in Italy. But because it suits an editorial purpose, a well-known untruth is paraded to point a moral. The crux of the editorial follows:

"Mexican oil development has not been brought about by American or British or Dutch imperialists walking in with big guns and black-snake whips to yank guitar-playing natives out of a state of primitive purity and chain them to derricks and tank cars. The foreigners bought their way into Mexico's oil fields with the consent of previous Mexican governments. They have paid Mexico royalties on production."

Every reliable authority on Mexico has given the proof of the gigantic fraud by which the oil lands were stolen from the Mexican people and the bloodshed and murder by which they have been held and exploited by American, British and Dutch interests. Every person who knows anything about Mexico knows about this business, but somehow it never enters the editorial offices of the jingo newspapers. When Hearst and Harry Chandler demand invasion of Mexico the reason is apparent: both are large land, mine and property owners there and fear socialization. But why should Joe Patterson publish such anti-Mexican propaganda? The largest American company operating in Mexico is the Huesteca Petroleum Company (one of the Doheny group). In the suit of Huesteca versus the Compania Mexicana de Combustibile it was testified that American corporations hired gunmen to murder the four Mexican owners of a well they wanted; that the last of the owners was shot, but not killed, and that the corporation sent a physician who poisoned the wounded man. "Probably ninety percent of the titles of the Huesteca company are usurpations," one of the documents in the case reads. Probably ninety percent of all the oil titles held by foreigners in Mexico are usurpations, and illegal.

But, continues the *Daily News* on March 31st, "the United States cannot afford to let Mr. Cardenas get by with his steal of Mexican oil. We use the word 'steal' advisedly. About $500,000,000 has been invested in Mexican oil development; and of this amount Mexicans put up only one percent. . . ."

Within a day or two after this declaration the American Secretary of State declared the Cardenas plan legal. It is not a steal. It is actually the carrying out of the 1917 constitution which restores the stolen mineral wealth to the nation and to the people—all the people—instead of the corporations.

The spectacle of that great imperialist nation, Tory Britain, protesting Cardenas' plan for repayment while refusing to pay her own debts, failed to impress Patterson's paper. Apparently private property, and not human life, is the utmost value in this materialistic world. I do not know how sincere Cardenas is; I have been in Mexico and praised Calles' plan which turned out to be nothing but another looting expedition, and I have seen other noted Mexican leaders betray their people for money, but on the face of it at this moment it is apparent that Cardenas is trying to do justice to the Mexican people. He is trying to do something that the author of "Confessions of a Drone" was hoping would be done in 1906. But in the editorial column published on May 23, 1938, by the author of the "Confessions" the red flag is pinned on President Cardenas. He is accused of acting on Trotsky's advice "to put over a Red readjustment." And, Patterson's paper concludes, "We don't see how our government can afford to side with or encourage Cardenas, as our liberals and radicals are insisting it shall. Cardenas grabbed other people's oil wells. . . ." And this is very bad for the British and our own navy. . . .

The Drone has now become metamorphosed. The little brother of the rich has become one of the lords of British and American imperialism.

※

Or take the Patterson editorials dealing with economics. On December 30, 1937, General Motors Corporation is dealt with and defended against a *Daily Worker* proposal that instead of declaring $64,000,000 dividends to men who have done nothing, the 30,000 workers who make G. M. cars and who were fired that day, should be retained. On February 6, 1938, maldistribution of wealth is dealt with. I will not quote either editorial. It is true that the *Daily News* is aimed at the less than fourteen-year-old mind but that is no reason for editorials being written by economic illiterates.

On the other hand the editorial writers of this same newspaper once they are free to step out of the labyrinth of economics and international politics, where they are lost through ignorance or ill will, are fearless in their attack on public injustices and even the hypocrisy of fellow publishers. The *News,* for example, is one of the three or four papers of the country which has declared the publishers' use of the term "freedom of the press" a pious fraud; it is one of the few newspapers which has denounced the A. N. P. A. for its dirty work in continuing child labor, and it is probably the only newspaper which has exposed and demanded the abolition of the press subsidy by the United States government.

Probably the bravest thing the *News* has done has been its editorial defiance of the pressure of the Catholic Church. This pressure is one of the most important forces in American life, and the only one about which secrecy is generally maintained, no newspaper being brave enough to discuss it, although all fear it and believe that the problem should be dragged into the open and made publicly known.

In January, 1938, the *News* realizing that the annual child labor amendment would again be defeated, blamed the Catholic bishops of the state, and especially Bishop Edmund F. Gibbons, of Albany; it derided the propaganda which called the freeing of children "regimentation" or "youth control" and called the bishops "misled." "Nearly all radicals and many liberals," it continued, "maintain that the Catholic hierarchy in this country tends to be more and more conservative; in some cases reactionary. Insofar as this is true, the explanation would seem to lie in the fact that many of these ecclesiastics are elderly gentlemen who administer the properties of their dioceses, both in real estate and in securities—a function which would tend to give some of them the cast of mind of the conservative business man."

To criticize the Catholic Church is to invite a boycott, the withdrawal of advertising, loss in circulation and in revenue. It is the same when a newspaper prints news favorable to the labor movement. Nevertheless it was the *News* which in the spring of 1937 dedicated the page opposite its editorials to a fair discussion of both sides of the labor problem. The "Economic Battle Page" was the logical successor to the "Presidential Battle Page" which had in 1936 given Democrats and Republicans equal space to make and answer arguments.

This is one of the most honest things that has happened in American newspaper history, and in a concluding chapter a challenge to the American press is based upon its willingness to open its columns to both sides of political and economic questions.

Throughout the Roosevelt administration the *News* has been one of the few papers exposing the hypocrisy of many of the campaigns against the President and his policies. Roosevelt was for taxation but publishers, being human beings, were opposed to paying. Most notable Roosevelt-haters are Colonel McCormick of the *Chicago Tribune* and the unspeakable Hearst. These men and the majority of publishers moved heaven and earth and ninety percent of the presses to attack the administration's taxation policy, using every argument which endangered pocketbooks and bought brains could produce, but Patterson said bluntly that almost the entire opposition to the President's taxation program arose from the selfish motives of the publishers: they are wealthy men, they feel that their money is menaced by proposed taxation, and they have therefore worked themselves up into the hysterical state of mind which confuses public welfare and their personal financial welfare.

When the 1938 Reorganization Bill was defeated the *New York Times* followed its usual custom of asking the leading papers of the country to give their editorial views. The general public of course never knows which views are accepted, which thrown into the waste-basket. But the *News* has not hesitated to break another journalistic taboo, which is to keep quiet about the ethics of fellow newspapers. It attacked the *Times,* saying:

We're annoyed with the *New York Times*—which always asks us for advance proofs of our editorials on New Deal developments, then consistently fails to print the editorial or any part thereof. The *Times,* however, prints the *Herald Tribune* editorial or part of it on the same subject.

Don't misunderstand us; we admire the *Times* greatly, and think it is one of the master newspapers of the world. But in this small and annoying particular, it is misrepresenting on occasion the reaction of the New York morning press to phases of the New Deal.

Maybe the *Times* feels that the *News* is not a newspaper. That doesn't bother us. We've been contempted by experts. But after all, the *News* currently has three times the circulation of the *Times* and five times that of the *Herald Tribune.* If the *Times* pretends to collect cross sections of press opinion on important national affairs and print them for its readers' full information, it ought to include the *News* opinion—or it ought not to telephone over to our newspaper shop for advance proofs.

Equally frank is Patterson regarding the publication of dirt which was once almost a monopoly of the Hearst press and which has lately been charged to the tabloid press. At the end of the notorious Browning case, which reached the nadir of filth when the Macfadden *Graphic* published "composographs" picturing the elderly Browning and the youthful "Peaches," the *Daily News* said editorially:

Far be it from us to pin a lily on our coat. The *News* also has gone too far. . . . As long as there is more newspaper circulation in more smut, some presses will be found to roll out the smut. We hate bureaucracy. We hate the suppression of free speech. But unless the minds of the children of New York are to be drenched in obscenity it seems to us that censorship of the press as well as of the theater must come. . . .

There are many sorts of fake news items in the world press: the accidental fakes which all the vigilance in the world cannot prevent, the willful fakes which are connected with editorial policy, and semi-fakes which can be argued for a lifetime. The matter of news-faking is never discussed in newspapers. But Patterson in this field is also an iconoclast. Said the *News* (April 28, 1936):

> We're afraid it was a fake.
> . . . we printed a story from a New England correspondent saying that $20,000 in Lindbergh ransom bills had recently turned up in Albany and in various Massachusetts towns.
> We are convinced now that the story was a fake. . . . We are sorry to have published the story.
> We mention it in this public manner because we want to make it clear that this newspaper does not knowingly or intentionally fake news. We think any newspaper that does fake news is foolish. It is so easy to expose a fake news story, and as soon as the public finds out about it the paper that published the fake loses some reader confidence. Repeat the process often enough, and the paper loses the confidence of all the readers except the natural-born and incurable suckers.
> We want our readers to know that the news published in this paper is always true to the best of our knowledge.

Nevertheless, on the following September 4th the *News* devoted almost its entire front page to the following sensation:

PLOT TO
KILL F. D. R.
NIPPED

L. I. Alien Seized With Bombs

The story, on page three, was headed: "Red bomber seized in plot to blow up F. D. R." and the story said that "an alien radical's plot . . . was nipped. . . ."

In the *New York Times,* that same morning, there was a mere quarter column story on an inside page. There was no mention of a plot to assassinate the President. But, on the other hand, there was the statement that "among articles found in the shack, it was reported, were Communist litera‹ ture and several copies of the *Moscow News.*"

By evening there was no plot to kill the President, no "Red," no Communists, no *Moscow News*—nothing but an old man suffering "apparently from a persecution mania" as the *Post* truthfully reported. But neither the *News* nor the *Times* apologized.

This is one of thousands of episodes which illustrates the case against the American press today. It is no longer a matter of mere sensationalism, of yellow journalism, which so perturbed our fathers; it is now more a matter of distortion, coloration, a recklessness, if not a sinister intention, to blame aliens, Reds, Communists—and in other instances, labor, liberals and progressives—for violence, plottings and all the ills of a disturbed epoch.

In the cases of the Hearsts, the McCormicks and the rest of the reactionary majority of the A. N. P. A., the intention is more obvious every year; in the case of Patterson it is not bad will but confusion.

Patterson still likes to pull down his slouch hat, pull up his coat. collar, play the workingman, go into the streets, mingle with common people, and find out what they do and what they want. He does not go slumming, like his sister Eleanor; he goes because of that old Socialistic urge.

"He has always had a social conscience; he is by nature, by action and by conviction democratic and equalitarian

. . . " writes Burton Rascoe,* who has known "J. M. P." for decades. "He is impulsive, erratic and impatient, unpredictable, a man who acts and works on hunches. He is devoid of all except the most elementary reasoning powers; and his mistakes have been made through the initial errors of assuming that he was thinking when he was merely feeling, and of attempting to apply a logical process to matters of pure instinct and emotion. His most charming quality is that of trying to live up to his principles. And half the time he does not know what his real feelings are, so numerous are they, so complex and so checked and leashed by obligations to his conscience, to his employees, to the handful of heirs of the *Chicago Tribune* properties, to his belief in his mission in the world and to his innate, half-repressed, half-satisfied quest for a full, free life of admirable action and true *noblesse oblige*."

Patterson passed through the Northcliffe phase when he too thought he could be either a great power in politics or, failing that, the secret manipulator of the mannikins who play in the front pages of the nation's press. Patterson's slavery to the Northcliffe complex has not been long or important. He has seen service for a year in the Illinois House of Representatives but he later quit his job as commissioner of public works in Chicago when he learned that he could not beat gang politicians. The Northcliffe phase of direct action was knocked out by dirty politics, and the second Northcliffe phase, that of being the secret manipulator, has not superseded his old democratic Marxian experiences.

In 1933 he went in as an ordinary reporter to interview the head of a New York bank on which there was a run. The great banker said the bank was sound. Patterson agreed. But suddenly he was back in his old soap-box days of Chicago Socialism. He turned on the banker and gave him a tonguelashing on the evils of the capitalist system.

---

* In his autobiography, "Before I Forget," Doubleday-Doran, 1937.

J. M. P. treats his employees better than ninety or perhaps ninety-nine percent of the publishers of America. He is one of the few owners respected and liked by the Newspaper Guild. No one has ever accused him of double-crossing, nor have briefs charging violations of the law been filed against him. Some of the self-announced great liberal newspapers cannot make equal claims.

The *News* is one of the richest newspapers in America and its publisher could well afford to defy all the pressures which prevent our country from having a free press. He does defy more of them than ninety-nine percent of his colleagues. But that is not enough.

And it is a great pity. The matter of money is the chief obstacle to a free press, and no one has been more outspoken than Joseph Medill Patterson in exposing just that fact about his fellow publishers. And it is not a matter of money that keeps Patterson from producing not only a great newspaper but a free newspaper. A great free newspaper demands if not a great mind at least a social sense back of it, and Patterson has only good intentions; otherwise he is confused. He is just as courageous now as he was thirty years ago when he defied the social-financial milieu into which he was born, when he became a Socialist. He has not grown reactionary as the majority of publishers, editors and famous columnists do when they gain fame, money and social standing. But somewhere between 1908 and 1916 there was a moral detour, and ever since then the Patterson psyche has been traveling nowhere amidst great confusion and spectacular headlines.

Somewhere between his ivory tower and his soap box there is still a chance that Joe Patterson will find himself.

CHAPTER 3

Power of the Middle West

COLONEL ROBERT RUTHERFORD MCCORMICK is the only American press lord whom I know fairly well. I was employed by the Army edition of the *Chicago Tribune* for a short time in 1917, and by the Chicago Tribune Foreign News Service from 1919 to 1928. I had never been to Chicago. Colonel McCormick required a weekly letter from each of his foreign service men and two or three times a year held a conference in a European capital, when he impressed us all by his willingness to listen to the views of his correspondents. He was modest, friendly, easy to get along with, and apparently one of the few press lords who had escaped the Napoleon-Northcliffe power obsession.

To us of the foreign service the daily proclamation that the *Tribune* was "The World's Greatest Newspaper" was a daily joke. In the old days we had in addition to the *Manchester Guardian* and the *London Times*, the *Frankfurter Zeitung* and the *Corriere della Sera*, the latter two alas now perverted by totalitarian systems. We also had a faint suspicion that the *New York World*, the *St. Louis Post-Dispatch*, the *Baltimore Sun*, the *Kansas City Star* and the *New York Times* might dispute the claim. When we asked our Chicago colleagues for the basis on which it was made they usually mentioned the campaigns against "Boss" Thompson and the fact the *Tribune* could not be bought by advertising or other interests.

Today most newspapermen, including numerous *Tribune* employees agree that if a vote were taken for the title "The

41

World's Worst Newspaper," with the Fascist press hors concours, the ultimate choice probably would lie between one of the Hearst journals and the *Chicago Tribune*. In fact in the mass demonstrations against the Hearst and McCormick sheets on election day 1936 it was becoming evident that the more hated of the two was the *Tribune*.

My relations with Colonel McCormick and the *Tribune* were always good. On only one occasion was I aware that orders on how and what to write were given in much the same manner as the Goebbels, Ciano and Hearst propaganda bureaus issue daily orders. I received from Chicago a request for a cable on the failure of government owned and operated railroads. Duplicates had been sent to all correspondents and so far as I know the responses confirmed the implication.

I knew nothing about the German railroads. I was not aware that Colonel McCormick was opposed to the continuation of government operation of the American railroads after the war and was bolstering his view with foreign illustrations. The information I obtained proved fairly well that the German government railroads were a success and I so cabled.

The next day I received a long message, this time from the Paris office, instructing me exactly in what I was to say, to wit: that the German railroad system was a failure, that the public was angry, that passengers paid too much, that freight rates were too high, that governmental bureaucracy was simply terrible, and that the whole idea of governmental rivalry with private money-making was simply not to the good. I could have taken these instructions, signed them and sent them back as a news story. It was just exactly what was wanted. But as this was the one and only case in which I realized that I was being intimidated and driven into that easy classification known as a "journalistic prostitute," I made a thorough inquiry into the railroad business, and finding that my first cable was more than justified, I wrote a tremendously long story giving facts and figures triumphantly proving that government ownership and operation was a thousand times preferable to private enterprise, and that it would be magnificent for all countries, including the United States, to take a lesson from Republican Germany.

Need I tell my readers that my cablegram was never published?

Moreover, in 1923, when I was finishing my visit to Russia, a colleague from the Paris office, temporarily presiding in Berlin, found to his venal delight that the German state railroads were bankrupt—to the tune of millions of quintillions —and promptly sent a story to that effect. It made the front page. What the story did not explain was the fact of inflation —the daily catastrophic change in the value of the mark, which fell from four to four quintillion to the dollar—and which only for a few months caused a fictitious or bookkeeping show of failure.

This same colleague had several years earlier visited Russia for the purpose of writing a series of articles denouncing the Soviet system. But every day of his stay convinced him of the value of the system he was sent to attack. On arriving in Riga he began the first of a series of cautious cablegrams expressing his change of attitude, but despite care and diplomacy, he was caught writing contrary to the *Tribune's* anti-Russian policy and ordered to Paris. There he was placed against the wall. He was told to change his tune, or else. . . . He tried to compromise with his journalistic ethics by offering to refrain from writing anything at all about Russia, but the *Tribune* bosses were not that easy. They not only insisted that he write, but that he write against Russia, and the poor devil, gray-haired, tired, his future unprotected and a family clamoring for bread, was forced to betray his friends, himself, and all the ethics of the profession for the price of his butter. The significance of the episode was not lost on the rest of the *Tribune* staff.

I am not trying to make myself out an angel by contrast with this poor devil; I am merely trying to illustrate one of the fundamental facts about American journalism today, the fact that the servants of the press lords are slaves very much as they have always been, and that any attempt at revolt is immediately punished with the economic weapon. But much more vicious than these cases is the majority of foreign correspondents who never have to be placed against the wall, who are never told what to write and how to write it, but who know from contact with the great minds of the press lords or from the simple deduction that the bosses are in big business and the news must be slanted accordingly, or from the general intangible atmosphere which prevails everywhere, what they can do and what they must never do. The most stupid boast in the history of present-day journalism is that of the writer who says "I have never been given orders; I am free to do as I like."

The German railroad order was the only one I received in my ten years with the *Tribune*. I was nominally head of the Berlin bureau although I spent about two years in Italy, two years in Russia, a year with the French armies in Syria, and another year in the Balkans. On arriving in Germany with the American Army of Occupation on December 13, 1918, I found that my sympathies were strongly for the victims of both the German monarchy and the Versailles Treaty, and this sympathy I brought to Berlin when I took over the office in 1920. The *Tribune* had been pro-German before we got into the war, and did not carry over the hatred which it helped create after we entered it. There was therefore nothing I could write about Germany which would offend the editors. In 1921 I went to Russia to spell Floyd Gibbons, who had scooped the world on the vastness of the famine there. My approach to the Russian problem was from an entirely different angle than all the rest of my colleagues, who were either prejudiced or favorable before entering the forbidden land. My father had been a personal friend of Prince Kropotkin's, and himself active in the Friends of Russian Freedom at the time of the Revolution of 1905, but my father was fundamentally a libertarian who believed in no party—although he had worked for the Single Taxer Henry George in 1886 and named me after him several years later. I was born and brought up in the libertarian tradition and my whole quarrel with Soviet Russia—which certainly had more important quarrels on its hands at the time—concerned freedom for oppositional minorities, which had helped smash Tsarism, but which refused to accept the October Revolution. My contentions were based on my assumption that Russia was no longer threatened from without.

I was told that the war was not over, that "the bourgeois capitalist nations" were plotting to smash the Soviet state, that Russia was surrounded by conspirators, that all the apparent anti-democratic and anti-libertarian measures still in force were necessitated by this unseen state of war which Russians felt then existed.

How true that is can be seen today in the Berlin-Rome axis, and the open conspiracy of the Fascist nations and Tory Britain to destroy Soviet Russia. But to me all looked peaceful, so I pooh-hooed the idea and departed from Moscow to write a series of articles saying that democracy was dead in Russia, that the Red terror continued to take a bloody toll, and that the Third Internationale was a Red plot to seize the world.

No one on the *Tribune* ordered me to write these stories in this way, nor was the intangible power present directing me to write in accordance with the Red-baiting policy of the owner of the paper. The great attack of the Hearsts, the McCormicks, the Rothermeres and the Beaverbrooks has always been against Russia as an enemy of profit and property, whereas I heartily agreed to the Soviet economic system which aimed at the co-operative commonwealth and the eventual liberation of mankind from every social, economic, political and moral chain. My criticism was of means, not ends. Nevertheless, it was criticism, and therefore it was played up in Chicago and I got a bonus of $500 and a gold

pin from Colonel McCormick which made me a member of
his "eagles."

In the course of my Berlin tenure all sorts of men came
in with all sorts of stories, some free and some for sale. A
White Russian offered a set of documents about some plotting in Europe. I cabled Chicago and was told the *Tribune*
was not interested because the locale was too far away.
Shortly afterward the White Russian appeared with documents about a Red plot in Buenos Aires for which he wanted
$5,000. He compromised I believe for fifty. At any rate the
story was accepted and published. Several years later when
H. R. Knickerbocker exposed the White Russian forgery
factory in Berlin it was revealed that the story was a complete
fraud.

This is but one of thousands of instances. A paper publishes what it wants to publish. If the story had been about a
White plot against the Reds, and if the documents had been
true (not forged) the *Chicago Tribune* would not have been
interested, although the locale might have been as intriguing
as Evanston, Illinois.

Outside of the German and Russian questions there were
none in Europe which might cause difficulties between correspondent and publisher. In the case of Vincent Sheean and
an amazing story he wrote about "the dogma of the tran-
substantiation of the Virgin Mary," it was a matter of pure
error. He certainly did not mean to bring down the wrath
of the Catholic hierarchy on himself and the paper. When I
came to Rome to extricate him and appease the church I
found that if one had taken the 6,000 word explanation of
the case as prepared by the monsignor who sold foreign
correspondents Catholic news, and condensed it to a 300
word cable, one was more likely than not to produce a false
impression and a news item offensive to the church. In 1925
when through an error which escaped my Catholic assistant
Cianfarra and my Catholic advisor, Lord Hemphill, I used
the words "dispensation" and "indulgence" as synonyms, a

boycott was started against the *Tribune* by a Catholic sheet called "Our Sunday Visitor" which caused me great annoyance. But when, a year later, I reported from Syria that there was an awful lot of religious intrigue in the political situation and the Druse rebellion which General Sarrail, the Catholic-hater, was fighting in the Near East, the *Tribune* published all my telegrams despite the fact that almost every newspaper in the world is scared to death when any religious sect is mentioned critically.

There are many more illustrative episodes. The reader may gain the impression from them that the *Chicago Tribune* is not as bad as it has been painted, and perhaps after all it should not be given worst place among American newspapers. The fact is that I have written considerably about my personal experiences to show that there is no personal feeling in the matter of criticizing this powerful newspaper and its publisher. I have studied the *Tribune* in America as any stranger from Europe would. I know of no newspaper which is so vicious and stupid in its attack on labor, no paper so consistent in its Red-baiting, and no paper in my opinion is such a great enemy of the American people. Here follow some of the reasons.

No newspaper in America has such an unbroken record of labor-baiting as the *Chicago Tribune*. Today its enmity to the vast majority which constitutes the laboring class is cloaked in many kinds of hypocrisy, but there was once a time when the *Tribune* was more honestly the organ of the rich, the employers, and the exploiters and when it demanded the shooting down of workingmen who wanted a better world for themselves, and recommended starvation for those whom the greed of the industrial system kept from exercising their "right to work."

Joseph Medill, it is true, was against slavery, and for

Lincoln. He supported the President in his bitter fight against the Supreme Court, not sparing the English language in his attack on the nine old men of his time, but when panic, the inevitable result of war, followed in 1873, and the country was overrun with the unemployed, whom the newspapers called "tramps," the *Chicago Tribune* * had a unique plan of dealing with them, "where one is not a member of the Humane Society." It was this: "To put a little strychnine or arsenic in the meat and other supplies furnished the tramps. This produces death within a comparatively short period of time, is a warning to other tramps to keep out of the neighborhood, puts the coroner in good humor, and saves one's chickens and other portable property from constant depredation."

In the great railroad strike of 1877 the *Tribune* editorially approved the police plan not to fire a warning round over the heads of the workingmen but to aim low. "Chicago is too far advanced to permit her bad elements to interfere with her interests," the *Tribune* wrote, and urged the formation of vigilantes to supplement the police and militia.

Ten days after the *Tribune* editorial favoring the murder by poison of unemployed, a mass meeting was held where Albert Parsons denounced the capitalist press for its attack on the working people, and particularly the *Tribune* which he declared always evaded the labor question by branding a mass meeting of workers as a gathering of Communists. At that time men worked twelve to fourteen hours a day and, said Parsons, the bosses took five-sixths of the profits. The use of new machinery was to blame. Wages were being reduced and men laid off everywhere.

The next morning the *Tribune,* which approved of the importation of scabs and thugs, demanded that the railroad men who would not take wage cuts and dismissal notices, "step out of the way. . . . If they will not step out voluntarily,

---

* Issue of July 12, 1877.

they must be made to by force." Strikers were called "the scum and filth of the city." It was an open class struggle, with no euphemism and hypocrisy. Capital and labor were at each other's throats. Parsons and others were arrested. On July 25th the *Tribune* reported that "Capitalists would offer any sum to see the leaders . . . strung up to a telegraph pole."

On the very afternoon in which this hope for hanging was expressed the police attacked a gathering of 3,000 workers at Halsted and Sixteenth Streets, killing two and wounding many. Over the story of this massacre the *Chicago Tribune* put the headlines:

RED WAR
Desperate Contest Between Rioters and Police on Halsted Street
An Assembly of the Communists Swiftly Smashed by the Police

In this news story the *Tribune* referred to the peaceful workmen as thieves and riffraff, cutthroats and bandits, who showed "all the elements of extreme viciousness incident to riots."

Throughout this epoch of unrest, the climax of which was the Haymarket bombing, the newspapers of Chicago, and principally the *Tribune,* were the chief instigators of class hatred, intolerance and warfare. Labor then did not exert any pressure on newspapers, and advertisers did not appeal to the poorer people. The press in those days made no pretenses. It was for the rich and against the poor.

Time after time the *Chicago Tribune* urged the authorities to break up workers' meetings with violence, with gunfire, and if necessary with dynamite. Police Captain John Bondfield frequently sent his men to beat up workingmen and arrest speakers because Mayor Harrison refused to call for Federal troops to do so. On May 3, 1886, at the McCormick reaper works, a fight occurred between the strikers and scabs, the police killing many of the former while defending the latter. On May 4th a quiet meeting occurred in the

Haymarket, the Mayor being present and instructing the police to return to their stations. Bondfield, to show his authority, kept them harassing both speakers and listeners.

The bomb which was thrown by a person who has never been identified killed seven policemen and wounded sixty-seven others, a sensational crime which aroused the whole country, but no emphasis was ever given in the news to another fact, that there were between two and three times as many workingmen victims as police victims. Whoever set off the bomb spilled more labor blood than police blood. But the newspapers eagerly started the Red-baiting hysteria; they yelled for bloody revenge, they faked news abut discoveries of plots and dynamite everywhere, they tried the case against the Chicago anarchists, not one of whom was guilty of the bomb throwing, found all guilty, sentenced all to death. The atmosphere was hysterical; it was made so by the press, and the leader in rabble rousing was Joseph Medill, who despite the historical fact that the Illinois industrial worker of his time had at his disposal an annual sum of $81 compared to the state's appropriations for individual paupers of $95, sententiously announced that the poor had only to blame "their own improvidence and misdirected efforts."

Half a century passed before the Haymarket affair could be judged impartially, the executed labor leaders raised to martyrs in the cause of justice and progress, and the newspapers of the time given their full share of the blame for the massacre. It took considerably less time, thanks to a news reel, to come to an honest judgment on the Memorial Day Massacre of 1937 outside the Chicago plant of the Republic Steel Company, and here again it was the notorious labor-hating *Chicago Tribune* whose conduct was more reprehensible than all the other newspapers of the country.

Every serious study of labor troubles in the history of the nation has proven that in the overwhelming majority of

cases the forces of law and order (so called) are responsible
for initiating violence. On the other hand every study of
the press shows that the newspapers generally lie when it
comes to reporting the war of capital versus labor. Some of
these lies are not told maliciously because in many cases
newspapers remote from the scene honestly publish lying
reports they believe are honest. Frequently it is impossible
to get at the truth. But the Chicago massacre was filmed by
the Paramount company and a description of the private
showing of the film before the La Follette Civil Liberties
Committee, reported in the *St. Louis Post-Dispatch* by Paul
Y. Anderson, forced the release of this news reel, and its
general showing also showed up the American press for its
complete failure to tell the truth about this bloody and
brutal event.

The *Chicago Tribune* praised the policemen, who now
stood revealed as ruthless murderers, because they protected
"life and property," but the Senate committee's report proved
that there was no call to protect life and property. The
police and the *Tribune* charged that the workers intended
to storm the Republic plant, but the Senate investigation
proved this charge false. The *Chicago Tribune* even after
the showing of the film called the police heroic, but the
official report called their actions more brutal than crimes
committed during the World War, and more cruel in the
treatment of wounded. The La Follette committee proved
that police officials lied both at the time of the massacre and
at the Washington hearings, but the *Tribune* remained
faithful to the police. The *Chicago Tribune* and the police
who needed a scapegoat to hide their murders, charged Reds
and Communists with inspiring or leading the workmen,
but this charge was proven absolutely false.

The *Tribune* continued to attack John L. Lewis, head of
the Committee for Industrial Organization. One of its
charges against the labor leader's style of living was sent to

Robert S. Allen, co-author with Drew Pearson of "The Washington Merry-Go-Round." Allen replied: * "The fact that such a story has appeared in the *Chicago Tribune* should be enough to stigmatize it as a lie. I wonder if that rag ever prints a word of truth about anything except racing and baseball results."

The *New York Times*, the *New York Herald Tribune*, and many more conservative and reactionary newspapers whose household gods are the same which business and the police worship, in the case of the massacre of C. I. O. workers in Chicago did condemn police violence and did call the police the instigators. Usually these papers blame the victims of violence and when that is too palpably a falsehood, ignore the matter of blame. The *Chicago Tribune* was the only big newspaper which stuck to its police guns. It thereby added another claim to the title of world's worst newspaper.

No newspaper has been as persistent in its Red-baiting campaign as the *Chicago Tribune*.

Red-baiting itself may be legitimate even if all baiting is unethical. Editorially newspapers have the right to attack and defend. But Red-baiting from 1917 to date has generally been accompanied by every sort of fakery that has helped discredit the press of the world, as was so amply proven by the Lippmann-Merz exposure in the *New Republic* in August, 1920. The paper chosen for a test was the *New York Times* which enjoyed a reputation for accuracy and honesty say about a thousand times greater than that of the *Chicago Tribune,* and the *Times,* in its chagrin, changed its policy. The *Tribune* did not.

In the old days, when no one dared criticize, it published the same sort of colored, distorted and fraudulent news

---

* *The Progressive,* August 28, 1937.

which Lippmann and Merz spotted in the *Times*. Much of it
had Associated Press credit lines and many items were based
on "well-informed sources" or "an official of the French
Foreign Office," but they were lies nevertheless, as history
has proven. On August 2, 1921, the *Tribune* published *
"what it said was a photograph of Soviet soldiers turning a
machine gun on a crowd of men, women and children. This
picture had been printed in the *Tribune* four years earlier,
and actually represented a World War scene, as the paper
acknowledged."

From the 1920's to the present day the *Tribune* has continued to print rumor and gossip, much of it proven false,
from Riga, Helsingfors, Reval and other places, all purporting to tell the uncensored story about Russia. Ever since
Colonel McCormick withdrew the present writer from Russia
in 1923 he has had no representative there, and has relied
upon sources outside the nation, which sources have been
generally discredited throughout the world.

Every man who worked for the *Tribune* in Europe knew
that it was not necessary to investigate a story if it was anti-
Soviet. Every fake, forgery and lie that appeared in the
European press, which in many instances was paid to lie,
could be copied and sent out to Chicago. Stories about other
nations and other economic systems required confirmation.
Not so stories about Russia—provided they were intended to
harm the enemy of the profit and property system.

Among the *Tribune's* enemies today is Professor Schuman
of Chicago University. The *Tribune* loves to bait him. Can
it be that this is petty revenge for a study of *Tribune* news
made some years ago? Professor Schuman found that in
October, 1925, the *Tribune* reported that "Soviet fights
famine as grain myth explodes"; that starvation threatened
the "doom of Soviet"; that Siberia had revolted. In 1926
some of the *Tribune* stories which history has proven false,

---

* Silas Bent, *Ballyhoo*, page 188.

exaggerated, biased, and colored, included one (on March 20th) in which a "secret report shows Russia near collapse." This was the year in which "Roumania hears of widespread Russian revolt," the same Roumanian revolt that brought us all to the frontier several months later and which turned out to be a Roumanian foreign office lie. The *Tribune* also scooped the world on "Odessa troops mutiny against Moscow regime" and "trade, industry totter." On August 10th the amazing story appeared that in Soviet Russia "Red factions grasp for power." Then the Reds were not in control, or what? Three days later the *Tribune* revolt had reached the heart of Russia itself. The Reds, believe it or not, "reinforce Kremlin fort as mutiny grows," and eight days later there was a crisis.

The year 1927 was a year of nothing but revolts in the *Tribune*. "Revolt against Soviet begins" (April 9th); the Red Army was fighting South Russia on the 19th; but troops were called home "as revolt rises" on the 21st; in July the *Tribune* manufactured a new famine; in October "industry faces swift disaster," and in November hundreds died "in Ukraine riots, Roumania hears." Roumania and the *Tribune* always heard the same stories. They were the same lies.

Concluding his study of the *Tribune*, Professor Schuman says "no inquiry into the factual basis of these news items would seem to be required. Suffice it to say that all of their reports of mutinies, revolts, and uprisings were wholly without foundation, so far as the writer has been able to ascertain, and that the remaining headlines differed only in the degree of their inaccuracy. The total picture presented is completely at variance with the facts and is obviously calculated to discredit the Soviet regime."

In August, 1932, the Finnish police found a group of insane grave robbers who performed obscene rites with dead bodies, whereupon the Helsingfors correspondent, aware that the Colonel loved such stories, added to it a line saying that the persons arrested "call themselves proletarians, and one is said to be a Communist."

During the excitement over the Weyerhauser kidnaping, the *Tribune* printed a front-page story purporting to be an interview with a Washington state police official who said that radicals interested in the lumber strike were being investigated for connection with the crime. The official may have said so, but it was a pure Red-baiting sensational story, which in time proved false.

In the North Pole flight from Moscow to the United States the *Tribune* saw nothing but a Red plot. First it reported that it was "timed to lend the greatest support to the waning C. I. O. movement," and later it reported in a terror-stricken editorial that John L. Lewis attended the banquet to the heroic flyers who "timed their flight to land in America when Lewis and his C. I. O. needed something to distract the public attention from their violent activities and take some of the curses off the Red purges which filled the world press. . . ."

On November 13, 1937, the *Tribune* reported from London the "discovery of a plot by German agents to assassinate Soviet Dictator Josef Stalin. . . . Confessions of two alleged German spies arrested in Leningrad early in the fall are said to have compromised Litvinoff, Soviet Commissar of Foreign Affairs, and to have been the real reason for the reputed arrest of three Soviet ambassadors." But despite the *Tribune* discovery Litvinoff has not been executed.

A happy combination of Roosevelt-baiting and Red-baiting was attempted by the *Tribune* in August, 1936, when it reported sensationally (but under a Riga dateline) "that Moscow has ordered 'Reds' in the United States to back Roosevelt against Landon."

To this story the *Chicago Daily Times,* only supporter of the President, replied with a front-page editorial saying: "If the *Tribune,* or any other newspaper, can prove to the satisfaction of the American Society of Newspaper Editors and the American Newspaper Publishers Association that the *Tribune's* dispatch from Donald Day, dated Riga, Latvia, August 8th, with its heading, is true, the *Times* will donate $5,000 to the work of the Freedom of the Press Committee of the American Newspaper Publishers Association" of which Colonel McCormick is the head, body and feet.

Moscow called the story a fake.

Colonel McCormick refused to make a statement. He never took up the challenge. But, acting under the freedom of the press for publishers, he ordered one of his cartoonists —who today are almost unique in upholding the tradition of prostitution of talents in newspaper offices—to draw a picture of Soviet Russia shouting orders to American Reds to "Stop Landon." And Landon's partner, Colonel Knox of the *Chicago Daily News,* published an editorial a week after the $5,000 challenge for veracity had been made, in which it was said that "in plain English, the Communist International at Moscow has authorized American Communists to vote for Roosevelt, in order to play up to other American radical groups and to defeat Landon and Knox." Needless to say Hearst played up the same hoax.

Colonel McCormick's sympathy with the reactionaries and the Red-baiters is also shown in his association with the Sentinels of the Republic, with Harry A. Jung, and his endorsement of Mrs. Dilling.

When Senator Black's committee investigating lobbying took up the Sentinels of the Republic it exposed, as the chief backer, a family named Pitcairn, and a series of letters. President Alexander Lincoln wrote to W. Cleveland Runyon that "I think that the Jewish threat is a real one," and Runyon replied that "the old-line Americans of $1,200 a year want a Hitler." The entire propaganda of the Sentinels was shown to be subsidized by big business, by Irénée du Pont, Alfred P. Sloan, E. T. Stotesbury of the House of Morgan and Raymond Pitcairn, a Philadelphia industrialist. The moral supporters, the Black committee found, were Al Smith, John J. Raskob, William Randolph Hearst and Colonel R. R. McCormick. McCormick hates Justice Black more than any man living.

Colonel McCormick's testimonial endorsing "The Red Network" appears on the cover of the third edition of this thoroughly unreliable Red-baiting collection of hate and prejudice. In his pamphlet "Plotting America's Pogroms," John L. Spivak names Harry A. Jung as one of McCormick's protégés who "supplies the Colonel with a great deal of his 'inside' information about Communists and Jews." The names Dilling and Jung are further linked by the La Follette Civil Liberties report, from page 321 of which I quote:

National Labor Relations Board Report
Patriotic Associations as Undercover Agents

Spy and strike-breaking agencies not infrequently assume the masks of patriotism, ultra-Americanism, or some form of public service. They sometimes set up affiliates under patriotic camouflage or sponsor citizens' committees for an alleged public purpose.

Conversely organizations actually or originally patriotic have been known to engage in industrial espionage and strike breaking.

The most insidious and reprehensible form of activities in this mixed field is that represented by certain "associations" whose purpose is private gain, and whose methods include making business by spreading scares or actually fomenting disturbances. The most frequent guise for these associations is some form of "Red hunting." The sustenance of such associations is usually from industry and finance, and its "services" may include strike breaking.

A typical concern of this sort is A. V. I. F., the American Vigilant Intelligence Federation with offices in the *Chicago Tribune* Tower Building, Chicago, which is the expression of its "honorary manager," one Harry Augustus Jung. Exposed frequently in the past dozen years by the Chicago Federation of

Labor, its record was written into the investigation of the Congressional Committee on Nazi and Other Propaganda, whose report, issued February 15, 1935, stated concerning certain allegedly patriotic associations, "Many are in reality the breeding places of racial and religious intolerance and their financial statements show them to be petty racketeers." The report names American Vigilant Intelligence Federation as one such.

Jung and his colleague, Nelson E. Hewitt, were associated with Mrs. Albert W. Dilling in compiling a book called "The Red Network."

McCormick's endorsement of this work says:

"I am glad to have it for reference and trust that the book will have a large sale so that Americans will know who are the enemies of society within our gates. You are to be commended highly for the patriotism and devotion to the welfare of your country that enabled you to publish this book."—Colonel Robert R. McCormick, publisher of *The Chicago Tribune.*

Europeans were fond of calling pre-depression America the land of unlimited possibilities, the land of unheard-of paradoxes, and it is still that in many ways. It is the richest land in the world, the only land outside Russia which can supply every one of its inhabitants with food, clothing and shelter in abundance, and it leads the world today in unemployment and misery.

It is also the land in which the publisher of a newspaper that violates all the canons of journalism is the Lord Protector of the Freedom of the Press. Sincerity, Truthfulness, Accuracy, Impartiality, Fair Play—these canons never thunder on the *Tribune.*

When Roosevelt was nominated for a second term, Colonel McCormick wrote to his excellent managing editor, E. S. Beck, a letter which *Editor & Publisher,* applauding, quoted under the heading:

COL. McCORMICK ORDERS STRICT IMPARTIALITY DURING CAMPAIGN

The letter was posted for all to read. It demanded "complete unbiased reports with an effort toward equal coverage subject to news value." But the letter also states that Roosevelt in his first term "tried to control the (Washington) correspondents" and it concludes with the remark that "there will be so much Roosevelt news created by his commissars that it will be necessary to see that Landon gets a fair share of that total. But the Roosevelt stories must be adequate and must be written without any animus against him."

What followed is pretty well known to everyone. Every day the *Tribune* editorial page was a biased attack on Roosevelt with the heading "Turn the Rascals Out"; every day the *Tribune* telephone operators said "Good morning. *Chicago Tribune*. There're only forty-three (or less) days left in which to save the American way of life." Every day truthfulness, accuracy, impartiality, fair play and decency were flouted in the most vicious campaign against the President.

On October 24, 1936 *Editor & Publisher* (which by the way draws a considerable amount of its revenue from *Chicago Tribune* advertising) courageously enough reported that the *Chicago Daily Times* had published the story of how the *Tribune* had faked a photograph and a news item in its attempt to hurt Roosevelt.

The President had visited Chicago. He had ridden through the streets, and he had spoken. But the *Tribune,* whose publisher is the spokesman for the freedom of the press, found that the public was not as enthusiastic as some imagined. It published a picture of a street filled with Roosevelt buttons apparently discarded by hundreds of persons to show their antagonism to the President. The caption read:

Roosevelt buttons intended for coat lapels land on ground.
A rag picker helping himself to Roosevelt buttons on a street
near the Loop yesterday. Apparently the buttons were tossed
aside by pedestrians to whom they were handed by women
members of Young Democrats of Cook County, who made wholesale distribution. (*Tribune* photo) (Story on page 18).

The rag picker shown in the *Tribune* photograph is
Charles Pelik. Charles Pelik has made a signed statement to
the effect that he was paid twenty-five cents to act in this
photograph. A witness has corroborated the story. The
Chicago Daily Times in addition published the statement
that the buttons were strewn about by the *Tribune* photog-
rapher for the purpose of producing a fake. But when
Editor & Publisher * asked Colonel McCormick for a statement all it was told is that *Tribune* photographs are always
authentic, nothing more.

Toward the end of the campaign President Roosevelt's
name did not figure in the news for days on end. Everyone
knows that the campaign was one of the filthiest in American
history, but few outside Chicago know how much responsibility for making it so lies with the *Tribune*.

On the day following the 1936 elections even Mr. Hearst
tried to make amends and cover up his stupidity, but the
Tribune was unrepentant. It began the campaign which it
now continues against every liberal and progressive measure
which the administration has proposed. Wrote William T.
Evjue, editor of *The Progressive:*† "The *Chicago Tribune*
is once more conducting a campaign against the Roosevelt
administration which for viciousness was only exceeded by
its memorable attempt to defeat Roosevelt for President. The
Tribune, which always hypocritically poses as the great defender of the highest standards of journalism, is now resort-
ing to practices which violate every standard of decent

---

* October 24, 1936.
† *The Progressive,* July 3, 1937.

journalism. . . . The *Chicago Tribune* is the most vicious and unscrupulous newspaper in the United States today."

Under the Medill Trust Colonel McCormick and Joseph Medill Patterson have become equal millionaires, and have increased their millions through their successful conduct of the *Tribune* and the *New York Daily News*. Three or four million dollars net profit a year has been a recent average; in 1933, when most newspapers were pretty deep in the red, Chicago reported $2,900,000 and New York (with the feature syndicate's profits included) $3,800,000 net; in boom years the profit has been $10,000,000.

McCormick and Patterson are so rich they could afford to provide America with two great newspapers equal and perhaps surpassing the *Manchester Guardian*. Patterson in fact does have a sort of social conscience, he is evidently a man of good will, and without having a Messianic complex he has a desire to help his fellow men. On the other hand in a period of ten years I have never heard McCormick express any concern for any one, and no actions of his newspaper have betrayed either a social conscience or even a social understanding.

There are of course the *Tribune* crusades.

A Safe and Sane Fourth of July. Lower taxation. Modified spelling reform. Big Bill Thompson. To bring the horse back to the farm. Americanism. Freedom of the Press. The Chicago School Board. The *Tribune* has conducted campaigns which have made the people of Chicago believe it is their great, fearless defender, devoted entirely to the common good. But as the *Tribune* has grown richer and richer the crusades have grown weaker and weaker: they no longer ever endanger a dollar of advertising money or any other profit.

The *Tribune*'s fight against the school board was always cloaked in altruistic verbiage. The board at one time included Jane Addams, Louis F. Post and Raymond Robbins, three persons whose integrity could never be questioned, but the *Tribune* for years continued its guttersniping journalism against them. It claimed it was doing a public service. But the few who knew the facts believe that the entire crusade was caused by the *Tribune's* disinclination to pay what the board thought a fair price for the land on which the *Tribune* downtown building stood.

The *Tribune* crusade against Senator Black becoming a Supreme Court Justice was said to be in the public interest. The public of course does not know that Black had previously attacked the *Tribune*. Here is the *Congressional Record* report. Senator Wheeler had just explained how subsidizers of the Liberty League made contributions in the form of loans so that the losses could be written off the income tax returns. Senator Black then said:

"Of course it is necessary to invent many new methods. The *Chicago Tribune* several weeks ago were required to pay back some three or four hundred thousand dollars by reason of the fact that they had had some kind of a corporation, and they had manipulated and managed it around until they thought they were not obliged to pay. . . . Perhaps they thought they could keep on doing that until there would be some administration which would not make them pay it back.

"Mr. Wheeler: The Senator does not intimate that the *Chicago Tribune* would do anything illegal?

"Mr. Black: On February 12 (1936) that was published in a press dispatch. Of course, I would not intimate that. But it was indicated—not only indicated but it was true—that they had been forced to pay this income tax by reason of the fact that the scheme and device which had been arranged had been stricken down by the Board of Tax Appeals."

The public reads the *Tribune's* attacks on Secretary Ickes and perhaps gets the notion that the paper is brave and unbiased, but it cannot know, because the *Tribune* has suppressed most of the story, that Ickes, who once was employed by the *Tribune,* has bitterly attacked it. Ickes, at North-western University, declared that he suspected Colonel Mc-Cormick of "suffering from political frustration," and added:

"I assert the fact to be that the *Chicago Tribune,* in giving expression to the envy and malice that poisons the mind of its publisher, has slandered the President of the United States; that it has deliberately made misstatements of fact with respect to his acts and purposes. Its news has been colored by insinuations, innuendoes and falsehoods.

"It is interesting to note that Colonel McCormick is now content to sit at the feet of his rival publisher, William Randolph Hearst, and eagerly pick up whatever journalistic crumbs may fall from that gentleman's table. The *Tribune* is erupting Hearstian front-page editorials. Every one of these ponderous and pontifical pronouncements that I have read has been based upon a false premise or has drawn a false conclusion.

"Colonel McCormick published a front-page editorial on October 11th, which sought to create the impression that Mr. Roosevelt and other members of his administration are 'allies' of the Communist party. This bogey-man with which to frighten the moronic mind was first raised by Mr. Hearst, so that here also we find Colonel McCormick sneezing when William Randolph takes snuff.

"In making this statement about President Roosevelt, I charge Colonel McCormick with insinuating what he knows to be false."

Of course it is safe and sane to campaign for a Safe and Sane Fourth of July, and there the *Tribune* was successful. The campaign to bring the horse back to the farm is a whim of the horse-loving Colonel, and although the McCormick cousins who manufacture farm tractors and the various automobile makers did not like it very much, there was no advertising boycott of the *Tribune.* In fact all *Tribune* crusades ever since McCormick took sole charge of the paper, in 1925, have not endangered a penny of profit although they may have sounded magnificently defiant to the Chicago public.

It is extremely difficult to come to a conclusion on the motivation of the McCormick *Tribune*. Although the Colonel may be politically frustrated, it cannot be said he suffers one of the Roy Howard, Paul Block, Hearst and Northcliffe complexes; he is too shy of contact with human beings and too arrogant in his dislike of the people ever to think of becoming a public figure, nor does he enjoy secret manipulation of political events. Power, money, fame, egotism, do not seem to be the Colonel's motives in making his newspaper what it is, and revenge may be the reason for the personal feuds with certain notable men. The *Tribune* used to advertise that it "is not a philanthropic institution. Nor is it a religious or a political institution. It is a commercial institution," and the Colonel himself has said that "there is venality in almost everyone's life," but both statements also fail to explain the *Tribune* completely.

The matter is perhaps one a psychologist should investigate; but the fact that confronts the Illinois public is that it must get its morning news from either the unspeakable Hearst or "from that unspeakable *Chicago Tribune* that even the newspapers themselves condemn," as it was recently referred to in the *Congressional Record*.

CHAPTER 4

Little Lord Northcliffe

PAUL BLOCK is a little man with a big complex.

Like Northcliffe, Hearst, and numerous others, some in high positions of sane respect, others in forgotten hoosegows, Paul Block has a nicely polished Napoleonic egotism.

This ego runs to things big. He cannot sleep in a little room, he cannot ride in an ordinary sleeper, or in a small automobile. When he stops over in a city he rents a suite of three to seven rooms for himself alone, he has his own private coach to attach to regular trains, and his automobile is the biggest made.

Paul Block, like his numerous colleagues, loves publicity. He loves his picture in the paper, loves to see his name in print, loves to read about himself, and when no one puts his picture in the papers, and no one writes about him, he buys space in papers throughout the country, and publishes his editorials broadcast, with his signature in nice big letters, the most readable part of the advertisements.

He also insists in basking in the flashlight. He is always present when the photographers let go their bombs, and if he is not the object of their bombing, he must be second high man.

On the occasion when Hoover, as President, paid a visit to Newark, Mr. Block in his easy neo-Napoleonic way, called up his city editor and said "Get me into the President's car for the parade tomorrow afternoon." But neither the city editor nor anyone else could get Paul Block into the Hoover car, and yet no one dared defy the pre-Waterloo dictator in the main office.

So someone brilliantly called up the police department and told the man covering main headquarters, an old-timer who had heart trouble and who never so much as walked up the stairs, to see to it that Paul Block got into the parade, and into Hoover's big car.

The reporter told the captain, and the captain detailed five men.

At exactly the moment when the parade reached the Newark building, the reporter shouted "Make way for Paul Block—Make way for Paul Block" and five policemen, with Block in the center of a flying wedge, broke through the crowds on the street.

As they rushed the Presidential car, at the head of the procession, the United States Secret Service operatives for a moment thought it a plot to assassinate the chief executive. Even the blue police uniforms did not disarm them.

"Make way for Paul Block," shouted the reporter.

The wedge got to the Hoover car. But Hoover would not stop.

For a second the wedge, with Block in the center, remained in the middle of the street.

Headed by Deputy Chief of Police John Harris, it finally broke through the crowd and got to the President's automobile, the Block police reporter still shouting, "Make way for Paul Block," but the police found the car full of notable persons. No one knew who Paul Block was. The police officer in charge of the safety of the President, Lieutenant William F. Gannon, of the Newark force, however, was impressed with the publisher's name, and Harris of course was doing his best to get Block into the car. But since this was physically impossible, it was decided that someone would have to be put out. The man chosen to be the sacrifice was Senator Joseph Frelinghuysen, of New Jersey, whom Hoover himself had chosen to ride with him. Frelinghuysen was put out; Block was pushed into his seat, and the procession moved on.

This is not the first instance in which Paul Block got what he went after. Every reporter who has worked around the country knows many towns in which there are these little press lords who exercise their authority in this fashion. As a rule they cause more laughter than harm.

Paul Block is the only publisher in America closely associated with William Randolph Hearst. In 1936 the *New York Post* called him a Hearst stooge, which he let pass, but in 1938, during the excitement over the appointment of Senator Black to the Supreme Court when Robert S. Allen wrote that "the expose of Justice Hugo Black's one-time membership in the Ku Klux Klan was a deliberate conspiracy. . . . Parties to the conspiracy were the Hearst stooge Paul Block" and others, Block sued Allen and the *Nation* for $900,000 libel damages.

Block and Hearst have engaged in numerous newspaper deals. *Time* claimed (April 4, 1938) that "partly with Hearst money, Mr. Block acquired nine substantial dailies by 1931," and for many years before becoming a publisher Paul Block Associates handled Hearst advertising. In 1927 Block and Hearst invaded Pittsburgh and the result was a slaughter of the press. In recent times the *Leader* and *Dispatch* had already been destroyed as rivals, and now Block bought the *Post* and *Sun* from the trustee of the late president of the Farmers National Bank and Hearst bought the *Gazette-Times* and *Chronicle-Telegraph,* two previously amalgamated newspapers owned by the Oliver family, which was associated with the steel industry and the Senate. The *Post-Gazette* became the unique Pittsburgh morning newspaper, and the *Sun-Telegraph* became the unique rival for the Scripps-Howard *Press* in the evening.

In 1937 another Block-Hearst deal took place, which *Editor & Publisher* reported involving more than $2,500,000 with Block obtaining complete control of the *Post-Gazette* and Hearst regaining possession of the *Milwaukee Sentinel* which he merged with his *Wisconsin News.*

Editor & Publisher (September 18, 1937) quoted Block saying that Hearst "helped finance" his purchase of the *Pittsburgh Post* and *Sun* ten years earlier, and that "when the Pittsburgh deal was consummated Mr. Hearst retained a 'considerable amount of stock' in the *Post-Gazette* on which Block had an option."

In 1931 Hearst announced that the *Los Angeles Express* would be merged with his *Evening Herald,* to be known as the *Evening Herald & Express.* He said "It was I who prevailed upon Mr. Block to enter the Los Angeles newspaper field. . . . As a competitor of mine in other cities I had learned to admire and esteem him highly. We are also pleased to announce that Mr. Block will become a director of the *Herald & Express.*"

In the following year Mr. Block's name came up in the case of the Mayor of New York, when testimony was given that the two had a joint stock exchange account. The *New York Evening Post* * reported the case as follows:

"Paul Block, newspaper publisher and intimate of Mayor Walker, prefers to wait until he is called by Samuel Seabury, chief counsel of the Hofstadter Investigation Committee before making an explanation of the joint account which he and Mayor Walker shared from February, 1927, to August, 1929, and from which the Mayor cleared $246,692.76 without the investment of a cent on his own part, as the Mayor testified before the committee yesterday."

The paper quoted a "person in a position to speak with authority" to the effect that Block received no favors in return, and added:

"Mr. Block feels, it was said, there is no reason in law or ethics why he cannot give earnings in cash or stocks to whomever he pleases. . . .

* May 7, 1932.

"Mr. Block was associated with State Senator John A. Hastings in a chemical company which planned to produce a tile for use in subway stations. . . ."

In the 1936 campaign Block was almost as partisan as Hearst in his defense of Landon despite the fact that the Republican candidate for President administered probably the worst snub ever given this "squat, sallow, bald little Punch," as *Time* called him, when he refused to let Block hitch his private car on the Landon special train. Nevertheless about seven weeks before election day Mr. Block let the Hearst *American* publish a scoop interview in which he said: "I have never felt more certain of anything in my life than the defeat of President Roosevelt. By mid-October people will wonder why they ever had any doubt about it.

"Roosevelt will be defeated by two things—high taxes and increased cost of living. Every workingman is now being taxed annually $200 in indirect taxes."

Block, like all publishers, is supposed to know what the people think and want.

He once wrote to Arthur Elliot Sproul who asked for his autobiography, that his hobbies were "newspapers and friendships." He said he had never started a newspaper. "I have another ambition which I probably will never fulfil, mostly because I cannot afford it, and probably am not capable of it, namely to *start* the publication of a newspaper. The reason for this is because I have bought a newspaper which was in a receiver's hands and have been lucky enough to build it up so it is successful. I have consolidated papers. . . . I have bought newspapers. . . . However, I have never started a newspaper. That would be a great thrill, if it would not break me. However, as already mentioned, I probably will never do it.

"I like progressive newspapers, but not sensational ones. I would not know how to publish the latter kind. However, for that matter, there are lots of things I do not know."

The modesty is false. Mr. Block thinks very well of himself. And while it is true that he has never started a newspaper, it is also true that he has killed off many.

His original business was advertising. Advertising is either the first or one of the first enemies of a free press. The transformation of a big advertising man into publisher has been no credit to the free press. But to his credit it must be said that Block has never made his sheets as bad as Hearst's.

CHAPTER 5

California Press and Landlord

THE story of Harry Chandler's rise to fame and fortune is usually told in the Horatio Alger manner, with the heavily emphasized moral that America is still the land of golden opportunity, and if one combines brain work and leg work it is still possible to become a millionaire—and in this case, a press lord.

The success story in brief is that of a New Hampshire Yankee lad who had to quit Dartmouth on account of his health. He went West in the days the West still called. Eventually he became a "circulation hustler" for a Los Angeles newspaper, came to the notice of Colonel Harrison Gray Otis who owned the *Los Angeles Times*, became general manager of the paper, married the boss's daughter, inherited the *Times*, the ranches, the Mexican acres, the millions, and the policies.

In those days circulation routes were bought and sold, and with his first money Chandler acquired a *Times* route with 1,400 names and supervised the delivery of papers. With the approval of this newspaper he later acquired the circulation route of the *Herald*, and also of the *Express*.

There came a quarrel between Otis and his partner, H. H. Boyce, who then started the *Morning Tribune* as a rival, and began to cut down on the income of the *Times*. And then it was that Chandler made the plan by which he became famous. As he himself boasts:

"I went to General Otis and told him the situation. He said I couldn't do it. I told him I could and not only that but for the *Times'* sake I should. My scheme was to starve out the *Tribune*. With two of the three morning papers' distribution systems under my control, it would be simple to play them together against the *Tribune*. If a *Times* subscriber quit we could swing him to the *Herald,* whereas he might have gone to the *Tribune* if left alone. If a *Herald* subscriber quit we could swing him to the *Times*. Of course, no one but General Otis would know of my connection. The *Herald* routes were to be handled through a dummy."

The scheme, which is legal and shrewd and supposedly good business, succeeded in two years in crowding out the *Tribune*. Boyce never knew what ruined him. When he was forced to sell out, he got no more than five cents on the dollar. Colonel Otis had tried to buy the defunct rival, but someone under an assumed name had succeeded in getting in on the ground floor. Otis was discussing the matter with Chandler, when Chandler admitted it was he who was now the owner of the *Tribune*. After that it was natural that Otis made Chandler his manager and finally his successor.

Harry Chandler continued Otis' policy of attacking labor, his antagonism to the Mexican republic, his general obscurantism. Otis made a policy of perverting the news concerning labor. He published every item which could be twisted and colored to misrepresent the trades unions and all movements by working people throughout the world which aimed at a better life for themselves and their children. Otis, of course, had a reason for his mad hatred. His paper had been bombed in the midst of a labor war. But Chandler continued the policy of labor-baiting, and also Otis' antagonism to the Mexican republic, and in fact all of Otis' reactionary and obscurantist ideas. And yet, according to *Editor & Publisher*, "The Chandlers, a visitor at the *Times* plant learns, are 'fine people with old time ideas.' "

Humanitarians, from time immemorial, have dreamed of the emancipation of men and women from the drudgery of daily work. The machine and power age of today has made that possible. With the ultimate development of machinery and the elimination of profits for a few owners, it will be possible to provide all the food, shelter, clothing and even luxuries for the entire American population, with the reduction of the working week to ten or less hours. At the present moment there are 13,000,000 persons who have not the opportunity to work even one hour a day; under the ideal system everyone will work only a few hours, and all will have economic security and leisure for physical and mental improvement. But so reactionary is the *Los Angeles Times* editorial mind that even a shortening of working hours is disapproved.

"The inevitable result of too much spare time in the case of at least the majority of the workers," the *Times* editorializes, "would be to steer them into the only diversions they know—pool, poker, drinking and petty agitation over fancied grievance. . . . It would be a tragedy to wreck the whole economic program for a few hours more 'leisure hours'— that nobody would know what to do with."

Evidently *Los Angeles Times* editors have never done a day's physical labor in their lives.

Being the enemy of labor, Harry Chandler has been the enemy of the Newspaper Guild since it began as an A. F. of L. affiliate, and more intensely since it joined the C. I. O. On September 22, 1935, the *Los Angeles Times* published from Portland, Oregon, a news story which is notable for its misstatements regarding the Guild. Most newspapers make at least a pretense of confining their unfair reporting, misstatements, and anti-labor bias to the editorial page. The *Times* states in its news columns that "Seattle radical organizers are at work here. The Newspaper Guild, one of whose purposes is to control news of radical activities by 'advising' editors, has about twenty members in one office." The news item boasts that recent Portland strikes have been "promptly

nipped in the bud . . ." and hints that "should the provocation be sufficient" the governor was anxious to see "just
how good the National Guard is."

So violent did Chandler become in his tirades against
Seattle labor dominated by Dave Beck that he painted a
picture of the city going to rats and ruin. This was too much
for Hearst's *Post-Intelligencer* where the Guild strike was on.
Publisher John Boettiger, defending Seattle, accused Chandler of being "grossly unfair and misleading" and "hitting
below the belt." The criticism is significant in that it comes
from a Hearst paper.

At Christmas time, 1937, the clerks of the May Department Store who had been trying to get more than thirty cents
an hour and some improvement in working conditions—
without of course the support of the press—thought it oppor-
tune to go on strike. The Los Angeles papers, led by the
Times, headlined this demand for better wages as "Assassination of Santa Claus" and "Murder of the Spirit of Christmas."
The liberal *News* participated in this anti-union campaign.
All these newspapers were carrying a full page of May Department Store advertising at the time. Naturally enough a
few newspapermen thought there was a financial connection
between back-page ads, editorial support and front-page
hysterics.

Old man Otis had 650,000 acres of land in North Mexico
which he got from Diaz, the dictator, at the time Diaz was
pocketing the money and literally and figuratively selling
out his country. When Diaz was overthrown Otis couldn't
get his cattle out in time. He immediately began a campaign
for the annexation of Northern Mexico. Failing in that, he
favored the formation of an independent North Mexican
Republic, a buffer state, in which his cattle lands would be
safe from the Carranza reforms. And Chandler consistently
has carried on a campaign against the Mexican Republic.
Upton Sinclair has told the story of how Chandler was once
indicted, charged with conspiracy to ship arms into Mexico,

and how he was acquitted. Chandler remains one of the largest landowners in Mexico and California. According to the conservative weekly *Time* (July 15, 1935) Chandler has proved himself "an inspired capitalist." In 1899 he "launched a syndicate which bought up 862,000 acres in Lower California. He and his associates built Hollywood, founded a vast agricultural colony at Calexico which produced $18,-000,000 worth of cotton in 1919. He owns a 281,000-acre ranch in Los Angeles and Kern Counties stocked with fine cattle, a 340,000-acre hunting preserve in Colorado, an interest in another 500,000-acre sporting preserve in New Mexico, is officer or director in thirty-five California corporations, including oil, shipping, banking. The whisper, 'Chandler's in it,' signifies a good thing to most California businessmen."

Throughout the valleys where Chandler and his associates own and control California crops there is terrorism and the nearest approach to Fascism in the United States (outside the Hague Domain in New Jersey). There is child labor and even peonage. There is starvation in the midst of plenty. There is vigilantism, tarring and feathering, bloodshed and violence. There is also big money for the Chandler crowd.

No one has ever heard Chandler say anything which could be interpreted even vaguely as humanitarian, altruistic, liberal or progressively intelligent. But there must be something in him outside the shrewd Yankee trader who slyly put a rival out of business so he could buy the ruins at five cents on the dollar and become a big shot. If you ask *Los Angeles Times* employees about the boss they answer that last Christmas he distributed a bonus of $197,000 among them. Somehow the question of money and human dignity get badly mixed up in Los Angeles.

CHAPTER 6

Lord Howard and His Empire

THE repudiation of the Hearst press, now general, is the climax of decades of criticism and doubt; the attack with rotten eggs, stones and curses against the *Chicago Tribune* and other reactionary Chicago papers on election night was a sudden outbreak of long repressed mass disillusionment and indignation. These facts indicate that the American people are following Europeans in realizing that the press is a powerful force affecting their lives, and that frequently it is an inimical force.

The time has not yet come when the enlightened, liberal and progressive American public will be ready to throw stones at the windows of the Scripps-Howard newspapers, call Howard the names they called Colonel McCormick, and boycott his merchandise—but the time surely has come when all of us who are interested in a free press—and not the publishers' association commercial idea of freedom of the press—should no longer fool ourselves by counting among the liberal and progressive forces in America the entire Howard outfit: the twenty-four papers, the United Press, the N. E. A. feature syndicate, the radio stations, forming what President Coolidge called "a world power, influential beyond the dreams of any of its founders."

To all these enterprises the time apparently has come for liberal-minded men to say hail and farewell. Individual newspapers, especially those in the more progressive Middle West and Far West, seem to follow the old Scripps ideal, but the management itself has gone conservative.

When Edward Wyllis Scripps founded the *Penny Press* (now the *Cleveland Press*) in 1879 he had to borrow the money. Today the empire Howard controls is worth about $100,000,000 (of which $28,000,000 is real estate) plus another $10,000,000 for good will. About a third of this empire was built up by Scripps who became a multimillionaire without ever losing his integrity. He realized from the first day that it was almost impossible to have a free press unless advertising was practically eliminated. He wrote Lincoln Steffens he intended to prove it was possible "that the people can have a free press, not only without having it subsidized or endowed, but a free press that will not only support but magnificently reward those who conduct its various units." Steffens found him sincere and not cynical. Steffens said that Scripps "avoided other rich men so as to escape being one; he knew the danger his riches carried for himself, for his papers and for his seeing." Throughout his lifetime Scripps stuck to his ideals, which were: public service, positive justice as between man and man as men, the promotion of the equality of opportunity, the putting into the homes of workers who had little time to read of honest, fearless thought in clean and concise form, impartiality incorruptible by social, political or financial influence, and the square deal all round without fear or favor.

United Press men for a generation said Scripps endowed the newspaper institution with a soul. They spoke of the Unipress soul without blushing.

The "soul" of this empire died in 1926.

Robert Paine Scripps, the frustrated, sensitive son of the founder, became the largest stockholder and apparently the inheritor of the liberal tradition. He said of the Scripps-Howard chain of newspapers: "The dictionary definition that appeals to me as applying to the kind of newspapers that my associates and I are trying to produce runs this way: 'Befitting or worthy of a man of free birth; free, not servile or mean; not narrow or contracted in view; broadminded, free from bigotry; not bound by orthodox forms in political or religious philosophy.' I would add economic to political and religious, so as to embrace all of the principal phases of life in this developing society of ours."

In Bob Scripps the liberal spirit, if not the "soul" of liberalism, flickered intermittently for a little while. None doubted Bob's sincerity but all realized that the other partner, Roy Wilson Howard, who in 1912 had become head of the United Press and in 1922 made a partner in the Scripps empire, was now its dominating leader and would-be dictator.

This is the same Roy Howard who told the Chamber of Commerce of Denver on the occasion of a banquet given him to honor the establishment of a Scripps-Howard newspaper that "We are coming to Denver neither with a tin cup nor a lead pipe. We will live with and in this community and not on or off it. We are nobody's big brother, wayward sister or poor relation. We come here simply as news merchants. We are here to sell advertising and sell it at a rate profitable to those who buy it. But first we must produce a newspaper with news appeal that will result in a circulation and to make that advertising effective. We shall run no lottery."

Here in the statements of intentions we have a pretty fair history of the rise and fall of the Scripps-Howard press. The elder Scripps twice tried ad-less newspapers because he knew that no free press can ever exist which owes a first allegiance to business; he supported labor unions in general and raised money for picketers, and he was not afraid to dedicate his press to the workingmen. The younger Scripps lived in the shadow of his fatal illness but he wanted a press befitting a nation of free men. And the present head of all the newspapers, news services, radio stations and other means of manufacturing public opinion in America, says "We are here to sell advertising."

That all-revealing statement was made more than a decade

ago. Then, as Silas Bent reported, Scripps-Howard men were "fighting editors," and "these papers not only fight on their own account but put their strength joyfully behind other fighters." Even today we hear of Ohio and other journals carrying on a crusade against corrupt politics or for a better economic world, but with the disappearance of the Scripps family from the directorate as well as the Scripps "soul," the fighting spirit is also disappearing, and many "crusades" recently engaged in become open to a search for a financial or political personal advantage as vital cause. No such doubts clouded the Scripps era.

The Grim Reaper has played the rôle of Santa Claus for Roy Howard. He has delivered him a new journalistic empire unspoiled by traditional journalistic idealism.

Free at last from the Scripps bonds, from the utopian idea of a newspaper defying advertising and business, Roy Howard has begun to follow Hearst in Red-baiting and labor-baiting. He has begun the suppression of his highly paid columnists, has altered their views, and he has gradually changed the policies of his papers from liberal to phony-liberal and eventually to a more honest anti-liberalism. He has done so at a critical time in our history when everyone with a minimum of intelligence, not only writers, is taking sides, and when it is easier to see the right side on which there is always butter, than the left, which is not only un-buttered but perhaps not enough to sustain existence. People take sides, and in the process a large number change view-points, so that it is fast becoming impossible to see the liter-ary and journalistic woods because of the thousands of lost leaders hiding among the renegade trees.

But in the case of Roy Howard no Browning can sing of his leaving us just for a handful of silver or for a riband to stick in his coat. Money and power, as shall be explained later, are the dominating motives in this man's existence, but it is not a matter of thirty pieces or, in fact, lost leader-ship. Roy Howard, the Scripps partner, as a leader of liberal thought and progressive politics in America, is and has been an accepted myth. Had he been that it would be easy to say he sold out, he abandoned his followers, he betrayed the usual newspaper slogan of Truth, Honesty, Public Service, the Welfare of the Common People.

But Roy Howard cannot be accused because he has never belonged to the Scripps movement with which he has always been associated and to which his only relationship was journalistic marriage. It is the public which made the mistake of confounding a marriage of convenience with a union of liberal minds. The Scripps-Howard "outfit" did have an ideal, a program which it respected, and a crusading spirit, but no one can accuse Roy Howard of giving more than a Bronx cheer sort of adherence to it during the Scripps lifetime. The Scripps "soul" and the Howard police reporter's soul co-existed for decades without influencing each other.

From his youth Howard devoted himself to making money and gaining power. Only so long as the old Scripps brand of liberalism paid, did he stick to it. After all, every newspaper and every affiliated enterprise which Scripps dedicated to "the common people" had paid six percent per annum or more and there was no reason to change the policy.

Not for a long time.

The change, which is now obvious, did not come, as many, including Howard employees, believe, with his opposition to the Roosevelt administration reforms, the NRA, the ill-fated (and hypocritical) publishers' code, the NLRB, the Wagner Act and other social-economic developments which directly affected the pocketbooks of publishers and drove them in a raging stampede against the New Deal. Actually the change came ten years earlier and was the result of the campaign of the elder La Follette for the Presidency.

The Scripps-Howard editors were for Robert La Follette in 1924. Their selection was natural, in harmony with Scripps family liberalism, but Howard went along reluctantly. No one expected La Follette to win, but it was a good

fight. The Scripps-Howard press had to its credit a fine showing in all its towns and a real victory in Cleveland where the
Press, the largest and most powerful of the journals—until
the formation of the *World-Telegram*—carried the city for
the Progressives.

The shouts and editorials of triumph made Scripps-
Howard men feel good—all but Mr. Howard. He was not
looking at the election returns, he was looking at the box
office. Business, advertisers (the supporters of the Republican
and Democratic parties) had attacked the chain in its vulner-
able spot, the till, and the *Cleveland Press* had lost a tremendous number of advertisements and a lot of money.

Howard learned in 1924 that it does not pay, in dollars
and cents, to be liberal. He learned then what all publishers
know now, that there is little money in the liberal center,
no money whatever in the liberal left, boycott and blackmail
for the radical left, and that the big money is on the right, in
the conservative, tory, and finally in the Fascist right. It
took Howard a longer time than most newspaper publishers
to find this out because up to then he had seen Scripps making millions under the banner of liberalism.

Scripps-Howard editors are supposed to have the right to
vote on their choice for President, and in 1928 the majority
declared themselves liberally on the side of Al Smith, but
Howard was for Hoover, and it did not take much maneu-
vering to bring the editors into line with the boss. The chain
supported Hoover. Four years later it would have been
suicidal to renew the support and Howard very wisely went
over to Roosevelt, to whom he remained faithful until
Rooseveltian legislation, alienating the affection of most big
business, made an enemy of between seventy and eighty-five
percent of the press in 1936 and at least ten percent more in
1938. In the final ten percent the most powerful element was
Howard's twenty-four newspapers.

And now it must be noted that Roy Howard has also been
playing a behind-the-scenes rôle in American politics. Up

to the time of the war, and for some years after it, he had been content with being a newspaperman. He still considers himself a "working reporter" and would not hesitate to cover a fire if he found himself exclusively present. But Howard is also one of many newspaper editors and publishers who suffers from the Northcliffe complex.

Northcliffe himself suffered from Napoleonic delusions and went entirely insane. Let me digress for a moment to say that while sane he wrote enthusiastic recommendations for a journalistic union, and after he went crazy he wrote violent attacks on the union, which the anti-Newspaper Guild forces, including *Editor & Publisher,* are quoting to-day, apparently not knowing the later quotations are the ravings of a man about to die. Northcliffe, the Napoleonic publisher, wanted to rule Britain, and the greatest disappointment of his life was not being named prime minister in wartime. But the Northcliffe phase which American editors copy is the make-or-break power behind the scenes, the rôle Northcliffe always excelled in and boasted most about, and whose chief hero and victim was Lord Kitchener.

Like Northcliffe, in the anonymous phase, Howard also is trying to make himself and his press so powerful that he can name Presidents and plot the course of administrations, with no one but his mirror to applaud him. He had tried, in 1932, to name as Democratic candidate for President his own company's attorney, Newton D. Baker, which would have allied him with the Wall Street movement to stop Roosevelt, and with Tammany, and a year later he was attacking Tammany in his support of La Guardia. *This was pure opportunism.*

However, it is more and more in the field of labor that Roy Howard pursues his Northcliffian—if not Hearstian—way. He is no longer content with publishing newspapers—and everyone knows that one of the greatest powers in the world lies in the hands of those men who have the right to pick and choose even truthful news—but he must play a part in pulling strings and shaping events, invisible like all gods. National politics was fun, fed the ego, and held out hope of profit, but ever since the labor movement began to open its political eyes, and especially from the day labor became a financial issue in editorial offices, Howard has been a maker as well as a teller of the news.

He instigated, for example, the blast against the Screen Writers' Guild which Rupert Hughes signed in May, 1936. Hollywood *Variety* takes the credit for this exposure of hidden activities and secret diplomacy which now characterize Howard methods. The Hughes pronunciamento is not only stale today, but its stupidity proven by passing time. What is important is the fact that Howard not only ordered it but suggested its tenor. He had telegraphed a request for 500 to 1000 words from Hughes stating that "Only about twenty-five words printed here — your statement — Screen Guild's closed shop policy would create writers' Soviet . . . this attempt hogtie and standardize creative writing." He likens the Screen Writers with the Newspaper Guild saying "net effect" of their success "would be Guild dictatorship of American press on parity with Communist, Fascist or Nazi unilateral press dictatorship abroad. Difference be here Guild would dictate policies owners retain responsibility and foot bills. . . . Would like you incidentally point out menace to democratic institutions of attempting limit editorial expression to proponents of any one school of political or economic thought."

When Hughes obliged, Howard repaid him by a telegram of thanks which concluded: "Am asking the press associations to watch your efforts tonight which I think are of vital importance to real liberty of the writing craft and honest to God freedom of expression." Hughes got the headlines, but the Screen Guild got a raw deal, and this seems to be part of the publishers' idea of "honest to God freedom."

The episode cannot be dismissed as picayune: it illuminates in fact the entire new economic and political policy of

Roy Howard, the triple policy of attacking labor, of manufacturing news, and of working the *deus ex machina* racket.

The four-year-war which Howard has waged against the
Newspaper Guild is likewise no intramural affair, but part
of the general policy.

When the Guild was started it was the natural expectation
of all concerned that the Scripps-Howard outfit would be
the first to recognize it. It is true that the minimum wages
demanded would go harder with this organization than with
most others because—as I can testify from personal experience on the United Press—newspapermen were paid in three
kinds of coin, two of which were neither negotiable nor good
for taxes. These were first the privilege of working for a
liberal service and therefore escaping the old-fashioned
charge of being "servants of vested interests" or as the phrase
went up to the 1920's, "prostitutes of the press"—and second,
the "by-line." Thus Westbrook Pegler in 1917 wrote war
correspondence at a minimum wage but via his signed
stories got a good-paying job with the *Chicago Tribune,*
from which the United Press had to buy him back at an
enormous salary. But we thought highly of Scripps-Howard
then because it did not suppress the news, or pervert the
news, and we frequently refused better money from reactionary papers.

The Guild minimums were not excessive; the Guild program seemed to be just the thing for the Scripps-Howard
outfit to make its own. But 1934 ended without any results
and February, 1935, began three years of shadow-boxing,
stalling, and straddling for which Roy Howard alone is
blamed. Hearst is considered a straight-forward, square-deal-
ing, pleasant, liberal-minded, fair dealer compared to the
evasive Howard.

So far as New York is concerned, the situation was dramat-
ically exposed in mid-summer 1935 when the *Post,* announcing its complete recognition of the Guild, published an
editorial openly suspecting the *World-Telegram* of hypocrisy

in its fight to change the Wagner Labor Bill and its attitude toward the newspapermen's organization. This editorial gave notice that the *Post* was willing to take the place of the *World-Telegram* as the one liberal newspaper of the metropolis, and that the wheel-horse of Scripps-Howard liberalism was decidedly on the opposite road.

A year later Howard was still issuing statements and making charges which the *New Republic* showed were nothing but straw men and inventions, and it exposed the fact that Howard had circulated his fellow publishers with these unfair diatribes. Hearst had used them as a warning to his employees given by a "liberal." Howard's idea was to bargain with his own men; in other words, he favored the company union, which labor and the liberal press then denounced and which has since been held unlawful by the Supreme Court of the United States.

(In the midst of all this headline making by Howard it may be noted that pay raises from about $2.50 to $5 a week were quietly made to United Press men without their asking for them.)

In April, 1937, the *World-Telegram* signed a contract with the Guild covering wages, hours and working conditions but omitting the preferential shop—or, as the majority of publishers inaccurately called it, the closed shop. In October, when United Press men voted 277 to 84 for joining up with the Guild, the *Guild Reporter* said the vote meant that "the publishers have failed to impress Unipressers with their falsehoods about the Guild threat to freedom of the press." From now on it was a pretty straight war of thousands of Scripps-Howard employees against Mr. Howard, and "falsehoods" is one of the mild terms now frequently heard. Ostensibly it was a conflict about the five-day week, minimum wages, lay-offs, pay-cuts, and all the other troubles which affect the hundred-million-dollar Howard empire just as they affect the two-billion-dollar Ford empire. And so we come to 1938 when the Guild by bitter experience has learned that its chief enemy is Roy Howard. And the Guild also sees the intriguing fingers of its enemy in many affairs and notably in its first metropolitan test of strength, the *Brooklyn Eagle* strike, when Jonathan Eddy, executive vice-president of the Guild, accused the big publishers of supporting the *Eagle's* Mr. Goodfellow for the purpose of breaking the unionization movement in New York. "Mr. Howard," Eddy wrote in the *Guild Reporter* (January 3, 1938) "is probably the greatest of the adepts at stirring up weaker (I refrain from saying 'weak-minded') publishers to pull his chestnuts out of the fire. . . . The picture today is one of the biggest publishers attempting to incite the smaller ones, whom they regard as suckers, into pulling the big fellows' chestnuts out of the fire as a matter of 'principle.'"

From fighting the C. I. O. Guild there is but one step to fighting the C. I. O. movement, and from there the steps become openly anti-labor, Red-baiting, reactionary and eventually Fascist. Howard has now taken several of these steps.

CHAPTER 7

The Light That Failed

EMPLOYEES of the Scripps-Howard newspapers throughout the United States were the first to realize that the Howard policy had won, that changes were being made, that the swing to reaction was definite. The public did not know much about it. There were and still are liberal and progressive editorials alternating with reactionary and obscurantist editorials, and frequently the spirit of "Lusty" Scripps pervades the news columns too.

When Howard engaged Benjamin Stolberg to write a series of articles purporting to expose the C. I. O. by charging Communist intrigue or control of the new great liberal labor movement, the organization's spokesmen replied by calling Stolberg a "poison-penman," the Communist organs labeled him "America's No. 1 literary stool-pigeon," and Robert Forsythe coined the phrase "parlor fink." Mr. Stolberg was deeply hurt and very angry, especially over the general accusation that he was a "renegade Socialist." He contends he wrote the articles to help certain C. I. O. leaders, his friends, purge the movement of the Communists in time. But that is not our concern here. Our concern is the motive of Mr. Howard. Howard advertised Stolberg as a radical who would tell the "inside story" of the C. I. O., the connotation being that he would attack, and attack he did.

Now, of course, under the American tradition every man has the right to speak and publish, although that right cannot be well exercised when it opposes a corrupt political machine such as those in Jersey City or Newark, or Fascist

87

groups such as the American Legion of Terre Haute and Tampa, and in thousands of other cases. Nevertheless Mr. Stolberg has the right to criticize and Mr. Howard the right to attack. And their critics certainly have the right to question the ethics of both. Mr. Stolberg's only possible excuse for doing these articles for Howard would be that he was unaware that Howard today is in the same class as Mr. Hearst. I cannot imagine any liberal writer doing such a series for a Hearst newspaper. It may be good business to have a literary agent sell one's output without consideration of the character of the journal which will publish it, but it is another to sell *oneself* to Mr. Hearst for the purpose of defaming a labor movement. There is an ethic of place as well as an ethic of words. If Mr. Stolberg did not realize he was being made the usual Howardian cat's-paw, and that the difference between Howard and Hearst today is frequently only in size of type, it would be nice to hear him make a public explanation.

The Stolberg series marked the emergence of Howard as one of the leaders in the anti-labor movement in America. The fitting accolade was given by Tom Girdler who was delighted to find "a radical like Benjamin Stolberg . . . pointing to the insidious Communistic influences in the C. I. O." as revealed in the Scripps-Howard press. The Girdlers and Weirs and Liberty Leaguers everywhere approved Stolberg and Howard, but there were, as expected, numerous protests and demands for retractions and correction from the unions.

How did Mr. Howard reply to the latter? Did he grant them the inviolable right of redress which is inherent in freedom of the press? Did he even make a pretense of publishing the rebuttal? The answer is, yes. He made a pretense.

In every city where one of the twenty-four Scripps-Howard papers is published there was a chance to test the code of ethics of the press. In New York City for example, Michael J. Quill, international president of the Transport Workers Union of America, informed Lee B. Wood, executive editor of the *World-Telegram* that Stolberg twisted facts and published "vicious and obvious distortions and untruths." Quill continued: "We request that you publish this letter. . . . We deem it our duty to allow an official spokesman designated by the C. I. O. to use an equal amount of space in your paper. . . . At a time when the progressive labor movement is waging a serious fight for organizational unity, economic security, industrial democracy and political liberty, its enemies are expected to produce their Girdlers, Hagues, Bergoffs and Stolbergs. . . . Your paper has chosen to share the disgrace of the Hearst press, serving as a channel for their hatred of labor and progress. If the *World-Telegram* does not make amends for the series of articles by Mr. Stolberg, it will remain condemned in the eyes and in the minds of its readers . . . as being guilty of suppressing the truth and of disseminating calumnies, lies and misstatements about the American labor movement and its most progressive leaders and institutions."

Mr. Wood (or Mr. Howard, or both) refused to give the C. I. O. the space requested. And worse than that, they printed only a part of Quill's letter, suppressing the demand for space and the paragraphs cited above.

In San Francisco Mr. Howard's *News* has always enjoyed the support of labor and with enthusiasm after the 1934 strike. When its managing editor, Frank A. Clarvoe, received the Stolberg series he cautiously prefixed the announcement that "The *San Francisco News* and other Scripps-Howard newspapers are publishing the Stolberg story of the C. I. O. as a matter of historical interest." But even that was not enough. The Stolberg articles dealing with the Pacific coast differed from the originals.

In the *World-Telegram,* for instance, Mr. Stolberg came to this conclusion about the situation on the coast:

"The resulting bitterness is incredible. It broke up the powerful Maritime Federation of the Pacific, which today is on its last legs."

Perhaps the union there is centipedal. At any rate in the *News* the Stolberg verdict of history is different. It reads:

"The resulting bitterness is incredible. It threatens to break up the powerful Maritime Federation of the Pacific." (There is no mention of last legs, not even penultimate ones.)

There are an additional score of instances in which supposed facts and stated opinions are changed or deleted in California. When Stolberg accuses Bridges of being "devious," of "playing both ends against the middle," of fighting the C. I. O., and California unions of being "up in arms against Bridges" and John L. Lewis "showing signs of regretting" the appointment of Bridges, all these references are missing in California. Obviously one of these two Howard papers is not publishing the facts, uncolored.

In Toledo, Ohio, John Brophy, national director of the C. I. O., told a huge meeting that "an erstwhile liberal chain of newspapers which has capitalized over the years on a reputation of being liberal and progressive . . . hires a renegade radical to do the dirty work of besmirching the labor movement," the labor movement must "serve notice to the newspapers which discredit labor." This speech was delivered on January 21, 1938.

It certainly was news in Toledo, but Howard's *News-Bee,* which carefully reported the meeting, suppressed all criticism of Stolberg and the Howard chain.*

Whether an Ohio speech is still news in New York is open to question. If the *World-Telegram* had never printed a line about it no professional newspaperman would have found fault. But what happened in New York was this: the *World-Telegram* did not print the news on the 22nd, the 23rd, or the 24th. But on the night of the 25th, after numerous C. I. O. and other publications had accused it of suppressing the news, the *World-Telegram* carried a few paragraphs. Here is one of them:

---

* The *Toledo News-Bee* suspended publication and the *Akron Times-Press* was sold in August, 1938.

Brophy's Speech:

"These papers claim to be liberal. But when the test comes, they capitulate to the doctrines of Hearst. They become anti-labor and anti-liberal. Well, we are finding out who are our enemies."

World-Telegram:

"He did not mention the Scripps-Howard newspapers by name, but described the group as 'an erstwhile liberal chain' which has now 'accepted the doctrines of Hearst' and said 'we are now finding out who are our friends.'"

Friends, or enemies?

In Akron the Industrial Union Council went on record "condemning the recent series of articles by Benjamin Stolberg in the *Akron Times-Press* and other Scripps-Howard newspapers as prejudiced, distorted and inaccurate" and charged that their publication was prompted by Mr. Roy Howard's intense hatred of the C. I. O. in general and the American Newspaper Guild in particular.

Elsewhere similar actions were taken. In the C. I. O. press the comparison between Hearst and Howard was made frequently, with the intimation that the labor boycott, which has caused Mr. Hearst a considerable financial as well as moral headache, might sometime be invoked against Hearst's would-be successor. But Mr. Howard has not been frightened. In fact it would not surprise anyone in the newspaper game to learn that the chain's advertising solicitors are using this threat from the C. I. O. as a means of selling more space to big business.

Red-baiting is also a means to good business. In the case of Simon W. Gerson, a reporter on the Communist *Daily Worker,* appointed to a city job by Borough President Stanley M. Isaacs because of his fitness and despite his political associations, the *World-Telegram* indulged in the usual Hearst style of journalism. In the office of the paper the order was given to "get" Gerson. There was no longer a pretense at publishing straight news, there was a crusade on, and news was manufactured in just the way Hearst, waging a campaign against imaginary "Reds" in the schools and colleges of America for several years, got his reporters to try every known trick to fabricate a story where none existed. But apparently the Howard boys have not yet learned all the Hearst tricks, their journalistic hearts may not be in their work, and their journalistic tongues are surely in their cheeks. About the most sensational item which Mr. Wood was able to show Mr. Howard was one saying that "two months before his appointment . . . Gerson wrote an article in which he urged the Communist party to continue an active recruiting drive after election, it was discovered today." One of Mr. Wood's great discoveries. And this is followed by another sensational discovery, namely, that Gerson is "under fire by the American Legion and numerous other patriotic, civic and religious groups."

For some twenty years the Scripps-Howard papers were among the few which from time to time showed up the excesses of the Legion, its provocation of violence, its denial of civil rights to minorities, but today it cheers the same organization which is notoriously the stooge of big business and according to General Smedley Butler the biggest strike-breaking agency in America. The "religious groups" are not mentioned, because the Howard sheet knows it will do its baiting campaign no good to say that certain reactionary Catholic organizations and publications are in this business. Nor are the professional patriots named, because in almost all cases such patriotic organizations are found to be the subsidiaries of labor-hating big business organizations.

Everyone who knows anything at all about politics knows that Red-baiting is not just Red-baiting: it is the first and sometimes the last but always the most important weapon of reaction. It is in fact so important that Mussolini invented a "Communist menace" in 1925 as a reason for his attack on labor and the co-operatives in 1919. Other dictators use Red-baiting, with or without reason. Hitler had at least some 7,000,000 Communist voters to blame for his party's anti-

Communist policy. But since we are no friend of Japan's we can see in her Red scare as an excuse for her attack on China the utter falsity and hypocrisy of raising the red banner in attacking one's enemies for egotistic, financial or political purposes.

So with Mr. Howard. The policy of "pinning the red label" on one's adversaries, which was also adopted by American business, and notably by the National Electric Light Association's fight against public ownership, is now a Howard policy in fighting the progressive labor movement. He has not yet reached the dictatorial heights of attacking all labor and all liberalism as Red and subversive, but he is undoubtedly well on the road.

An indication can be seen in the distorted reporting of all recent campaigns in which labor, the labor parties, and especially the progressive C. I. O., has participated, and the general attack on pro-labor legislation. Thus, in recent months, the Scripps-Howard papers in many cities have burst into violent attacks on secondary picketing—that is, picketing of advertisers, which is a matter much closer to the newspaper pocketbook than picketing in general—and all the pro-labor legislation which has marked the halting march of the New Deal.

In all the recent election tests the Scripps-Howard headlines and the Hearst headlines could well have been substituted, because they tell the same story of "C. I. O. Plowed Under," "Lewis Rebuffed in Bid for Power," "Labor Turns in Pennsylvania" and "New Deal Repudiated." Should the New Deal, labor or the C. I. O. make any progress somewhere, that fact is not suppressed but so minimized that the lay reader will not be impressed by it. He is either muddled or misled or left ignorant of the facts, when the facts are available to every reporter.

The *World-Telegram* headline "C. I. O. Candidate Trails Martin in Oregon Vote," May 21st, was soon enough corrected when Hess defeated Martin. But in Pennsylvania on

May 19th the paper saw Earle's victory as the "political pluck-
ing of John L. Lewis' eyebrows." The "political menace" of
the C. I. O., the editorial continued, is over, and so is Mr.
Lewis' hope that "he could scowl his way to political power."
The election, the paper suspects, "is a turning point in
America's labor movement, a turning away from the false
path of politics and back toward unionism's true objectives."

The facts are that a swing of 33,000 votes would have
elected C. I. O.'s Kennedy. The fact is that Kennedy carried
the entire state of Pennsylvania except the two reactionary
cities, Philadelphia and Pittsburgh, where the old "corrupt
and contented" Republican and Democratic party machines
have seldom been routed. Kennedy carried the rural population but did not do too well in his own mining towns where
he felt the antagonism of the A. F. of L. But generally speaking the labor movement in politics, despite all its defeats,
is getting along remarkably well, and ten times faster than
the British Labor Party went in its long fight for power.
The Scripps-Howard press can speak of nothing but labor
defeats, but an inquiring reporter at the United States Chamber of Commerce or the National Association of Manufacturers will hear quite a different story about the march of
labor into national politics. Big business is scared. But it is
willing to face the situation rather than distort the news
about it.

The test of a free press is its resistance to pressures. Money,
usually in the form of advertising, is still in my opinion the
medium of greatest pressure, but, on the other side, reader
pressure is becoming more and more apparent. There are
racial, religious and patriotic groups as well as political
groups which either directly influence the press or by the
very fact of their existence scare our editors into euphemism,
hypocrisy or silence.

Pressure need not necessarily be sinister. Surely the labor

unions which began a peaceful boycott of Hearst in 1934 were acting in their own defense and merit the applause of all people who believe in the economic weapon rather than the violence which is usually the employers' weapon. Today the labor pressure on newspapers is growing, and will become powerful when labor grows more aware of the fact that the press has in most cases been its greatest enemy while pretending to be its greatest friend. But the biggest pressure group in the nation today is Catholic.

When Heywood Broun was fired from the old *World* ten years ago it was for writing a piece beginning "There ought to be a place in New York City for a liberal newspaper" and ending with a description of selfish pressure groups which make cowards of editors and destroy the courage and tenacity of the press. "Admitting the danger of generalities," concludes Broun, "I would contend that the Irish are the crybabies of the Western World. Even the mildest quip will set them off into resolutions and protests. And still more precarious is the position of the New York newspaper man who ventures any criticism of the Catholic Church. There is not a single New York editor who does not live in mortal terror of the power of this group. . . . If the Church can bluff its way into a preferred position the fault lies not with the Catholics but with the editors."

Ten years ago the Catholic Church was on the defensive. Today it is on the aggressive, and there is ten times the fear of it there was a decade ago. Father Curran, of the International Catholic Truth Society (God save the mark), changed the policy of one newspaper because he controlled $20,000 of business (*New Republic,* December 30, 1936) and had the effrontery to boast of this outrageous attack on the freedom of the press. But it is general Catholic pressure, not $20,000, which frightens if it does not wholly corrupt many other newspapers.

It was no surprise, then, to see Roy Howard's newspapers suppress Pegler's column (Spring 1938) in which this pugnacious writer, himself educated in a Jesuit school, very rightly attacked Franco. The Catholic Church in America with few exceptions, has supported that child murderer, and two cardinals have defended Franco—Hayes prayed for him— at a time the Pope openly demanded that Franco stop the murder of civilians. "If I were a Spaniard who had seen Franco's missionary work among the children I might see him in hell but never in church," concluded Pegler in the column the Scripps-Howard papers did not have the courage to publish.

Fellow newspapermen sympathize with Howard in the Pegler case, because every reporter knows how deep and vicious is the hatred which press criticism of any religious sect always causes. The *World-Telegram* is no braver than the old *World,* which lived and died a liberal newspaper, in withstanding Catholic pressure—or other pressures for that matter—and no one expects any American publisher to do otherwise. But it is quite a different matter when the Howard papers begin suppressing their columnists because of liberal views which differ from that of our silk-hatted and white-spatted Napoleon.

Most of the daily columnists are conservative and reactionary, a necessary requirement for getting into the big money. Most of them speak as oracles of Reason, Common Sense, Good Sense, and of course, straight American Liberalism. Only once in a while do they write that way too. In many newspapers which buy several of the notable columns there is usually an editorial foreword absolving the publisher of sharing in the views of the writer.

In Mr. Howard's papers there is no such foreword, but there is, on the other hand, considerable suppression. Thus when General Hugh S. Johnson, for once forsaking obscurantist fields, writes of John L. Lewis—that same Lewis of the C. I. O. of which the Howard-hated Newspaper Guild is a part—that he is "one of the best" and that the American people "would be better off if more of our leaders in both political and business fields were more like John Lewis," Mr. Howard promptly suppresses General Johnson.

The public of course did not know of this. But a still greater mystery is General Johnson's statement about a week after this suppression in which he claimed he is uncensored. On April 28, 1938, he boasted that although he had split with Roosevelt he had not joined forces with the Roosevelt-haters, and added: "I don't have to. In the freedom of the American press, which still prevails, and the liberalism of the Scripps-Howard newspapers of which I am an exponent, I am permitted to say whatever I please. I may be backed up against the front door . . . but I have at least the assurance that what is said here is influenced by nobody. I wouldn't trade my job for anybody's. It couldn't happen in any other country. That is why I think the relatively new institution of columns is worth while. I read all my contemporaries. . . ."

But apparently not his own. At least not the suppressed columns.

Heywood Broun, one of the few syndicated non-reactionaries, is not only suppressed from time to time for expressing ideas which Howard doesn't approve, but his daily copy is actually censored by Lee Wood. So crude is the Wood pencil that *World-Telegram* employees have numerous samples of paragraphs which don't make sense because Wood has not censored well, and also another "Before and After" series in which Wood (or Howard) has mowed Broun down between the first and second editions.

Raymond Clapper, Washington columnist, and Dorothy Dunbar Bromley (who has just left Scripps-Howard for the more congenial atmosphere of the *Post*) have also been suppressed for expressing the mildest of liberal ideas, and even the artists have felt the reactionary whip. In fact the troubles which Kirby and Wortman have had may illustrate perhaps better than the news columns the fact that Roy Howard has developed an anti-social conscience. When a Wortman picture is suppressed because a strike breaker says "even a good scab can't find work now," such action must put the suppressor in the class of scab employers. And according to the *Nation,* Rollin Kirby, a very forceful cartoonist who thoroughly believes in middle-of-the-road liberalism, has been forced to share in Howard's anti-Gerson Red-baiting campaign by drawing a picture "for which he later apologized in a letter to a friend."

The public never knows about news censorship. But when columns are omitted even laymen begin to ask questions, and the letters are beginning to worry Howard. He has been forced to make personal replies. Here is one of his typical explanations:

If by the terms "curtailed or blocked out" you mean to inquire whether columnists writing for the *World-Telegram* are having their matter submitted to a censorship calculated to controversial statements or statements in opposition to the editorial policy of the paper, will say that the answer is no.

The *World-Telegram* has available for its use each day the signed product of some twenty-five columnists whose stuff is contracted for by the paper. Space limitations make impossible use of any given day of much more than half of this stuff.

In the selection of that matter used the same test of quality, importance, interest and readability is applied as in the case of all other editorial matter. . . .

. . . As publishers of an independent paper, which is our objective, the *World-Telegram* welcomes the presentation of conflicting ideas and viewpoints, the presentation of which we regard as the most desirable function of a truly independent press, which must be the foundation of an intelligently functioning democratic system.

It is no use going to the length of refuting this statement. When Mayor Hague raved for an hour at a recent mass meeting it was a *World-Telegram* representative, Edd Johnson, who involuntarily spoke the one word which destroyed the entire Hague oration. Mr. Johnson said "Nuts." And to Mr.

Howard the newspapermen who have seen this letter simply
say "Nonsense."

Life does not give most men any choice whatever; but to
few and notably to leaders of public opinion, it frequently
offers the alternative of loot or laurels. For editors and publishers the choice is hard because the newspaper business has
become a big business, and the basis of big business is loot
and not laurels.

The greatest documentary exposure of the financial corruption of the majority of the newspapers of America is the
seventy-two-volume report of the Federal Trade Commission
which accuses the National Electric Light Association, the
propaganda and bribery department of the public utilities, of
poisoning the mind of the entire people through its $25,-
000,000 a year newspaper advertising fund. The N. E. L. A.
at its annual conventions boasted that it had "reached" four-
fifths of the press, but this figure may be slightly exaggerated.
They did "reach" a majority.

The corruption fund, it was disclosed at one of these conventions, was actually taken from the victims' pockets. The
managing director of the N. E. L. A. urged his associates to
spend lavishly because the public, perennial suckers, always
footed the bill. His actual words were: "All the money being
spent is worth while. . . . Don't be afraid of the expense. The
public pays the expense."

The head of this organization, which the Federal Trade
Commission so thoroughly exposed, was Merlin H. Aylesworth. When the N. E. L. A. was disbanded Aylesworth went
into straight selling of advertising, and he has been so successful in advertising that a few months ago Roy Howard
appointed him publisher of the *World-Telegram*. If Roy
Howard had searched the whole world over for a gesture to
show the world of big business that it had won and the last

trace of Scrippsean idealism was gone, he could not have done better than to choose the former director of the biggest propaganda fund that ever fought the free press of America.

Under the Aylesworth regime, for example, a story which makes the front page of the *Post* becomes merely financial news on page 23 of the *World-Telegram:*

Post, Page 1:	*World-Telegram,* Page 23:
State Bars Brokers in	Bennett Files Suit to Restrain
16 Million Fraud	41 Names in Trust Conspiracy
Paine, Webber Enjoined	Paine, Webber Among
From Stock Trading	Defendants in Proceedings

Under the Aylesworth regime the *World-Telegram* makes a weekly hero of Bruce Barton who in addition to being a Congressman is the chairman of the board of Batten, Barton, Durstine & Osborn, distributors of enormous advertising money. I have not kept a file but recently noticed the following items:

May 2: "Barton Backs Plan to Reduce Taxes for Job Creators."
May 11: "Nation Must Take Middle Road Now, Barton Believes."
June 1: "Barton Demands Wide Reforms of Auto Insurance."
June 6: "Barton Urges Recess Study of 'Seven Deadly Sores'."

Mr. Barton is also public relations adviser of the Republican National Committee, and according to the *Guild Reporter* he has sent Republican propaganda to editors with his advertising card attached "and doubtless the publishers got the idea."

I cannot give the details here of the Scripps-Howard wars against Governor Davey of Ohio and certain whiskey distillers, nor do I care to speak in favor of Davey, but the Governor produced the letters from the *Cleveland Press* to Schenley Distillers to back up his statement that "it is fully evident that the motive back of the Scripps crusade was not a moral regard for the political welfare, but it was a strictly cash register crusade."

It is hard to imagine Scripps *père* or *fils* ever being mixed up in such events and charges, with all their crusades in behalf of labor and the underdog and clean politics and a better America being challenged as inspired by the money till and not the Scripps "soul," but it is the expected behavior of an Aylesworth-Howard regime.

I have no space for many more examples which show how this great newspaper chain which E. W. Scripps founded in his quest for the laurel has become under Howard's rule a means of dragging in the advertising loot. But one more interesting fact must be stated: Many years ago, when *Collier's* was fighting the bad medicine men, it branded the Proprietary Association of America, which controlled $40,000,000 worth of newspaper advertising, "an organization of quack doctors and patent medicine makers." Now* the national advertising department of the Scripps-Howard newspapers has become an associate member of the Proprietary Association for the purpose of co-operating with the advisory committee on advertising.

Mr. Scripps said there could not be a free press if it depended on advertising. Mr. Howard joins the medicine ad men.

Mr. Scripps founded a newspaper to serve the workingman. Mr. Howard attacks labor.

The younger Scripps restated the policy of liberalism. Mr. Howard suppresses the liberal columnists.

The elder Scripps shunned the rich, but through a consistent and honest policy built up a thirty-million-dollar business. His present successor has achieved a pinnacle of fame by being listed with the Mellons, Du Ponts, and other multimillionaire legal tax dodgers.

---

* *Editor & Publisher*, December 12, 1936.

There is almost nothing left of the Scripps empire. Buildings, business, machines, material things worth millions but only a few cents worth of spirit; and that flickering in few of his twenty-four cities.

And the symbol: the lighthouse. It still stands on the editorial page of all the Howard newspapers, casting two dimensional beams, Right and Left. But that light years ago showed Howard that the loot was to be found at only one end of the beam, the Right, and he has never returned to either Left or Center.

The light itself, the Scripps light, is dead, another light that failed.

CHAPTER 8

A Jewish Press Lord

THERE is only one metropolitan newspaper which was founded neither for money nor the hope of making money nor the personal advancement of its owner. It has a circulation of more than a quarter million copies daily, is worth at least a million dollars, has given away about a million dollars, paid its scrubwomen $37 a week, encouraged genius and the arts, and once didn't give a damn for advertising.

This paper, one of the few non-commercial journals in the world, is the *Jewish Daily Forward*. Abe Cahan, its elected editor and publisher, can be discharged by a vote of his colleagues, but in every sense of the word Abe Cahan ranks as one of the press lords of America.

He was born in Vilna, Russia, the son of a Hebrew teacher, in 1860 and arrived in the United States in 1882. He had no intention of becoming a Jewish editor, his first ambition being to shine in the English language field, and the second, and greater ambition, to devote himself to novel writing. He wrote "The Rise of David Levinsky," which in addition to being an important contribution to Americana is a good novel, and also "Yekl." These works of fiction show that he was on the road to becoming a major American novelist when the insistent pressure of all his friends who knew he was a journalist of the first rank, forced him into the editorship of the co-operative *Jewish Daily Forward*.

He had tried the *Sun* first, then the *Evening Post*, then the *Commercial Advertiser*, where Lincoln Steffens gave him the job. On these three newspapers he learned the American style of journalism, and it is precisely because the *Forward,* under his direction, was American in spirit despite its foreign language, that it became so great a success.

The *Forward* was founded in 1897. In the previous year Daniel de Leon in Chicago split the Socialist and labor movement by moving far to the left, whereupon Meyer London, Dr. Isaac Hourwich, Abe Cahan and a few others organized the Social Democratic Party and began publishing the *Forward* as a counter attack to De Leon's *Arbeiterzeitung.*

No stocks and bonds were issued. A board of nine managers formed the Forward Association of 200 persons. Only members of the Socialist Party can be elected to the governing board when they are approved by a two-third majority of its members. No one can invest in the paper, and there are no dividends. But there is an enormous profit. In good times it runs up to a quarter of a million dollars a year. This money has been used to make the *Forward* a better paper, to publish a Chicago edition, to help great men in need, and in the distant past to help the labor movement in the United States. In other words it once gave its readers, mostly trade union men, the money it made from advertising and from their subscriptions.

Mr. Cahan did not remain as editor once the paper was started. He quit in order to write novels, but in 1902, when the circulation was only 7,000 he was asked to save it from ruin.

He called the board together and berated it for filling the paper with polemics, with Marxian dialectics, with nothing but abuse of the capitalists, and with a lot of propaganda. A third of a century later, reminiscing for a reporter of *Editor & Publisher,* Abe Cahan told what a sensation his introduction of American style journalism created in the East Side of New York.

"We sent out after human interest stuff and played it up," he said. "We started a sports page. What a hullabaloo that raised! We made the paper as lively as possible, and made a complete metamorphosis from the dry political tract it originally was.

"People like our paper and read it. I can remember one story I got about an Italian barber down on Broome street who fell in love with a Jewish girl. She was very pretty and he was just crazy about her. But her mother was religious and wouldn't hear of it. Finally the mother gave in and said they could be married but the barber would have to become a Jew. And then the old lady made him learn Hebrew and pray every morning with a cap on his head. The poor man couldn't get his breakfast until he prayed.

"But the girl had a brother named Joe who was born here in America and he didn't pray. The barber said, 'Why doesn't Joe have to pray before breakfast?'

"That made a great stir when we printed it. Some people were shocked at reading such a story in a Socialist paper, but people talked about it, and it brought readers.

"It was fascinating work."

Abe Cahan combined human interest news with crusading. His first big campaign was against the sweatshop in the needle trades. The needle trades unions today are still the largest supporters of the *Forward*. One day he published a feature story urging mothers to give their children handkerchiefs. But indignant Socialist leaders demanded of him what the relationship was between the "Manifesto" of Karl Marx and handkerchiefs for East Side children. Cahan replied: "And since when has Socialism been opposed to clean noses?"

Cahan invented Letters from the Lovelorn. His department in the *Forward* was called *"A Bintel Brief,"* meaning a bundle of letters, where men and women told their troubles and got advice. In addition to marriage and divorce there were thousands of letters discussing the problems of behavior of immigrant Jews in the new world.

In recent times Cahan has been attacked bitterly by the more radical labor movement, and by various Socialist and Communist organizations who do not believe in his Socialist program. His journalistic and political policy is as follows:

"Things should speak for themselves. The first thing to report is the truth.

"The *Forward* is a party paper, but it is first of all a newspaper. I think that party affiliations of newspapers are compatible so long as the newspapers remember their primary purpose.

"Compared with Yiddish, the English language is like a millionaire compared with a pauper.

"When I was young Socialistic ideas were considered as dreams. Now you hear them from our most renowned representatives in public life. . . . The New Deal was excellent as far as it went, but it did not go far enough. It will come up again because *there will be another depression sooner or later. Capitalism spells depression, and the number of people on relief is bound to grow.*

"It is possible that this country will work its way into Socialism without a party. But there will be a third party and it will be the greatest one. Things are developing in that direction and a progressive spirit is noticeable in the land.

"We are working for a change to a better organized economic system. But we are willing to work at a reasonable rate. We aren't damn fools. We don't think the whole building can be pulled down and changed over night."

But despite lip-service to socialism, Cahan and his paper have taken the road to reaction. They had always represented the conservative wing, had fought De Leon, Debs, Haywood, Norman Thomas; they first supported, but from 1921 on attacked Soviet Russia, using all the propaganda and Riga falsehoods long before Hearst and McCormick. At the same time wages of the big editors increased regularly. Cahan now gets $20,000 a year.

Worse yet, the *Forward* has become commercialized. It publishes the usual bad medicine and other advertising and it has accepted the ads of corporations whose union men were on strike. On more than one occasion workingmen have smashed the *Forward* office windows.

In 1922 Editor Villard of the *Nation* called the *Forward* the most interesting paper in America; in 1935 the *Nation* said that those who had praised Cahan and his sheet were usually unable to read Yiddish and pass judgment. The *Nation* now compared the *Forward* to the Red-baiting Hearst rags, and said Cahan had learned little in forty years.

In 1936 Cahan and his old guard were expelled from the Socialist Party. Liberals have long ago given up the *Forward;* radicals regard Cahan as a typical rich bourgeois renegade.

In the past year Mr. Cahan has faced a great problem in the trades union situation. The young radical of the 1880's had come up against the C. I. O. industrial union idea, militant labor, the sit-down, and a new radical movement which he would have been the first to support in his youth. Now, celebrating his seventy-eighth birthday in midsummer, 1938, he was unable to bring himself to the point of endorsing John L. Lewis, but he joined with the straddlers and Red-baiters in hinting at Communist "control" of the new labor organization.

In the Amalgamated Clothing Workers Union, one of the largest component parts of the C. I. O., there was considerable anger over a statement Cahan made to the *New York Times* directed against Sidney Hillman, the union's president. Cahan was reported saying, "I feel that Mr. Hillman's attitude toward the Communist movement is objectionable and irresponsible. Mr. Hillman is not a Communist, but he does not mind playing with Communists when he considers it to his political advantage to do so." This statement was used by all that part of the press trying to make the C. I. O. appear "Communist-dominated" and by the Red-baiters who had tried to smear Hillman and other progressive labor leaders.

The radical of forty years ago hasn't kept up with the times. Only those who expect miracles nowadays are surprised and shocked.

CHAPTER 9

Lord Baltimore

IF INTEGRITY is a luxury, it was well exemplified in the case of Van-Lear Black and the *Baltimore Sun* papers.

The *Sun* and *Evening Sun* of Baltimore have always been prominent among the few really great newspapers in America which can be compared with the *Manchester Guardian,* the old *Frankfurter Zeitung,* the dead *New York World.*

(All these papers, by the way, were rich men's newspapers: the *Guardian* owned by C. P. Scott, the *Frankfurter* by Sonnemann, the *World* by Joseph Pulitzer, and the Baltimore papers by Black.)

Black was probably the richest individual in the state of Maryland; he was president of the Fidelity and Deposit Company of Baltimore, director of the Consolidated Coal Company, the Massachusetts Mutual Life Insurance Company, the American Ship and Commerce Corporation, American Sugar Refining Company, the Chatham-Phenix National Bank and Trust Company of New York.

But did Mr. Black present his editors with a list of these corporations with instructions to treat them as "sacred cows"? Did he instruct his editors to color the news to suit the sugar company or the shipping company? He did not. He not only told his editorial writers, editors and reporters that they must cover the news truthfully—as most editors do—but he proved to his staff that he was not bluffing—as so many others are doing.

The question of the man's integrity is well illustrated in one of the West Virginia coal strikes where the worst features of labor war in America were to be found, with violence, bloodshed and murder commonplaces. Mr. Van-Lear Black was not only a stockholder in one of the companies, but he was an operator in this field. But that did not deter him from sending two men, a staff reporter and a radical labor advocate, to write the story of the strike.

Mr. Black made a bet that when the stories came in, the one from the regular staff man would turn out to be more radical than that of the radical labor advocate, and he won. But it is to be noted that (1) the staff man knew he would not be fired no matter what he wrote as long as he was convinced it was the truth and (2) that the coal operator published in his own newspaper damning (but truthful) reports against his own profit interests.

Van-Lear Black began life as a clerk. In his youth he was interested only in business and finance; he became director of banks, shipping companies, insurance firms—he insured himself for $750,000—and his hobbies were yachting and airplanes. It was as chairman of the board of A. S. Abell Co. which published the *Sun* papers, that he became identified with journalism. He never interfered with the capable men he hired to run the papers. It is quite possible that he would not have interfered had the editors made the paper reactionary and servile, but since it is the natural habit of American reporters to produce as free a newspaper as the owner permits, and since in this instance the owner was sympathetic, the result was two great newspapers.

Unfortunately Van-Lear Black disappeared from his yacht one night in August, 1930. Alive he had furnished the world press with many stories, notably his 130,000-mile flight to all parts of the world, but in death he furnished a sensation. However, it was soon proved that although he was a drinking man he had not been drunk and there was no probability of suicide.

The accident had tragic effects on the *Sun* papers.

In the autumn of 1936, when the reactionary papers joined

like howling wolves around a single victim (the New Deal), the two most important deserters from the liberal democratic camp were the *St. Louis Post-Dispatch* and the *Baltimore Sun* papers. Said the *Sun:*

"The *Sun* now states that in this campaign it is unable to advocate the re-election of President Roosevelt.

"The statement is made with regret. . . .

"The *Sun* stands for competitive capitalism. It is the system which most effectively uproots the unfit, the unworthy, the lazy. It is the system which gives place to the vigorous, the competent, the purposeful. It is the system which constantly provides room for originality and thereby constantly enlarges achievement. It is the system which carries technological advance to its rational conclusion of lower prices and increased mass consumption. Even as distorted in recent periods, it has produced in this country a degree of well-being which has never been equaled, and in that well-being all classes of men have shared. . . .

"Within this system labor may organize and exercise its rights to bargain collectively. . . .

"This system of competition is, moreover, the protection of political liberty. It is the best protection for the ordinary citizen, the workingman. . . . It is the economic freedom of competition which guards political freedom. . . ."

Six weeks later, or just before the dawn of election day, the *Baltimore Sun* announced that it could not support Landon either.

But reaction has run the chariot of the *Sun* ever since.

One of its signs was the appointment of H. L. Mencken as editor of the *Evening Sun*. One of Mr. Mencken's stunts was to publish six columns of dots on the seven-column editorial page with the announcement that there were 1,000,075 dots, one for every Federal government's "immense corps of job-holders. . . . If there were no jobholders at all every tax-payer's income would be increased twenty-seven percent. Such is the bill for being saved from revolution and ruin by Wonder Men."

In midsummer 1938 Mr. Mencken, retiring as editor, but continuing as columnist, went to Germany for his holiday.

The *Sun* papers still produce excellent pages, still employ numerous editors and correspondents noted for liberalism and intelligence, but there is no millionaire owner today to encourage the staff to produce a great newspaper at the price of disagreeing with the forces of that "competitive capitalism" which the staff approves and which it claims uproots the unfit, the unworthy and the lazy and which in practice has always kept the American nation a third ill-fed, ill-clad and ill-housed—even in the good old days of the liberal Van-Lear Black.

CHAPTER 10

The American Thunderer

MANY persons in addition to its owners believe the *New York Times* is the best newspaper in the world: they point to its leadership in international news, its completeness in national news, its impartiality, decency, honesty, and other virtues; but the more they pile on the praise for this newspaper the more they condemn the press in general, because, all in all, the *New York Times* is not good enough.

The *Times* does not color and suppress the news in the way most papers do but it knows how to bury unpleasant items and play up pleasant ones—which is a confession that bias and partiality weigh the news there just as they do in the Hearst press.

The editorial page, Mr. Sulzberger assures me, is purposely kept weak and dawdling so as not to affect the news. If a strong editorial stand is taken every employee from Washington to Moscow will be influenced in how he writes and what he sends. If no editorial policy is emphasized the staff will be unprejudiced. That is Mr. Sulzberger's theory. He thinks it is working well. Others think it is not working at all.

I am absolutely sure that Mr. Sulzberger has convinced himself that he has made the *Times* completely free, liberal, and impartial. He not only says he is a liberal, he is devoted to liberalism, he is impassioned for democracy, and he cannot possibly see that he is a conservative, and that there is much about the *Times* that is not only conservative but tory, and toryism means prejudice, bias, unfairness to liberalism and democracy, unfairness to labor, to all progressive movements and their news, and to the forward march of civilization.

It is perhaps a job for a psychologist to explain the behavior pattern of the publisher of America's most important and powerful newspaper, to relate education, environment and upbringing of the man to his confession of liberalism, his delusion in believing that he is producing a great liberal journal, his transcendental failure to do so and his magnificent success materially. As a reporter it is merely my job to try to get at the facts, and the most interesting in my opinion is the fact that the publisher believes in his own liberalism. No liberal in the past or today has ever considered the *Times* or its owners as fellow travelers. The evidence has been against them.

A test for not only a liberal press but a free press can be made by an examination of its news on labor. It is not required that a newspaper claiming to be liberal should also be pro-labor, although that exists among magazines, and would not be held against newspapers. When, however, a newspaper slants its news or its headlines or selects news and plays up news which is inimical to labor, it can be said that that newspaper certainly is not liberal; it may not even be fair. As for Red-baiting, that attitude puts the Hearst stigmata on a newspaper and requires no more condemnation.

How then shall we judge events of May, 1938, when big business, which the La Follette committee had proven the enemy of labor, and William Allen White had admitted engaged in class warfare with labor, began to demand the revision or repeal of the Wagner Act, the annihilation of the National Labor Relations Board, the outlawing of secondary picketing—and perhaps all picketing—and sit-down strikes, and in short the repeal of all the gains labor had made not only under Roosevelt II but in a century. The American press, with the exception of a small minority, fell in with the plans of big business. A resolution "tentatively adopted by the Chamber of Commerce" for an investigation of the National Labor Relations Act made the front page of the *Times* with a three-line head. The same day when Knudsen of General Motors predicted a governmental curb on industrial unionism the *World-Telegram* went into three-column hysterics—the *Post* published only a one-column head over a short piece—and Hearst went saffron with a story headed U. S. MUST STOP VIOLENCE BY UNIONS, SAYS KNUDSEN. The *Times* the next day (May 6th) again front paged the story LABOR ACT REPEAL ASKED BY CHAMBER which was followed on June 3rd with a front page story ROOSEVELT IS REPORTED PLANNING REVISION OF NATIONAL LABOR ACT. This last story was immediately denied, but all are overplayed anti-labor news items.

Meanwhile the Supreme Court had decided several cases in favor of the law. In the Mackay case the court recognized the "continuity of employment" while workers are on strike. The *Times* said editorially that certain provisions of the Wagner Act had been held legal, but "The country, it seems clear, is coming more and more to recognize that it is the Wagner Act itself, rather than merely its administration by the Labor Board, that is fundamentally in need of change." If by the country the *Times* means its clients and supporters, the editorial is a fact; if it means five million organized workers, every liberal thinking man, it is talking nonsense. However, it is a tragic fact that the anti-labor press of the country has built up quite a powerful revisionist following even among ignorant workingmen for whose benefit the law was made. Nor is this the first instance in which a majority of newspapers has so influenced public opinion that the people have acted against their own good or selfish interests.

In the general strike of 1934 when the publishers of San Francisco (with the exception of the Scripps-Howard *News*) conspired to break labor, Hearst ordered the press to play up the story of how Britain broke its general strike in 1926. If one searches the columns of the *Times* one will find the coincidence in its use of the British story and an editorial on how it was done. Moreover the *Times* went the Hearst crowd one better with a story headed

CLEVELAND BROKE
STRIKE WITH ARMY

On every possible occasion the *Times* writes an editorial against picketing. And now that labor has taken to picketing advertisers the *Times* joins with the cheap newspapers in a concerted battle to outlaw this weapon. The *Times* bias goes over into its letter department. Here are some samples clipped in November, 1937:

W. K. A. writes that the public is annoyed "by silly demonstrations . . . foolishness . . . nuisance." Richard Janes says the Automat picketing is not justified because the strikers are a minority. W. H. B., who should get a high post when Fascism arrives, declares he makes it his business to patronize struck establishments. R. J. Derby writes: "I have been doing the same thing." M. F. F. says "Neither yea nor nay." R. C. O'Brien says picketing promotes disorder. Cyril Brown proposes licenses.

Only one letter takes the side of labor.

Can it be that no *Times* readers are pro-labor? The present reader wrote numerous letters under numerous names and got many friends to write in. But not one letter out of twenty favoring picketing was published. Here is one of the suppressed letters:

To the Editor of The New York Times:

Reading all the letters from *Times* readers protesting picketing I begin to wonder whether an impartial poll of public opinion would agree with them. All the courts where the issue has been raised have ruled picketing legal. One higher court has ruled picketing legal in time of no strike. There can be no question that those who would deny labor the right to picket are advocating illegal methods.

More interesting I find the mentality which expresses itself in patronizing struck shops to show a contempt for labor and its methods. I have never been able to find an American who admitted himself a Fascist but this is obviously the Fascist mentality and the Fascist method. After all it was "squadrismo," or the violent arm of Mussolini's Fascist Movement, which smashed strikes and picketing and the co-operative movement in Italy, while in the employ of the employers' associations. I am indeed surprised to find so much Fascist mentality in America proclaiming itself American.

Grant Singleton.

New York, November 28, 1937.

The *Times* had no room for pro-labor letters, but it found room for a story headed "J. L. Lewis to Move Near White House," beginning, "John L. Lewis will move three blocks nearer to the White House Monday." This story, it must be admitted, is a good story in the Hearst style. It means nothing. But a Hearst writer could make a sensation out of rumors of Lewis' alleged desire for political power, and the *Times* makes the insinuation.

Again, on the occasion of a Lewis broadcast in which he spoke of "The slaughter of workers paralleling the massacres of Ludlow and Homestead," the *Times* asked editorially why he did not include Herrin. Why should he? The La Follette committee had supplied the evidence (which the doubting *Times* puts in quotation marks) of massacres of workingmen by police and by company forces. The fact that workmen had once fought among themselves is totally irrelevant: that was not part of the labor struggle.

Anti-labor and Red-baiting go together. The *Times* is anti-labor, and there is a lot of evidence with which to build up a case of Red-baiting. Here is an example. On August 26, 1935, the *Times* had a story:

SEE CLUE TO FIREBUG IN NURSE'S NOTEBOOK

Denver Police Find Leaves at Three Blazes and Suspect Communist Group.

The police chief, Captain James E. Childers, was quoted saying "It is possible that a Communist organization with a hatred of religion and of men who own large buildings and hotels is attempting to spread a reign of terror." Three Catholic churches had been set on fire.

To publish such charges against a legal, recognized political party is not good journalism. One cannot imagine the Democratic *Times* ever referring to a Republican organization as engaged in arson. And to publish the true story the next day without reference to the Red-baiting lie of the previous day is not fair journalism. The fact was that a pyromaniac, a boy named Warren Cramer, confessed setting twenty-four fires for fun.

Again the *Times* (October 14, 1936) had a scoop with a wild tale about hundreds of Communists running wild in the textile district. Commissioner Valentine, who in his time had conducted numerous "Red" raids, called the stories "a lot of bunk." The *Times* kept quiet.

A later *Times* scoop, with the two-column head, "Miss Poyntz's Disappearance Laid to 'Kidnaping' Here for Soviet," made the front page in the midst of a spy scare. There were columns of sensationalism credited to the Italian radical leader Carlo Tresca who is anti-Soviet. Miss Poyntz's attorney, Elias Lieberman, is also quoted. The next day the *World-Telegram* quoted the attorney saying the story was "purely imaginative" and by the time Tresca came before the investigating grand jury the *Times* polished the story off with about six inches of police reporting. There was nothing to the story. The Red-baiting boomerang did the *Times* no credit. Neither did its December 17, 1937, story of the arrest of a burglar which it headed "Red Leader

Arrested in Social Tax Thefts." It was a good story, but as Cyril Brown once said in Berlin, "The best stories are not necessarily true."

There are many other illustrations. Nevertheless I would not say that the *Times* is now "one of the most impassioned Red-baiters," as Oswald Garrison Villard found it was in reporting the 1919 steel strike, nor is it consistently Red-baiting today as it was when campaigning against Charles A. Lindbergh, Sr. It has dropped its Red-baiting campaign against Russia. But it somehow cannot escape fits of Red-baiting. The test will come soon because labor is inevitably going left and business corporations, as well as cheap jack politicians, purposely confuse militant labor with Red ideology.

One of the tests by which a reader can tell whether the press is not only liberal or conservative, but fair to its customers, is the manner in which it reports Congressional and Federal trade commission investigations.

Throughout our history—and we have only to think back to those of most recent date, notably the Teapot Dome, the Nye Munitions and the La Follette Civil Liberties investigations—these extramural activities by committees of the Senate and the House have unearthed tremendous scandals, the worst corruption, the most flagrant examples of injustice and law breaking, and they have also supplied the press with many of its most prolonged sensations.

It would have been natural to suppose that the newspapers, many of which also engage in attacking vice, corruption and law breaking, and all of which protest their aim is to serve the American public by telling it the truthful facts of public life, would have welcomed all Congressional investigations and notably those which supplied the biggest headlines.

But the opposite is more often true. Of course the exposure of the $25,000,000 press corruption fund operated by the National Electric Light Association got little if any space in the newspapers because so many of them were directly involved, but when merchants of death were exposed, and a member of the cabinet caught taking a hundred-thousand-dollar bribe, that was news that sells the papers, that rivals wars and lovers' quarrels.

The press has not been friendly. Senator Wheeler, during the Black lobby investigation, invited his colleagues not to "get too excited about what the newspapers say about these investigations and investigating committees," suggesting that an examination be made of the cartoons and editorials which were published about Senator Walsh which would show "that the press of the country was almost unanimously against the committee and strongly denounced my colleague. Yet after the investigation was over and after the situation had been exposed and it was known that Fall had accepted money from Doheny, then the same respectable press which had denounced Senator Walsh during the time the investigation was going on, after the public had been aroused by the exposures made by the committee, all proclaimed Senator Walsh as a great man.

"Likewise in the so-called Daugherty investigation, which I helped to conduct, every paper in the United States, almost without exception—both the old guard Democratic papers and the Old Guard Republican papers—denounced me, denounced the investigation, and wrote editorials upholding and supporting Harry M. Daugherty. Until after the investigation got to the point where the papers could not any longer stand it, that continued; and eventually they were compelled to switch over.

"As a matter of fact, during the investigation the Associated Press would carry what the committee brought out during the hearings, and above that they would carry every night a story as to what Daugherty said, and what his comment was upon the committee's hearings. They repeatedly through the press denounced me for not calling Daugherty; and when I finally did ask him to come before the committee, and he refused to come, there was hardly a single editorial denouncing him until after he had been reluctantly thrown out of office by President Coolidge. . . . Almost the entire press of the country was against both the Walsh investigation and the Daugherty investigation.

"If it had not been for those investigations, most of those men would have continued to hold public office. Most of them would have continued to carry on their thievery. . . . Most of them would have gone on exploiting public domain, and most of them would have gone on debauching the government of the United States; and yet I say it is a sad commentary that the press of the country, both Republican and Democratic, denounce every investigation carried on by the Congress of the United States.

"I wish to say, for my part, that I feel that one of the most beneficial things the Senate has done since I have been in Congress has been to expose corruption and crookedness in high places, and likewise to expose the corrupting influences that are used to oppose the passage of legislation in the interest of the masses of the people of the United States.

"The Senate has done more, in my opinion, to preserve a democracy in this country through those investigations than almost anything else. . . . If it were not for the investigatory powers of Congress and the fear of exposure on the part of some individuals high up in some of the industries of the country, our government would not last very long.

"I think the members of the Black committee are to be congratulated upon the work they have carried on, and I do not think they should take very seriously what Mr. Hearst says, or what the owner of the *Washington Post* (Eugene Meyer) says. . . .

"The people of the country desire to have these things exposed, and they desire to have crookedness shown up. . . ."

Senator Wheeler's statement can be backed up by historical facts. The Pujo, the Pecora, the Nye Munitions, the Walsh and the present La Follette investigations, to name but a few, have produced the evidence of corruption and frequently resulted in good laws. A crook named Fall went to jail but the big business men who bribed him were unfortunately not discovered by the Teapot Dome investigation.

Yet in this instance, as in almost every instance without exception, the *New York Times* has begun by ridiculing the investigation committee and ended by minimizing its findings. I know of no big newspaper in America which has so bad and consistent a record in opposing investigations. I cannot imagine why this is so except perhaps the fact that every investigation exposes the corruption of men and organizations who represent power and riches and the *Times* is fundamentally the paper of the people of the same class of society.

I have already told in "Freedom of the Press" how Mr. Ochs had boasted that "American newspapers, with whatever faults and defects they may have been charged, are not open to the accusation of venality" just before a Senate committee heard Frederick Bonfils of the *Denver Post* admit he had blackmailed oil men for a million dollars to suppress the first news of the Teapot Dome scandal, and John C. Shaffer, then owner of the *Chicago Evening Post, Indianapolis Star, Muncie Star, Terre Haute Star* and *Rocky Mountain News,* testify he had received $92,500. Ochs' *Times* even then declared that the Senators making the investigation acted "like men who at heart are enemies of lawful and orderly government," suggesting that the object of the probe was "to paralyze the administration, to terrorize members of the cabinet, to break down the efficiency of the government." Mr. Ochs' *Times* called the investigators "scandalmongers and assassins of character." This was absolutely false. The investigators as we now know sent criminals to jail and saved the oil reserve for the United States Navy. If the *Times* was at fault in the Teapot Dome case, it was even more culpable in the Nye Munitions investigation when its great and good friend, the J. P. Morgan company, was discussed and found an important factor in bringing America into the World War. This is a complicated subject and I offer an enormous documentation to any student seeking material for an interesting thesis. Here I can give only a few facts concerning the *Times*.

In the autumn of 1935 Senator Nye recalled the fact that President Wilson had admitted that the World War was a commercial and industrial war. "To state that America went into the last war to help American commercial and banking interests is in itself too bold a statement to command a hearing," Nye continued in a radio address, adding that it was necessary "to state the step-by-step course through which these commercial and banking interests led us to war." This he proceeded to do. He discussed at length the "Morgan credits" and the tie-up with the State Department. Finally he read the famous Page telegram which warned of a great panic because "the approaching crisis has gone beyond the ability of Morgan" and urged "our going to war" as "the only way in which our present pre-eminent trade position can be maintained and a panic averted."

"And so," concluded Senator Nye, "into the war we went. Not to make the world safe for democracy but to prevent a panic."

The Morgan firm was scheduled to give testimony early in January, 1936. In December, 1935, Kenneth Crawford, staff correspondent of the *New York Post,* wrote a story with the banner line ALLIES LOANS PUT U. S. INTO WAR and Raymond Clapper, Scripps-Howard staff writer, appeared in the *World-Telegram* under the headline INQUIRY TO SHOW MORGAN STRONG FACTOR IN WAR. From that time on the *Times* began its defense of Morgan.

Take for example the papers of January 7th. The *Times* has "Morgan Defends Financing in War" and the *Post* has "Morgan Accused of Hampering Probe." The testimony of the 8th was worth headlines in every newspaper that night and the next morning. Here they are:

Post:
Morgan Gave U. S. Secrets to English in '15, Nye Says
World-Telegram:
Morgan Interests Bared in 363 Million Wars Sales
N. Y. American:
Morgan Arms Sales Aided War, Senate Probers Charge
N. Y. Sun:
Senators Read Morgan Cable Inviting Britain to Buy Arms
  Plant Here in January, 1916
N. Y. Tribune:
Morgan Shown Averting Tie-Up in War Supplies From U. S.
  to Allies in '16
N. Y. Times:
Allied Financing Arms Plant Deals Told by Morgan

The *Tribune* published no editorial. The *Post* said "We don't believe that J. P. Morgan & Co. deliberately set out to involve this country . . . Morgan was merely the instrument by which the United States was linked to Europe's cataclysm." The *World-Telegram,* asking for measures against a repetition of a world war, says that Morgan showed how the fortunes of his house "deeply rooted though it was and is still in the economic life of this country, were involved with the war fortunes of the Allies." The *Times* on the 8th tried the comic approach. In its "Topics of the *Times*" column it said: "It really wasn't the munitions makers and bankers who took us into the war on the side of the Allies, but the theatrical managers and Equity." Because there were "nearly a dozen English shows recently in town." But the next morning there was a leading editorial:

Senator Nye may be an amiable and sincere gentleman, but he is a little on the credulous order. He swallows scandalous rumors greedily, and puts the plate of evidence away untouched. In several addresses during the past summer and autumn he recited charges against J. P. Morgan & Co. That firm had, according to the Senator, followed an iniquitous course all through the first years of the Great War, and had finally, in a desperate effort to collect its foreign loans, dragged the Wilson administration and the country into the war. When the actual test of these assertions came before the Senate committee a plain tale put most of them down as wild or ridiculous. . . .

The editorial attack on Nye and defense of Morgan continued almost daily. In "The Committee's Discoveries" the sensational disclosures which were making banner lines throughout the world were called "familiar history" and the proceedings "possibly . . . a little wearying." In "Instructive Irrelevancies" it was stated that the "committee delving into the affairs of the Morgans" . . . "has taken up questions which are irrelevant and immaterial. Everybody can see that and infer what was the motive for it. . . . Some Senators still believe in a kind of political demonology. To them it seems impossible that important events can have happened without a sinister and wicked person controlling and directing them for his own nefarious reasons. . . ." In "Inquiry Unlimited" (January 16th) the *Times* suggests that the hearings having proven dull, be discontinued. "One reason," states the editorial, "is that their personal and financial sensations have all been exploded, with little or no damage." It maintains that "the endeavor to prove that only the profit motive drew the United States into war in 1917" left the committee "confused and baffled." Of the falsification regarding the secret treaties charged to Wilson the editorial said "irrelevant if true" and "more matter of that kind will soon justify the committee in putting up the shutters."

That same day the "Topics of the *Times*" said with its usual elephantine attempt at humor that "the shrewd men on the Nye committee will not be deceived" by Morgan's statement in favor of the purple heather and grouse shooting in Scotland; "this grouse situation must be looked into."

In defense of the *Times* it could be said that its treatment of Morgan was not as servile as that of other newspapers—if that fact can be a defense. The *Sun* (January 15, 1936) reported that "Nye Exonerates Morgan of Wrong" and the *Herald Tribune* (on the 19th) in a leading editorial, "Morgan Turns the Tables," said:

Mr. Morgan, to his credit be it said, has turned the tables on Senator Nye and the other inquisitors who, during the last few weeks, have been doing their best to prove that he was a liar, a scoundrel, a traitor and a bloodthirsty and greedy knave. As the committee's work is approaching its end Senators Nye and Clark are the discredited ones, and Mr. Morgan's integrity and character have been blazoned before the nation. . . . May their (the Senators) experience serve as a warning that the country is tired of "smearing" campaigns—even when the objects of vilification have for so many years been maligned, misrepresented and manhandled, as is the case with the members of the House of Morgan.

The climax to the *Times* campaign against Nye came when the inquiry ended and the Senator gave the lie direct to a *Times* editorial. This paper had said (February 9, 1936) under the heading "An Inquiry Ends Well" that Nye had predicted he would prove *inter alia* that the Morgan firm "in order to save its own loans, had used its powerful influence to induce the Washington government to take this country into the struggle against Germany." The *Times* adds: "The prolonged and searching investigation utterly failed to prove that there was any real foundation for these charges. . . . Indeed the inquiry ended on a sort of jovial note of congratulations between Mr. Morgan and his friend Nye.

"Such an outcome is of great public benefit. It verified the statement made by one of the committee's own examiners. . . . 'I don't see that the Morgans did anything wrong at all. . . .' It is easy to imagine the disturbing effect if a contrary result had been reached. People would despairingly have concluded that there was something rotten in the whole banking business. As it was, the firm under scrutiny was shown to have conducted its affairs honorably. . . . The way in which it emerged from the investigation without the smell of fire upon its garments is a good thing not only for J. P. Morgan & Co., but for the country."

This editorial is at variance with the Nye statements, acts and reports, as well as historical accuracy. Senator Nye electrified a large audience by publicly denying the *Times* statements and views. Morgan was not cleared; there was no whitewash; there was no jovial note of congratulation but a formal diplomatic handshake, and exactly every item the *Times* said was not proven had been proven.

"There appeared one day last week," said Senator Nye to an audience which applauded him and booed Morgan and the *Times,* "in the greatest independent newspaper in the country, the story that our examination of the Morgan partners was concluded with a handshaking all around and a general agreement we had wound up by whitewashing the Morgan interest. . . .

"There is not a single member of the Senate committee of inquiry that believes the inquiry has afforded a clean bill of health to the House of Morgan.

"It would not be fair to say that the House of Morgan took us to war to save their investment in the Allies, but the record of facts makes it altogether fair to say that these bankers were in the heart and center of a system that made our going to war inevitable."

Essentially this was the report of the committee. It found that the House of Morgan held a key position to influence government policy in the first years of the war and while it did not "drag" the country in, it helped steer the nation into a position which made its entry inevitable. Two historians who are expert on this subject agree. Walter Millis writes that "great sections of American industry and finance led by the Morgan firm . . . devoted themselves to establishing the economic complex which tended constantly thereafter to thrust the nation more and more deeply into an economic alliance with the Entente and consequently nearer and nearer to war with Germany." And Dr. Harry Elmer Barnes, who believes that the Communists must have shouted with joyous derision when the Morgan testimony ended, says that the evidence produced by the Nye committee and Baker's latest volume on Wilson "make it perfectly clear that no single factor was so powerful in bringing the United States into the World War as the bankers' pressure on the government to permit the extension of unlimited credit to the Allies."

Obviously there is no personal devil. Obviously it is not J. P. Morgan who took America into the war, but something even bigger than Morgan, and that something of course is a combination of big business, finance capital, and the profit motive. Since it is a fact that the Morgan House has no financial interest or any control over the *Times* it is only fair to infer that it is the *Times'* general interest in the same ideals which Morgan represents which drove it editorially to the limit of distortion and unfairness in discussing the Nye investigation.

Coincident with that event was a series of letters begun by the Morgan partner, Thomas Lamont, which sought to exonerate the bankers. I can state on my own authority that the *Times* suppressed numerous letters taking issue with Lamont and published over a long period many letters supporting him, all of which Morgan republished and distributed. Some of the letters dealt with a matter of historical fact: did or did not Woodrow Wilson in his St. Louis speech in July, 1919, admit that "this was an industrial and commercial war." I had first come across this statement in "Falsehood in Wartime," by Lord Ponsonby, and verified it in the columns of the *New York Times* of September 6, 1919, where the story is on the front page and the text on page 2, column 4. I sent this important fact, which would have decided the controversy, to the *Times* and my wife wrote another letter which she signed "Helen Larkin" and mailed from another town. But the *Times* suppressed both and let the controversy continue although it had the solution in its own files. The solution, however, was not gratifying to those who want to preserve the myth of patriotism about the World War and who are fearful of having economic truth published.

On April 8, 1936, the *Times* made an occasion for again denouncing investigations in general. It said that "in the long run the abuse of powers of investigation carries precisely as great risk for the 'radical' or the 'liberal' as for the 'reactionary' or the 'conservative.' Today it is the 'power trust' or the 'bankers' lobby' that faces an investigating committee which makes its own rules and intimidates its witnesses. Tomorrow it may be a Socialist newspaper or a strike committee."

The investigation of the power trust, it so happens, brought out the evidence of the $25,000,000-a-year bribe fund to corrupt the American press. The investigation of the lobbies, of the banking system, of the munitions industry, of big business and its employment of thugs and murderers as strike breakers, and in fact all investigations of the recent past and present have had the approval of all liberal elements and nothing but the disapproval and at times sabotage from conservative and reactionary elements, notably the press. Socialist papers, strike committees, have nothing to fear from a Congressional investigation. The *Times* argument is nonsense.

But the meanest of all *Times* editorial attacks was made in December 24, 1937, when the La Follette Civil Liberties Committee, having published fourteen volumes of testimony and documents which constitute the most complete indictment of American big business as a law breaker (through the employment of thugs, the use of violence, and the denial of civil rights to American labor) added to the evidence a list of 2,500 individuals or companies using spies. There were exactly eight challenges of which six were immediately answered by the documentary evidence. One case was admitted as mislisted: the company should have been charged with employing a "guard" not a "spy." In one instance the committee was looking up the facts. At most the committee could have made 2 mistakes in 2,500 investigations.

But the *Times*, traditionally hostile to all investigations, attacked without getting the facts or reading the documents. The Senators would not let the challenge go unanswered. Here in parallel columns slightly abbreviated, is the *Times* editorial and the reply:

Hair-Trigger Charges

The La Follette two-man committee accused 2,500 business firms of employing labor spies. It mentioned these companies by name. Several of them immediately protested that they never used spies of any sort. . . .

In reply to these protests, Senator La Follette blandly admits that he never really checked the matter up. . . .

The committee, in short, admits that no careful check was made regarding any individual firms; yet it did not hesitate to defame each individual firm by accusing it of employing spies. . . . In the face of this amazing admission, what confidence can any one place in the committee's report?

Defending the Industrial Espionage Report

This wholly unwarranted effort to impugn the credibility of an eighteen-month study by this committee, so fully and accurately reported in your news columns, is based upon the inference that "numerous employers" have successfully denied statements in the report. . . .

Since the middle of last March to the publication of the report . . . only one firm protested to this committee that it had been improperly listed. . . .

In the investigation of such magnitude, where the very nature of the activities examined were shrouded in secrecy and duplicity, so small a number of complaints is in itself evidence of the thoroughness and care with which the committee has undertaken its work.

That more protests were not filed is surprising . . . the information ... has been checked against all available data. . . . The committee has additional data in its files.

Out of the eight firms either denying the accuracy of the committee's list or requesting further information, six were found in the committee's records either to have used industrial espionage or to have contributed to an association making espionage services available to its members. . . . The others had used guard services.

In view of this record and the report of the committee, we can see no basis for the unwarranted inferences drawn by the *New York Times* in its recent editorial.

(Sen.) Robert M. La Follette, Jr.
(Sen.) Elbert Thomas.

Moreover, the *Times* charge that La Follette blandly admits he never really checked the matter up is not true, neither is it true that the committee admits no careful check was made regarding any individual firms.

But it so happens that the list of 2,500 firms represents what has been called "a blue book of American industry." It includes the largest advertisers in the *Times* and other papers, notably General Motors, Chrysler, General Electric, Borden, Kellogg, National Dairy, Quaker Oats, Swift, National Biscuit, Frigidaire, Aluminum Co., Lever Bros., Parker Pen Co., Standard Oil, Bethlehem Steel, Pennsylvania Railroad, Consolidated Gas, Radio Corp., American Locomotive, Pullman, A. & P. Tea Co., F. W. Woolworth, Montgomery, Ward & Co., numerous big advertising department stores such as Gimbel Bros., Lord & Taylor, John Wanamaker. But I would not accuse the *Times* of venality. Neither would I say that it is just a dozen coincidences that in a dozen cases the same paper has been defending men and corporations who are the outstanding symbols of the big business system, and who are almost always guilty of unsocial acts.

Surely it is no exaggeration to say that the *Times* policy in all these instances has been that of a reactionary paper. The liberal press, notably the *New Republic* and *Nation*, have in all these instances accused the *Times* of unfairness. I bring this matter to the attention of Mr. Sulzberger as refutation to his claim, made to me personally, that the *Times* is a liberal newspaper. It is not. It is a reactionary newspaper. Moreover, it is at times even worse than reactionary. At times it is obscurantist.

Mr. Sulzberger repeats Mr. Ochs' statement that the press is not venal. The point need not be argued so far as it affects the *Times*. The *Times* is not venal. It does not suppress news at the request of advertisers, it does not violate the ethics of journalism for pay, and it frequently prints news which both advertisers in the *Times* and the wealthy class with which the *Times* is associated would have preferred to have suppressed.

How then account for the following facts—for the few examples which I quote out of a dossier of several hundred, all gathered since 1935 when the *Times* was criticized in "Freedom of the Press"?

On the morning of November 25, 1937, readers who bought both the soi-disant Democratic *Times* and the Republican *Herald Tribune* found these items

Herald Tribune:	*Times:*
CHRYSLER CUTS PAY ROLLS, AUTO PRODUCTION OFF	Chrysler Cuts Work.

The *Herald Tribune* heading in three lines, in large type, was followed by a long story and most important of all, was sensationally played up on page 1. The *Times* story was a single-line head, followed by three or four inches of news, and completely buried alive on page 32, bottom.

If the *Herald Tribune* can be accused of overplaying the story because of its hatred for the administration, the *Times* on the other hand can justly be accused of semi-suppression of an important news item. Whether this was done out of friendship for the administration or respect to a big advertiser we do not know. But the episode is typical.

Continuing the comparison of the "liberal" *Times* and the tory *Herald Tribune*, here are two more startling instances. One concerns the arrest and imprisonment of Heywood Broun, president of the Newspaper Guild, during a strike in Milwaukee. Both papers carry the same Associated Press report. But the *Times* did not have courage to include this paragraph:

"Anyone who thinks we have a free press is not a wise newspaper reader," he (Broun) said. "Newspapers are the first line of defense of entrenched capital and William Randolph Hearst is the epitome, the symbol of entrenched greed in the United States."

Of course this statement may have been cut for lack of space!

In reporting the suicide of George C. Hanson, famed American diplomatic "trouble-shooter" and former consul general in Moscow, the *Times* had about twice as much room as the *Herald Tribune* to reprint Hanson's last letter, first published in the *Bridgeport Times-Star* in which "he accused New York bankers of meddling in State Department affairs for their own advantage." But the *Times* suppressed the name of the bank.

Times:	*Herald Tribune:*
The sources and motivation of these charges I can only conclude are not disinterested. I would hesitate to believe that the — — — Bank is attempting to interfere with American Government appointments. . . .	The sources and motivation of these charges I can only conclude are not disinterested. I would hesitate to believe that the Chase National Bank is attempting to interfere with American government appointments. . . .

May Day is always a difficult time for the *Times*. On that day rather than Labor Day organized labor generally marches in New York City, and the left wing elements of labor usually predominate. In 1936 the *Times* reported 40,000 MARCH HERE IN MAY DAY PARADE, QUIETEST IN YEARS, whereas the *Post*, favorable to labor, reported that between 200,000 and 250,000 marched.

May Day 1938 was even worse for the *New York Times*. Mr. Ernest Meyer of the *Post* suggested that the tabulators should have gotten together on this because the results were: *Times*, 50,000; *Sunday News*, over 100,000; *Herald Tribune*, between 50,000 and 100,000, and the Communist *Daily Worker* a triumphant 200,000. Mr. Meyer said that the matter was of no tremendous significance because "Among papers of such various shades of political slant, one cannot expect a united front of adding machines."

In December, 1937, the Federated Press, the *Guild Reporter* and the *New York Post* joined in accusing the *Times* of suppressing that part of the speech by Marriner S. Eccles, chairman of the Federal Reserve Board, in which he expressed opposition to the repeal of the undistributed profits and capital gains taxes, two things which both Mr. Sulzberger and the *Times* editorial policy are bitterly decided upon. It is interesting to note that both the Associated Press and the United Press placed Eccles' remarks on profits and gains first but the *Times* leading paragraph said: "Labor and industry were warned today . . . that restrictive practices raising cost . . . were responsible for the present decline. . . ." It is also interesting to note that other newspapers opposed to the administration and the taxes carried fair headlines. Here are some examples compared to the *Times:*

> *Baltimore Sun:* Eccles Urges Retention of Profit Tax Principle.
> *Washington Post:* Save Principle of Profits Tax, Eccles Pleads.
> *New York Times:* Eccles Urges Cut in Building Costs. (!)

In all primary voting and elections since the labor movement began to enter politics the *Times* has also had considerable difficulty in reporting the facts and commenting on them fairly. In Pennsylvania in May, 1938, for instance, the headlines and editorials of the bluestocking *Times* and yellow Hearst sheets were almost identical. Apparently their anti-C. I. O. policies do coincide. But comparing the *Times* with the pro-administration *Post* it is obvious that one of the two is far from being fair or accurate. The *Times* headline was:

PENNSYLVANIA RESULTS BLOW
TO NEW DEAL AND ITS CHIEFS;
REPUBLICANS SEE NEW HOPE

Lewis Prestige Hit.

and editorially the *Times* said: "Another C. I. O. campaign has come a cropper. . . . The attempt to use industrial unionism as a means of acquiring political power has failed ingloriously. Mr. Lewis has been rebuffed by the Democratic voters . . . his candidates ran behind even in some of the coal-mining districts. . . ."

The *Post,* denouncing the "pitiful efforts of the tory press to find a New Deal defeat in the Pennsylvania election," put forth these claims:

The New Deal gained ground: . . . no vestige of a new Deal reverse can be found. . . .

Almost 1,300,000 voted in the Democratic primary. The highest previous Democratic primary turnout, in 1934, was 569,000. *The C. I. O. made a sensational showing:* . . . try to find this in the reactionary press—Kennedy carried the entire State outside of Philadelphia and Pittsburgh. Most startling, the C. I. O. candidate carried the rural counties. . . . He lost the election by less than 66,000 votes. . . . Kennedy lost solely, because of the (opposition) machine's power and labor's split. (Other unions did not support C. I. O.)

The *New York Daily News* has already exposed the *Times* "Opinion of the Press" department for failure to print the *News* editorials after asking for them repeatedly. A similar charge against the *Times* could be made regarding its letter department. It is not conducted fairly. I have mentioned this fact to Mr. Sulzberger and found he is under the impression that there is no gerrymandering going on in those columns, but from personal experience as well as the reports of numerous persons I can produce considerable evidence that the same sort of editing, of selection and of suppression, goes on in this harmless (?) field as elsewhere. Needless to say the majority of letters published are innocuous, favorable to the policies of the *Times,* or generally reactionary. Liberal letter writers have the utmost difficulty in crashing the *Times*. Is Mr. Sulzberger aware of the fact that Malcolm Cowley, of the *New Republic;* John Langdon-Davies, the noted British writer; Lillian Hellman, James Waterman Wise, Richard Watts, Jr., of the *Herald Tribune;* H. V. Kaltenborn, and others have been refused permission to answer Ellery Sedgwick in the letter columns of the *Times?* Then there is the matter of delay. The *Times* news columns called the International Labor Defense "a Communist left-wing organization." Its head, former Congressman Vito Marcantonio, immediately wrote to say: "This statement is incorrect. The I. L. D. is not affiliated with any political party nor does it inquire into the political affiliations of any of its (300,000) members. . . ." Ethically this statement should have been given the same space and place as the original story. It certainly should have been published the next morning. But the *Times* letter editor kept it seven days until its timeliness was over.

Under Mr. Ochs the *Times* valiantly defended the American oil interests and attacked the liberal-labor reformist anti-dictatorial regime of Carranza, Obregon and Calles. It did not demand invasion and annexation, as the *Chicago Tribune* did, but it upheld the dollar sign just as vigorously. Mr. Ochs probably did not know that one of his correspondents in Mexico City was accused by the Mexican government of telegraphing biased anti-Mexican news because he had been refused an oil concession.

In 1927 Mr. Charles Merz, who had collaborated with Walter Lippmann seven years earlier in exposing the perverted news and downright lies about the Russian Soviets in their first three years, made a survey of the news from Mexico. He showed that the *Times* story, "Spread of Disorders Alarms Mexico," was nothing but a murder and two holdups in three days, a record far below Chicago's. When the oil laws were put into effect the *Times* headline was "Mexico Is Pictured on Brink of Revolt." January 24, 1927, the *Times* had a story of a big effort to overthrow the regime which was nothing but a statement from Adolfo de La Huerta who was in exile in the United States.

On March 31, 1938, under the liberal Sulzberger regime, I find this story: PEOPLE OF MEXICO HELD MISLED ON OIL. The Cardenas government had finally put into effect the constitutional rights of 1917, which Calles made a bluff of enforcing in 1927. British and American oil interests whose holdings had been proven ninety percent usurpations, and who were now legally dispossessed, were attempting to use the Foreign Office and the State Department and to threaten with armies and navies if their private property was harmed.

It was the old story of private property vs. human rights and as usual all the material interests, including of course the press, were aligned against human interests. Fortunately, however, the Roosevelt administration is not playing the game of the British foreign office as regards Mexico. But the *Times* is still anti-Mexican.

Under the headline quoted which does not say who "holds" the Mexican people "misled on oil," the *Times* news columns after stating that there is a censorship and that the people do not know the facts adds that "This is the conclusion reached by oil companies here yesterday." There is no further indication of what oil companies or what officials. The story remains anonymous. It is moreover tendentious and purely propagandistic, as any members of the Institute for Propaganda Analysis at Columbia University can testify. It ranks with Hearst's anti-Mexican tainted news.

The *Guild Reporter* calls attention of all American newspapermen to the fact that the *Times* headline HIGH COURT PASSES CLOSED SHOP ISSUE on March 1, 1938, was absolutely correct and that in a late edition this head was changed to TRANSIT WORKERS LOSE IN HIGH COURT which (says the *Reporter*) "created a false impression."

Dorothy Dunbar Bromley tells the story of the Keep America Out of War congress of 1,000 delegates in Washington at which American diplomatic intrigue with British tories was incidentally exposed. The Associated Press sent out the news. The *Times* is of course pledged to Anglo-American friendship.* It failed to mention the event for three days. The *Herald Tribune* did publish a story following cabled requests from noted participants.

The *Times* also likes to minimize scholastic peace movements. Its April 26, 1936, editorial said that the anti-war demonstrations that year "were not so large and impressive as had been predicted," whereas the facts announced later

---

* But it is not connected with British interests, as is frequently charged.

showed that 500,000 had participated, or double the number of 1935 and considerably more than predicted by student organizers.

For a final example of the handling, or rather mishandling, of news here is the instance of a famous speech by Senator Borah. Credit must be given the *Times* for publishing Borah's statement that "the most revolting instance of mass murder in all history" was that committed by the Catholic General Franco who sent his aviators to kill innocent women and children in Guernica. "Guernica," he added, "was not a single instance, it was simply a culmination of a long line of unspeakable atrocities" by the Spanish Clerico-Fascists and their German and Italian fellow ·murderers. Credit must also be given the *Times* for publishing that part of Senator Borah's statement in which he avers that the advocates of Fascism are insidious, subtle and powerful·in America; that Fascism "has far more supporters in this country than Communism and they are much more active and much more adroit," but the fact still remains that the *Herald Tribune* published the following paragraph and the *Times* did not. It read:

The centralization of wealth and the centralization of political power go hand in hand to form the basis for Fascism.

Here, in other words, was an instance where the·tremendous pressure being put forth by the American Catholic hierarchy to suppress all news unfavorable to Franco, whom even the Pope himself has rebuked for his massacres, has failed to operate, whereas "wealth" and "power" which have no official or organized pressure group working in the *Times* office, but which nevertheless pervade the very air, were effective in editing the news.

The *Times* is of course a big business. It represents an investment of millions, a gross income of between twenty and thirty million dollars a year, and a net profit of several millions a year. But that fact is not as important as the fact that in addition to being a big business organization it is the organ of big business.

To be liberal a newspaper need not be the enemy of big business but it must at least be free to criticize. The *Times* has never attempted that. It takes the part of attorney for big business.

Whatever laws are the enemies of big business are the enemies of the *Times;* whatever actions are favorable to big business receive the applause of the *Times*. It opposes every Congressional investigation. It opposes the laws which the American Federation of Labor and the Committee for Industrial Organization favor, and when the Chamber of Commerce and the National Association of Manufacturers express a wish the *Times* turns a somersault. Can all these things be coincidences?

Every employee in every department knows that the *Times* is the organ of big business. When the editor of the letters department destroys ninety-nine percent of the letters favoring picketing and fills his column with letters ninety-nine percent of which oppose picketing he is not doing so under instructions from Mr. Sulzberger or Colonel Adler. He is doing so because he is a smart man and knows where the capitalistic butter is churned.

Very rarely is the bias flagrant. The lay reader may not notice it at all. The *Times* for example can give nice space to Tom Girdler, one of labor's chief enemies ("Girdler Says Foes of Capitalism Err"—June 5, 1938), and no space to more important minds. The *Times* has tried to explain away its failure to publish the news of the impending failure of the Bank of United States but it had nothing to say when "Guy Fawkes" in the *New Yorker* caught it protecting the successor to Charles E. Mitchell at the National City Bank by misquoting him. The *Times* believes it is "good news" that the Roosevelt administration is settling its controversy with the public utility industry, and on May 26, 1937, the *Times* published a column report of a statement by its financial editor under the heading:

CAPITALISM IS SEEN
ON FIRM BASE AGAIN

Sound Working System Held Responsible for Recovery and
Advance by A. D. Noyes

God's in his heaven,
All's right with the world—and the *Times*.

In concluding my criticism of the *New York Times* in "Freedom of the Press," I said that: "A wonderful opportunity presents itself to Messrs. Arthur Hays Sulzberger and Julius Ochs Adler whose names now grace the masthead of the *Times:* if they have the character and courage and an enlightened intelligence they can easily surpass their predecessor. They must not, as so many *Times* men do, merely worship at the shrine of Adolph Ochs. Ochs did many things to make the *Times* the most important paper in America, and that is no mean accomplishment; but there are still vast improvements to be made, not so much in quality of news but under the headings of the Canons of Journalism: Sincerity, Truthfulness, Impartiality, Fair Play. I hope to see the *Times* some day as great as it is important."

I think that the *Times* today is a greater and more influential newspaper than it was under Ochs. One reason for its advancement is the retreat of many other great newspapers. The number of journals which want to be great, instead of great money makers, grows fewer every day. The pressures increase. Fear increases. Political activity of publishers increases. The free and independent journals decrease. The *Times,* despite all its faults, grows more powerful because while it is not the liberal leader its owners say it is, it is not retreating with the majority of rich newspapers.

Without denying Mr. Sulzberger's sincerity and intentions

I still think it fair to say that the *Times* is not liberal or impartial, and open to hundreds of questions under the canon "Fair Play."

I do not ask of Mr. Sulzberger that he publish a liberal paper; I ask him only to publish a newspaper. I ask him to publish a newspaper which will make it impossible for me or anyone else five years from now to publish another chapter of criticism such as the foregoing.

CHAPTER 11

The *Sun* Grows Cold

WILLIAM T. DEWART, publisher and president of *The New York Sun,* is a commendatore of Fascist Italy and a Litt.D. of Union College of Schenectady.

In making a doctor of letters of the eminent journalist Dr. Dixon Ryan Fox read the following citation: "A publisher—rising from a minor clerkship to command an enterprise of national influence, an instance of what sheer ability and ambition can accomplish in the American environment; now developing a great newspaper to new levels of public usefulness, not only as a diary of events, but as a medium of cultural instruction and an instrument of investigation, throwing the light of the *Sun* upon sinister obscurities in our political and social practice; bearing great responsibilities with poise and patience and discharging them with courage and understanding."

Otherwise William T. Dewart's name is rarely seen in his or anyone else's newspaper. He is an avoider of publicity. He has no political ambitions, does not want to rule anyone nor enjoy secret power behind the scenes. He is content to make money.

On one occasion, however, Dewart was very much in the news. He was recently listed among the numerous multimillionaires in America accused by a Senate committee of setting up holding companies for the purpose of avoiding taxation. (It was surprising how many administration-hating tax-hating newspaper owners there were in that list.)

Dewart replied with a front-page statement in his own

paper which was not without prejudice. It stated that the *Sun* was incorporated in Albany in 1926 with 30,000 shares of preferred (or A) stock and 20,000 second preferred (or B) stock, par value $100 a share and 100,000 shares of common. Dewart had bought the paper from the Metropolitan Museum of Art to whom the arch newspaper wrecker Frank Munsey had willed it. Employees of the *Sun* were permitted to buy preferred stock at eight percent, and 350 now own some. The second preferred and common stock have never paid dividends. "The facts," concludes the Dewart statement, "are repeated here so simply that anybody with a greater intellectual capacity than a Mongolian idiot can understand them. Even a treasury expert should grasp the truth about The New York Sun Inc. . . . ."

Three days later Under Secretary of the Treasury Roswell Magill informed the Congressional Tax Avoidance Investigating Committee that tax experts were "absolutely correct" in listing the New York Sun Inc. as a personal holding company. (He made the same statement about Consolidated Publishers, Inc., a Paul Block company.) "We of course cannot tell what the motives of the owners were in organizing these companies," Magill said, "we know only what the result was: substantial savings on taxes."

Besides the Dewarts—William T., William T., Jr., and Thomas W.—the following persons own one percent of the *Sun* stock or more: Frank M. O'Brien, editor; Keats Speed, managing editor; Edwin S. Friendly, business manager; Franz Schneider, Jr., Gilbert T. Hodges, Herbert B. Fairchild, Edwin A. Sutphin, and Robert H. Davis. The C. W. H. Corporation owns all of the stock owned by all the previously mentioned Dewarts plus Mary W. and Mary Dewart. There are no bondholders or mortgage holders listed in the sworn statement which the paper files annually but Ferdinand Lundberg in his "America's Sixty Families" challenges these affidavits. He states that "The *Sun* executives are understood to have obtained the money to buy the paper for a reputed $11,000,000 in the form of a loan, a large part of which is still said to be outstanding, from the Guaranty Trust Company. This loan does not appear among the admitted obligations of the Sun Publishing Company because it was privately made to the leading stockholders."

Franz Schneider, formerly financial editor of the *Sun* and the *Evening Post,* is president of Newmont Mining Company and, while still a journalist, was on the J. P. Morgan list of privileged characters who could buy Morgan offerings cheaply. He bought 1000 shares of Morgan's Standard Brands and many other stocks while financial editor of the *Sun,* enough to make a profit of almost $60,000. The *Sun,* says Lundberg, is regarded as a Morgan house organ. No one in Wall Street disputes that charge.

In appearance the *Sun* is the most conservative newspaper in the metropolis. But this sobriety of type, this restraint with headlines, does not mean that Dewart cannot beat Hearst at his own game. For example, the well-known chain tax hoax of the 1936 Presidential campaign. It was during the Republican propaganda attack in which regimentation and dictatorship were charged to the Democrats that John D. M. Hamilton accused the Social Security Board—which by the way had been sponsored by both parties—with planning to tag and chain every workingman and woman in America. There was no truth to the story of course. But the photographs of men wearing chains and license tags with numbers, one of the greatest newspaper hoaxes in history, is generally discredited to Hearst, whereas the *Sun* was equally if not more guilty. In fact the *Nation* charges the *Sun* with first publication. Its November 2 issue had as headline "New Deal Will Tag Workers." The *Sun* used two photographs, one of the metal tag itself and one showing a tagged worker. The difference between the *Sun* and numerous corrupt newspapers which used the photographs was that the *Sun* used probability in its captions, the yellow press used certainty. The *Sun* said: "Such a tag has been prepared and submitted to the Social Security Board for approval," the totally corrupt press inferred the tag was already approved.

Throughout the campaign the *Sun* ran a "'boondoggling" department. It chose an activity of the New Deal daily for attack or derision. It ridiculed the expenditure of ten thousand dollars for a dam at Boulder, Colorado, because it would take a tidal wave more than a mile high to reach the town. An investigation showed that raging floods had menaced the town every spring. It ridiculed the expenditure of money to renovate reference books in libraries. It sneered at every public welfare undertaking. Two years later an impartial survey of work from land reclamation and power plant construction to sewerage systems installation—not to mention the salvation of human material in the CCC, PWA and WPA—testified to the magnificent achievements of the *Sun's* boondoggling.

Probably the nadir of the ridiculous was reached by the conservative *Sun* in a story which indignantly told how one man tried to pull a Landon sunflower button off another's lapel. A big head and almost a column text! That was not yellow journalism, Hearst style, but something new in bluestocking sensationalism.

The *Sun* also accepted a paid advertisement from a cockeyed cartoonist named Percy Crosby who stated that "a vote for Roosevelt in 1936 is a vote for bloodshed in 1937"; who called the President the keeper of a "Washington reptile house"; and who concluded: "The time may come when defense is imminent; that time when we must fight for our very homes. If such time comes . . . then it would seem that the best philosophy under such a condition would be: NEVER WOUND A SNAKE, BUT KILL IT." For printing this advertisement the *Sun* was paid $3,200.

The Wall Street bankers and brokers commuting to Montclair, New Jersey, and Bronxville, New York, read the *Sun* almost exclusively. I have traveled in coaches where ninety percent of the passengers were of this type and a large part of the conversation was wish-fulfillment. I have heard bankers openly advocating the assassination of the President.

Such hatred, publicly expressed, such bloodthirstiness, I have never heard in the trenches. Perhaps a mob of Southern gentlemen intent on lynching speak that way when they are drunk and hysterical. But these men are the aristocrats of America—at least the commercial aristocrats. They are members of the same class whom Heywood Broun describes as listening to one of Roosevelt's fireside chats and using language which he could not reprint in his daily column.

In the letter columns of the *Sun* one can find some of this obscurantism and hatred. There the men who sit at radios and curse the administration of our nation can voice their opinions, provided of course they do not violate the law. They must restrain themselves. So every day with almost no exceptions there are letters abusing Roosevelt, Wallace, Ickes, Hopkins, and all the New Dealers in every printable term. If, as a test, a reader should every day for a month—as a journalism student has done—send in a letter in praise of a New Deal action, he will find that none will be printed.

In the *Sun* the reader will find a letter saying that "labor is tired of strife caused by the one-sided Wagner Act." Labor, in other words, is tired of the Magna Carta of labor. In the *Sun* letters defend Mayor Hague of Jersey City. Just before the Supreme Court declared leaflet distribution part of the freedom of the press, one John Eoghan Kelly wrote a letter to the *Sun* defending the forceful deportation of "outsiders" who had come to the Jersey town "interfering with legitimate business." Efforts at unionization become "Communistic intrusion," and labor becomes "Reds." The demand for civil rights is called "simian chatter" in a three-quarter-column letter in the *Sun* which says free speech is not denied in Jersey City because C. I. O. organizers are allowed to speak freely if they retire to their own headquarters. And as for literature distribution, Jersey City has a city ordinance

against it, and that's that. A letter protesting that leaflets
have the same rights as copies of the *Sun* was not printed.
If you bait the Reds you make the *Sun* letter columns; if you
uphold the Constitution and the Supreme Court in favor
of a baited minority, you do not.

Where Hearst is vulgar, the *Sun* is bluestocking in its Red-
baiting. Like Hearst, Dewart is for the Fascists in Spain. The
Sun headlines and the Hearst headlines speak of the Loyalists
as "Reds," whereas no newspaper in the world which can
make any claim to journalistic ethics has ever done so.

The *Sun* reporters are stockholders. They share the anti-
labor bias of their bosses. The Newspaper Guild has made
no headway in their reactionary stronghold. In its place
there is the Sun Editorial Employees Union, a makeshift
organized when the Wagner Act made a company union
illegal. Numerous concessions were made by Dewart—but
Sun employees refuse to recognize that it was the Guild's success as a powerful national body which forced the concessions. However, Dewart, thanks to this union and the stock-
holding feature, has succeeded in isolating his men. No
sound of the march of progress can enter the ivory towers
on which the sun never sets.

Generally speaking it may be said with fairness that the
Sun is the leading anti-labor newspaper in the East. In the
West the *Los Angeles Times* had an established law to publish all news inimical to labor and to labor unions and to
suppress all news favorable to unions or to the liberal-labor
movement. Under General Otis it was without doubt the
most perverted big newspaper in America. On the *Sun* there
is no general order to blacken labor but any reading of
headlines and stories will show that of all the New York
newspapers the *Sun* is most consistently inimical in every
way.

If, for example, there is a dispute among the taxi drivers
and acid is thrown, the *Sun* headline does not accuse a rival
union or a non-union man, but it accuses labor. "Labor

Vandals Attack 41 Cabs" reads the two-column front-page heading on a relatively unimportant item in the May 6, 1938, issue. "Labor Vandals Deface House" reads an item in the November 22, 1937, issue. The juxtaposition of labor and vandalism creates more than an implication.

In truth there is no justification in the stories themselves for the headlines. Vandalism has been committed. In no instance are the vandals known, and the reporters who wrote the stories, although unfriendly, are not faking. In the first instance the victim is the Allied Taxicab System, but only the headline suggests who the aggressor is. When on the following day Eugene Connolly, director of the Transport Workers Union, taxicab division, protested the *Sun's* headline and stated that "anti-union fleet operators have in the past resorted to such tactics (acid throwing) in an attempt to turn public sentiment against the union but in this instance the acid thrown may well have been committed by racketeers trying to muscle in to convince operators they need gangster protection," the *Sun* did not publish the story.

In the case of the house defaced by twelve splotches of red aniline dye the *Sun* told sympathetically the story of a Doctor Welton who claimed he treated the poor free and was hurt by the fact anyone should attack his non-union, picketed, $20,000 redecorating job.

An even better example of colored, half-true, prejudiced, tendentious and propaganda news was the *Sun* coverage of the Seattle labor situation in 1936. The employees of the Hearst *Post-Intelligencer* had walked out for good cause and the paper suspended peacefully. There was no violence. Everyone knew that if violence could be provoked it would help Hearst. But the *New York Sun* actually published a news item which was an approval of planned violence. It said (August 13th): "Something is going to happen soon and it promises not to be pleasant. The (conservative) citizenry is slowly gathering its forces and the day is not far distant when those forces will strike hard. Seattle is still American." To

strike hard—in other words, to use violence, break the law—
is in the mind of the *Sun* a symptom of Americanism.

In this same dispatch it is reported that a new daily paper
is planned in the Northwest. Liberal and progressive forces
were behind it. But the *Sun,* without any evidence, begins
by calling the proposed rival to Hearst "a Communist-
affiliated newspaper," proceeds to "the projected radical
Communist organ" which is an untruth and concludes with
"the new Communist daily," which is a falsehood.

In its summary of the situation on October 10th the *Sun*
headline said, "The Forces of Law Still Abet New Deal Racketeers," and the story opened with a remark about "New Deal
labor racketeering forces." The writer, Guy W. Beardsley,
then attempts to link the New Deal with Communists, then
predicts that "This is Republican weather along the Pacific
coast" and quotes a professional straw vote proving "that
there is a decided swing to Landon" and gives his own opinion that "Hearst made many Republican votes throughout
the state the day the New Deal racketeers closed his newspaper and every day it stays closed Republican prospects
throughout the state get brighter." The election proved the
whole *Sun* story ridiculous.

On the home front, here are *Sun* typical anti-labor headlines and stories:

November 30, 1937:
Police Smash C. I. O. Attempt to Get Foothold in Jersey City
December 16th:
Labor's Friend Berates Labor
December 17th:
U. S. Committed to Open Shop Labor Policy
January 10, 1938:
Frey Links C. I. O. to Communism

The first item refers to the violent attack on a group of
union men who were kidnaped and deported after being
arrested for distributing leaflets, a Jersey City "crime" which

the Supreme Court held legal. The news story referred to the "C. I. O. and so-called 'liberal' organizations." When in January, 1938, Mayor Hague called a meeting in the armory to listen to his bad-grammar Fascism, the *Sun* reported 75,-000 persons present. This was untrue because it was a physical impossibility. As Heywood Broun reported, the "hall was filled, but 15,000 persons would be a fair estimate as to its capacity." The *Sun* always slants the news in favor of the most reactionary mayor of the country.

The item headed "U. S. Committed to Open Shop Labor Policy" is a phony. The United States is not committed to an open shop labor policy. The other two items are typical cases of the *Sun* using any and all items as whips against labor and especially against the C. I. O. Never friendly to the American Federation of Labor, the *Sun* now employs their reactionary leaders whenever it can to abuse the more progressive union.

How far prejudice and unfairness can be carried were illustrated when the *Sun* took a full page advertisement in the *Daily News* to advertise a story headlined

THE MOST
HORRIFYING MURDERS
OF THE CENTURY
IN AMERICA

which turned out to be an account of a fight between miners in a labor war of fifteen years ago. It was known as the Herrin massacre. The purpose of the *Sun* rehash of stale news was merely to harm John L. Lewis who is head of the miners' union.

The *Sun* is so rabidly anti-labor that it goes in for crusading. Crusading has been from the earliest days of American journalism associated with public welfare, the objective being the exposure of evils, whether in men or in systems. The *Sun* is probably the unique example of the reactionary crusader. It exposes, for example (issue of November 17, 1937), the fact that "labor reaps its first fruits since election of La Guardia." In this story it is said that the estimates of a tunnel contract exceed the original by $7,000,000; "that sum represents the first fruits plucked by labor" due to an increased wage scale. The *Sun* claims the wage scale will be higher than elsewhere and "because of the labor costs the tunnel will stand the city's taxpayers approximately thirty percent more than had been anticipated." It will cost those taxpayers who have found no way of dodging taxes. In the issue of April 18, 1938, the *Sun* boasts of the firing of a Negro C. I. O. picket in Harlem because of "alarm" over "the *Sun's* recent exposure of picketing abuses."

These are the only two "crusades" this *Sun* reader has been able to detect in as many years, but perhaps they are enough to warrant a Litt.D. for "throwing the light of the *Sun* upon sinister obscurities in our political and social practice." Who knows?

In establishing "The Voice of Business" edition, Dewart declared that "Many of us have been led to believe that serious and constructive journalism is losing ground, that playing up the frivolities and foibles of humanity is the formula of the day. Well, here is the answer, written in a manner to give heart to the newspapermen of America. . . . It is a lesson which should not be lost on those who would worship the false gods of journalism."

The special edition runs to about 150 pages and is a magnificent advertising scheme because it gives steel corporations, cannon makers, bridge builders and great utilities which have nothing to sell direct to the public a chance to spend money in what is known as "good-will advertising." Who can tell whether it earns the good will of the public? But it certainly does of the publisher.

In the *Sun* business edition (January 4, 1936) it was announced that "outstanding authorities would present the facts and philosophies of the American system of industrial democracy (sic)." Here is a sample fact and philosophy written by an eminent authority:

TWO PERCENT CONTROL THE WEALTH!
WHAT OF IT—IF THEY DO?

The point the eminent authority, one Charles H. Franklin, makes, is that control does not mean ownership. That should make it all right with the third of a nation which has nothing. The eminent philosopher continues:

"You and I know from actual experience that nine out of ten of the poor, among whom we were reared in this city, remained so because of their refusal to accept their opportunities and because of their own vices. We know that nine out of every ten rich, middle class or poor, who made a go of things have done so because of their initiative and honesty."

On another page another eminent authority, Preston S. Krecker, writes on "Depressions! Wars and unsound business policies are causes." Rufus S. Tucker, on "The Profits and Who Gets Them," claims only ten percent of the total receipts of corporations go to stockholders and managers in good years. Byron D. Miller, of Woolworth's, writes in favor of private enterprise; A. W. Robertson, of Westinghouse, on "Federal policies delay recovery"; E. T. Weir, of National Steel, "sees politics as business hindrance"; Edward Seubert, of Standard Oil, "urges stable money . . . balanced budget"; John J. Raskob sees "revival of heavy industry retarded by taxation"; and David Lawrence discusses the barriers and impediments "the government has erected" against "an enlarged volume of business." Irénée du Pont demands that the administration get out of business, "but if they keep on trying to Sovietize the United States and are successful in so doing, it will end either in civil war or the United States being reduced to a scale of living of Russia."

But why go on? Such is *Sun* philosophy and economics.

The best thing that can be said in favor of the *New York Sun* is that it is not a hypocrite. It does not, like the majority of newspapers, pretend to be the friend of the common people, the upholder of the rights of the workingman, the defender of civil liberties and American democracy. The *Sun* is the organ of Wall Street, and in Wall Street money rights stand above human rights.

Such honesty is amazing in this journalistic transition era, this third stage of newspaper history in America, where business rather than traditional idealism has become the end as well as the means.

Being the voice of business the *Sun* naturally adopts the policy of business. Business today is openly anti-reform, anti-administration, anti-labor, anti-Wagner Act, anti-union (especially the militant unions), anti-co-operatives and generally anti-social.

There is no press law, no moral obligation or established custom by which a conservative newspaper becomes a tory newspaper, a tory becomes reactionary, and a reactionary becomes mean, intolerant, prejudiced, so that all its actions are biased and unfair and its achievements the perversion of men's minds, but in actual practice that is usually the case in every nation in the world. Even the great conservative *London Times* has on many occasions been caught slanting and coloring the news, while lately its conservatism has led it right up to Hitler's back door where it has joined with the conservative British "statesmen" in licking the boots of Fascism. The *Sun* would not feel uncomfortable if the Hague style of Fascism were to cross over from New Jersey.

In newspaper circles the *Sun* is regarded as a tragedy. It was once the journalists' journal. The impress of Dana, the publisher who said, "What the good Lord lets happen I am not ashamed to print," prevailed for a long time, even under Munsey the Wrecker. Under Dewart the *Sun* has become not so much a newspaper as a special pleader for a special class.

Under the law it has every right to do so.

Under the canons of journalism it is, of course, another matter.

Nevertheless in the summer of 1938 the School of Journalism of the University of Missouri awarded its medal of honor "for distinguished service in journalism" to the *New York Sun*. The citation read by Acting Dean Roscoe Ellard said in part:

"For the excellence of its literary style; for its urbanity, high journalistic craftsmanship and intelligence in selecting, as well as in handling, its news; for its unqualified intellectual honesty in conducting a newspaper for a highly intelligent and discriminating newspaper audience; for its treatment of the liberal arts, political correspondence and financial and commercial news by outstanding authorities; for its Saturday issue, which, in the scope, character and quality of its articles and its general informative value, is unusual among newspapers of the United States."

The *Sun* should also have a medal for the most dignified and refined violations of the canons of journalism to which the University of Missouri once dedicated itself.

CHAPTER 12

Stern's Fight for Liberalism

J. David Stern is one of a tiny minority of owners in America who really wants to publish a free newspaper.

From bitter costly experiments he has learned what most of his colleagues have not even been interested in, namely, that freedom is quite impossible. But he is a very reasonable and realistic human being, and he has frequently said that he intends to publish as free a newspaper as possible, without going into the red. "Lusty" Scripps said and did the same thing. But that was a generation ago when liberalism still paid dividends.

Mr. Stern knows just who the enemies of his dream are. He knows that to run a free newspaper it is necessary to publish news which advertisers will not like. He is a strong believer in strong editorials, and an editorial stand on almost any question outside the viciousness of the man-eating shark and the Bengal tiger means antagonism from pressure groups, advertising agencies, big business, and the great gods of finance.

Mr. Stern has therefore faced the choice of publishing as liberal and free a newspaper as possible, with the necessary compromises, thereby breaking even or making money, and publishing a completely free newspaper for a short time and having to go out of business because of a sit-down strike of advertisers, finance and big business in general.

A completely free newspaper, for example, might compare the Ford, Chevrolet and Plymouth cars, just as Consumers Union does, and as a result lose two-thirds of its automobile advertising; or it might publish a scientific report on poison in cigarettes and lose all its tobacco advertising; or it might investigate wages in department stores, and lose so much advertising that it would have to suspend even if it had a million dollars behind it and a million readers. Such things are out. No newspaper in America will ever compare automobiles from the consumers' viewpoint, and the *Christian Science Monitor* is probably the only metropolitan daily which will tell the truth about tobacco. And department stores, the main source of city advertising, are the most sacred of sacred cows in journalism.

On one occasion, however, Mr. Stern has even lassoed and thrown that animal—and incidentally shown up the suppression of news by the *Philadelphia Evening Bulletin* and the *Philadelphia Inquirer*.* The employees of Gimbels, Strawbridge & Clothier, Lit Brothers, Snellenburgs and Frank & Seder had gone out on strike just when the five stores were gaudy for the Thanksgiving and Christmas trade. Union recognition, better working conditions, and more wages were demanded, one of the pickets' placards announcing that salesmen cannot live on $12 a week. Trucks were overturned, deliveries were stopped, hundreds of customers refused to enter the struck stores and went to Wanamakers, and a million dollars' worth of business was lost. One official called it a "miniature revolution," but revolution or no, it was a front-page news story if ever there was one.

To those defenders of the American press who claim that department store advertising no longer influences newspapers I present the fact that Stern's *Philadelphia Record* was the only paper which for a week refused to suppress the news of this strike.

Stern has consistently tried to publish all the news and also to crusade in the public's behalf. His first newspaper was the *New Brunswick Times,* a small-town New Jersey sheet

* As *Time* also reported, November 30, 1936.

which he acquired in 1911 for $2,500. He immediately began
exposing the corrupt political boss. The town sat up. Corrupt
New Jersey politics sat up, too. Attempts were made to buy
Stern off, but he continued his campaign. "I wouldn't sell for
all the money in the world," he said. But he sold the paper
for $25,000 and was thereby enabled to buy a bigger paper in
a bigger town and start bigger crusades.

In 1920 he got the *Camden Courier*. Camden had been in
the hands of a corrupt political machine for twenty years, a
machine so corrupt and entrenched that it had passed through
the great muckraking era which began with the century and
which Lincoln Steffens fathered. The best citizens of Camden were among the crooks. When Stern entered the Camden
Club he says that "everybody stopped talking because they
had all been cursing me."

He hired expert municipal accountants. He found that
"Camden had the lowest per capita expenditure for the
health service of any similar city in the East . . . and the highest infant mortality rate, the lowest allowance for visiting
nurses and health work, with hundreds of thousands of dollars spent wasted on political drones." He spent from Christmas night to New Year's Eve making a drama out of the statistics. The result was sensational.

"It took me three years to go from Public Enemy No. 1 to
chief champion of the people of Camden," Stern says of his
experience.

In December, 1933, he took over the apparently moribund
New York Evening Post. He said to his staff:

"I want to run a newspaperman's newspaper. If you like it
the public will like it. . . .

"I am for the Newspaper Guild. I am for controlled credit
inflation."

It is said he paid $300,000. It is also said that the New
York publishers of evening newspapers had pledged a fund
of a quarter of a million dollars for the purpose of buying
and destroying the *Post*. This is the system the publishers

used in Pittsburgh to reduce rivalry, and it is the system
being employed in more and more cities. And when Stern
outmaneuvered them, the evening paper publishers, who had
a "co-operative" trucking system for paper delivery, served
notice on Stern that the *Post* would be dropped. This meant
a raise in the cost of suburban distribution of 400 percent.
This was the salute which the great "co-operative" publishers
of the great metropolis gave their colleague.

Just before entering New York, Mr. Stern wrote a defense
of the editorial page in which he pointed out the fact that
the 1929 depression had awakened the people, that they were
"hungry for courageous analysis and definite guidance." He
continued:

"The sad truth is that many newspapers have not shown
courage in serving sincerely and intelligently this new army
of serious readers because of wholly imaginary inhibitions—
because of a fear of offending that was wholly unwarranted.
The average newspaper is twice as free as it ever dares to be.

"I have been a newspaper publisher for twenty-five years,
and have owned six newspapers in various parts of the country. I have never been approached with an offer of money for
editorial support, nor has any banker to whom I owed money
ever attempted a squeeze play. I am in the humiliating position of the woman who was insulted because she had not
been insulted.

"Too many newspapers suffer from the fear complex. They
are not only afraid to offend important interests, but they
are afraid of writing over the heads of their readers. They
'edit down.'

"I have found that it is impossible to write over the heads
of the readers, if the writing is sincere, and in simple language. . . .

"Not half a dozen papers in the country make a practice
of running daring editorials on the front page, where such
editorials rightly belong."

In 1935, when the *Post* was attracting the support of all

liberal and intelligent elements, Mr. Stern, addressing an association of national advertisers, said he had learned from experience that "the public is sure to recognize sincerity and guts, and to pay well for it. . . . These are qualities in a newspaper that can't be bought or faked. They have to be in the heart of the publisher. You can't fool the public any more than you can fool the children at home. . . .

"Sooner or later an editor who is insincere reveals himself, and the public senses that insincerity with an intuition as quick and uncanny as that of a child."

(But it took the public forty-five years to begin the boycott of the Hearst press.)

Nothing he has done has won more admiration for J. David Stern than his exposure of the hypocrisies, inconsistencies and frequent falsehoods of other newspapers. In a metropolitan manner he has revived some of the audacity which marked journalism of an older day on the Western frontier. His most important gesture was his resignation from the American Newspaper Publishers Association.* At that time he was joined by Patterson's *New York Daily News* in the charge that the A. N. P. A. had set itself up as a supreme court to judge the constitutionality of the Wagner Labor Act before the Supreme Court itself had had a chance to do so. When the A. N. P. A., on the advice of attorney Hanson, had declared the law unconstitutional, Mr. Stern denounced this action.

He realizes what all newspaper owners know, that the press is a great force, for good or evil, for reaction or progress. He does not, as do most of his colleagues, exempt the newspapers from his praise or attacks, knowing that they have a large hand in political affairs nowadays.

* Chapter 1.

Thus, when Colonel McCormick was making a fuss over the anniversary of Peter Zenger, Colonial fighter for a free press, Stern said that "the same kind of tories who sent him to jail now gather to do him honor." There was a *Chicago Tribune* reporter present. It was at a time this paper was running a Red scare, and linking the administration with Reds. The *Tribune* man asked Stern to explain. Stern replied:

"You tell Bertie (McCormick) that he is seeing things under the bed. . . . Lip service from autocratic steel barons and Red-baiting publishers is no honor to Zenger."

McCormick, who is the head of the freedom of the press committee of the A. N. P. A., had a cheap revenge on Stern in May, 1938, when the leading American Fascist of the time, the Mayor of Jersey City, suppressed the *Post*. Said the *Chicago Tribune:*

"A Federal judge has issued an injunction to restrain Mayor Frank Hague and his Jersey City police from stopping the display of the *New York Post* on Jersey City newsstands. Perhaps some of our readers expect us to sound off about the gallantry of the little New York newspaper in defending the freedom of the press against a rapacious politician. If so they are going to be disappointed." The reason? Because the *Post* supported the Roosevelt administration at the time the publishers were trying to write a code, "the most dishonest, weasel-worded and treacherous document" ever offered to General Johnson.

Stern replied editorially that the publishers' code "had no more to do with freedom of the press than the State laws regulating the hours of women workers, fire laws calling for adequate staircases and traffics laws compelling newspaper trucks, like all others, to stay on the right side of the street." But, he asked, "did American publishers join in the great effort that most of business was making? They did not, by and large. They put themselves in a special class. They wrapped the mantle of freedom of the press about them to fight the code, when what they really feared was freedom of their employees to organize!"

In March, 1936, the *Post* began a series of editorials on "The Facts of Life for Newspaper Readers" in which it showed up its contemporaries by contrasting their headlines and stories. The series was occasioned by a letter from E. K. Merat, of the Advanced School of Education of Columbia University. Mr. Merat is a Persian but his interest in truth in the news exceeds that of at least ninety-nine percent of the American people. Mr. Merat asked the entire New York press whether news is separate from opinion; if the papers permit their editorial policy to affect their news policy; if they allow editorial sentiments and opinions to influence the news and the presentation of news in the news columns, or whether the two policies are kept separate.

The *New York Times, World-Telegram* and *Daily Worker* replied, but Mr. Merat considered their answers confidential. The *New York Herald Tribune, Sun, Daily News* and *Journal & American* did not reply. The *Post* was the only paper to publish the correspondence.

Said the chief Stern organ:

"We don't know who has been handing you this line about 'the theory of American journalism that news is separate from opinion,' but we'll bet it wasn't a working newspaper man. . . . The theory . . . not only isn't true but it couldn't possibly ever be true, on any paper. . . .

"Men, not machines, report news stories, and men, not machines, edit and make newspapers. . . . Editors have to use their judgment. Judgment, dear E. K. Merat, is opinion.

"A certain proposed constitutional amendment comes up at Albany. The *Post* headlines: CHILD LABOR AMENDMENT IS UP FOR VOTE. The *Herald Tribune* headlines: YOUTH-CONTROL AMENDMENT IS UP FOR VOTE. Both papers are reporting the news. Or are they, dear E. K. Merat?

"A Democratic convention meets. The delegates storm at each other for three hours, then pass a harmony resolution.

A Republican paper headlines: DEMOCRATS RAGE FOR THREE HOURS IN WILD SESSION. A Democratic paper headlines: DEMOCRATS MAKE PEACE; HARMONY VOTE PASSES. Both papers are honestly reporting the facts as they see them, but . . . Republican eyes are not Democratic eyes. . . .

"Such stuff as the *Journal's* constant reference to the Spanish 'Reds' when they mean the government forces is becoming rare. We're talking about the honest judgment that an editor has to make to get up an edition. . . .

"The *Times* is a great paper. We think the *Times* could make any issue fairly important by putting it under a four-column head on Page 1 often enough. The *Times,* a newspaper of 'record,' tries not to editorialize. But it doesn't pick its headlines out of a paper bag either. . . .

"We think it's good for newspaper readers to know the facts of life. . . ."

On May 25, 1938, the *Post* took the *Times* over the hurdles. Under an editorial heading, ADD FACTS OF LIFE—NEWS UNFIT TO PRINT, it said that "the Supreme Court must be a trial to the editors" who more valiantly than Justices Butler and McReynolds "have fought to keep the Court in the anti-New Deal column." Instances are then given: in every one of them a decision favorable to the New Deal was played down in the *Times,* a decision unfavorable played up by being given either the front page or big type, and four specific cases in one day are mentioned:

Item 1. Chief Justice Hughes sharply questions an attorney for Girdler's Republic Steel Corporation.

Item 2. The National Labor Relations Board wins three cases, including the one ordering Remington Rand to reinstate 4,000 men.

Item 3. Hughes rebukes a circuit court of appeals for trying to prevent an investigation of Associated Gas subsidiaries.

Item 4. The Court rejected an appeal of utility companies which questioned the right of PWA to finance the Santee Cooper project, biggest public power project next to TVA.

What happened to these four big news items? The *Post* reports: "Tom Girdler's slightest snort makes page 1 in the *Times,* but Item 1 was nowhere to be found in Tuesday's *Times.* Item 2 was buried in the fifth paragraph of a story on page 6 headed HIGH COURT HEARS NLRB ARGUMENTS. Item 3 was put back on page 33. And Item 4 wasn't in the paper."

But still more important is the *Post* investigation of what happens in the Republican, tory and self-styled liberal press of New York City when there is a news story extremely at variance with the general anti-New Deal policies of the press.

For years the papers have published the released summaries sent them by *Fortune,* the big business magazine. At the end of May, 1938, after five years of pounding by the press, it was found that the popularity of the President was holding firm, "that the chances of any important number of Mr. Roosevelt's men will be defeated in the primaries this year are very thin," that 54.7 percent of the people back Roosevelt and only 34.4 percent disapprove. This was of course good, big news for the Roosevelt papers, few as they are, but it was nevertheless news for any paper. And what happened in this case? The *Post* investigation showed:

New York Times, Wednesday: Not hide nor hair of it anywhere. But the *Times* found room for a column-and-a-quarter account of a sectional bankers' conference, way out in Springfield, Illinois, in which the New Deal was attacked. (The actual figures on *Fortune's* poll were reserved for afternoon papers, but the important editorial was available to the morning papers.)

New York Herald Tribune: Nothing on Wednesday, but on Thursday half a column no page 15. The *Herald Tribune* used the figures on Roosevelt's popularity, but omitted *Fortune's* editorial criticism of business and *Fortune's* defense of the New Deal.

New York Sun: Nothing at all.

New York Journal: Nothing at all. But there was room for a full column quoting a group of Chicago business men against the New Deal.

New York World-Telegram: Two-thirds of a column on *Fortune's* release, under a two-column headline,' Page 5; adequate handling.

New York Post: A bit more than a column, Page 1, first edition; Page 4 later. We're for the New Deal and so we have a sharp eye for New Deal items. . . .

New York is served by the best papers in America. But something pretty darn funny has been happening lately in the heat of the fight against Roosevelt, and we think the local press ought to have a few moments of solemn communion with itself.

When an important story from a major source is omitted and readers are kept in ignorance of a significant pro-Roosevelt poll, are kept in the dark about our leading business magazine's rebuke to business, it is time for a checkup.

What would have happened to that release had it shown an anti-Roosevelt majority?

Very properly Mr. Merat, whose innocent Persian question began all this discussion, concluded it with a letter in which he stated it was apparent to him that newspaper owners and editors can be a great deal more objective, more unbiased and more insistent on the presentation of both sides in a controversy if they were willing to make the necessary effort and sacrifice. "It may be possible," he continued, "that prejudice and suppression are not altogether due to human equation, but they exist because some newspaper owners and editors do not care to be objective, to be fair and impartial, and to present arguments advanced by both sides in any given controversy.

"No phenomenon is more menacing to the foundations of democratic ideas than the adulteration, suppression and distortion of facts by particular groups and their settled convictions and by the refraction of facts through propaganda and censorship."

When the rebellion broke out in Spain the newspapers reported the facts to the best of their ability. In time of revolt, as distinguished from a war of nation against nation, it is extremely difficult for journalists to get both sides of the story, but the news from Spain was told honestly or with intended honesty. There were many honest errors and omissions.

The fact that Germany and Italy were part of the conspiracy to destroy the Spanish Republic was not known at the beginning. But it was obvious that the plot included only the officers of the army and the leaders of the Catholic and Fascist elements, notably Robles, the Catholic, and Lerroux, the reactionary, whose regime had been upset by the elections of February, 1936, the generals Sanjurjo, Mola, Queipo de Llano and Franco.

The rebellion was put down generally throughout Spain in the first few weeks. Although the generals took eighty or ninety percent of the military with them, the armed population was able to retake the seized barracks and public buildings in all the principal cities except Burgos, Seville, Salamanca and a few others. It was obvious that an overwhelming majority of the people—and Spain is ninety-nine and nine-tenths Catholic although there are millions of anti-clericals—were for the republic and against the Clerico-Fascist rebels. Certainly no one can doubt that the trades unions, which have more than 5,000,000 members, were and are a hundred percent against the rebels.

By the end of July, 1936, however, Franco was able, with the aid of Italian airplanes and German equipment from the ship *Kamerun,* to land Moors from Africa, equip them, and march on Toledo and Madrid, stopping in the working-men's sectors of Badajoz and Seville en route to murder many thousands. The war became a war of foreign troops and foreign equipment against the vast majority of the Spanish people. The press of all journalistically free countries so reported.

But a new element entered into the war: the Catholic Church. It sided with the rebels. The rebels had sworn to restore the Church to power. That was one reason for the Vatican's sympathy. The other was the fact, which the republic has admitted, that in the first weeks of street fighting in the civil war, when there was no authority, no central power directing the Loyalists, anti-clerical and anti-Catholic elements killed numerous priests. Some of these priests were killed in the churches in which arms were found and which were used as strong points by the Clerico-Fascist forces. Some were killed by outraged peasants who claimed that the church engaged in usury in the land. Some were killed for other reasons. But not one priest was killed by the republican government, and from the moment the government restored its power it has protected churchmen and churches.

The American press got its first facts fairly straight. Its errors were unintentional. But from the beginning of August, 1936, the Catholic hierarchy in America—as distinguished from the hierarchy in Europe where no such attempt was made—began a crusade against the newspapers which truthfully reported events in Spain.

Naturally the pressure was hardest against the liberal press which had editorially supported the legal, recognized, liberal republican coalition. The Stern papers were the leaders. The *Philadelphia Record* and *New York Post* published powerful and brilliant editorials whose veracity cannot be questioned. Here are extracts of one of them entitled DEMOCRACY IS AT STAKE IN SPAIN, which resulted in a conflict with the Catholic Church.

The struggle in Spain is not a struggle between Communism and Fascism.

Two groups are battling for supremacy.

On one side are Republicans, Socialists, Communists, Syndicalists, and Anarchists. They differ widely on many questions, but they are in agreement on one. Each regards the *preservation* of

Spanish democracy as the first and essential step in carrying out its own particular program.

On the other side are equally diverse elements, Carlist, Alfonsist and Juanist Monarchists, feudal land owners, Conservative Republicans, Fascists. They differ widely on many questions but they agree on one. Each regards the *destruction* of Spanish democracy as the first and essential step in carrying out its own particular program.

Between these two groups believers in democracy can have but one choice. Their sympathy must go to the forces supporting the Spanish Republic.

Its government is neither Socialist nor Communist.

It was elected by an overwhelming majority of the Spanish people.

It was seeking a peaceful solution of Spain's economic and political questions when the Right took up arms and precipitated a bloody revolution.

Law and order in Spain are menaced not by the Left but by the Right.

The Right represents elements which have proved their bankruptcy by their misgovernment of Spain for generations and their exploitation of her people.

They represent only a small minority of the Spanish people, and those the most backward.

The Right has no popular support.

The Right is to blame for the Spanish government's Left swing since the civil war broke out.

Democracy is at stake in Spain.

The civil war is between a Government supported by those defending democracy and rebels out to crush democracy.

This is a fair editorial opinion. It tells facts. But even if it could be called a biased editorial opinion, it is in keeping with the right of editors to express themselves on the editorial page, so long as they keep their news columns free from editorial opinion. But as a result of fair editorial opinions whose facts could not be disputed, a campaign to boycott the *Philadelphia Record* was "urged in Catholic pulpits throughout the city." * The official diocesan newspaper, the *Catholic Standard and Times,* said in its July 24th issue:

"Because of the censorships and claims and counterclaims, it is still almost impossible to know what is going on in Spain. It would seem however, that the 'rebels' are made up of all factions opposed to Communism, and the 'Popular Front' party is made up of Communists, anarcho-syndicalists, and the more radical Socialists. This group is fanatically determined to completely destroy the Church and it is for this group that the *Record* wished 'more power.' Catholics rightly have resented this. Catholics moreover, cannot consistently support—even to the extent of two cents a day—a paper that supports Communism. The *Record* owes an apology, or at least an explanation, to its Catholic readers."

This Catholic newspaper's description of the Popular Front is false. The majority of the Popular Front is not composed of Communists, anarcho-syndicalists and Socialists, but liberals, republicans and democrats. The Popular Front is not "fanatically determined to completely destroy the Church." It is, however, determined not to permit the restoration of the Roman Catholic Church to temporal power —which was ended in 1931—nor to permit it ever again to control education in Spain. It is determined to treat the Roman Catholic Church in just the same manner the United States treats the Roman Catholic Church.

How effective the boycott against the Stern paper was I do not know. But every newspaperman knows that the most powerful pressure group in America today is the Roman Catholic Church. I do not know whether it succeeded in curtailing the *Record* circulation or inflicting a financial blow through the withdrawal of advertising by Catholic business men. But on August 10, 1936, Publisher Stern addressed the following humble letter to Cardinal Dougherty:

---

* *Editor & Publisher,* August 22, 1936.

"On Wednesday July 29th we ran an editorial entitled NOW THE SPANISH REGIME LOSES ITS HEAD. . . . .This second editorial denounced the Spanish government's action against the Catholic Church.

"We had hoped that it would offset any unfriendly impression created by the first editorial. But this second editorial was overlooked by an editorial writer for the *Catholic Standard and Times,* which, on August 7th, denounced the *Record* because of the first editorial.

"I very much regret this situation, especially because we have hurt the feelings of friends on religious grounds. I need not tell you that the *Philadelphia Record* stands four-square for religious freedom and tolerance and is bitterly opposed to Communism, Fascism or any form of government which denies its citizens complete protection in their worship.

"You have always been fair to the *Record.* I would very much appreciate your advice as to what I should or should not do in the matter."

Cardinal Dougherty accepted the apology. He wrote:

"It is a pleasure to hear from you that, when this editorial was published, the *Record* was not aware that the so-called Rebel, or Rightist party, in Spain was really battling for religious rights; and that as soon as you learned this, you published a second editorial to offset the impression derived from the first editorial.

"Your further assurance that the *Record* stands four-square for religious freedom and tolerance and is opposed to Communism is also gratifying."

I believe that every newspaperman in America who really values freedom of the press, no matter what his religious beliefs may be, will deplore this episode, and especially the *Record's* genuflections.

We have the testimony of Heywood Broun concerning the Catholic pressure against the old *New York World.*

We have the evidence of the *World-Telegram* and the

other twenty-three Scripps-Howard newspapers suppressing
Pegler's column critical of the mass-murderer Franco (for
whom Cardinal Hayes prayed every day).

We have Father Curran's boast that he changed the policy
of a Brooklyn newspaper through the $20,000 worth of print-
ing or advertising business he controls there.

And now we behold the publisher of a chain of four newspapers, four of the very tiny minority of liberal, free, independent newspapers left in America, bowing before the pressure of the Church when in fact his editorials on Spain had
been true, honest, favorable to the anti-Fascist movement in
Spain and applauded by all fair, liberal and intelligent men.

Caught between the advertising pressure of big business
on the one hand, and the political pressure of a religious organization on the other, the *New York Post, Philadelphia
Record, Camden Courier* and *Camden Post* have had to
make the usual compromises.

I know of no better illustration of the fact that there is no
completely free press in America.

When Stern bought the *New York Post* there was considerable metropolitan rejoicing. It was at a time the *World-
Telegram,* grown rich and conscious of its power, had begun
to shed pretensions of liberalism, and the hope of survival of
the old *New York World* spirit was dead. But Stern had been
preceded by the fame of his *Philadelphia Record* and a real
liberal newspaper was expected.

In this New York was not disappointed. There was a time,
however, when Ernest Gruening, editor for only a few
months, resigned amidst rumors which caused great questioning, but the matters involved were the usual difficulties with
advertisers and financial backers of the paper. People were
more than willing to give the new liberal journal a better
than even break.

The circulation rose from some 40,000 to 100,000 in the first year of Stern management, doubled the next year, rose to 300,000 in the third, a phenomenal growth even with contests and book bargains discounted, and proving that the metropolis appreciated journalism which aimed at the old *World* and the *Manchester Guardian* standards.

In 1936, when I went to Spain with *Post* credentials, I sent Harry Saylor, the editor, a series of stories aimed to tell the fundamental truth about the whole situation. One of the articles dealt severely with the part the Catholic Church was playing in the civil war. It was then twenty-seven years since I had started in journalism, by which time I had learned the first lesson, namely, that one must never write on controversial subjects, the first of which was religion, and that one must never report even the truth in any case in which the Catholic hierarchy might be offended. Nevertheless I tested every word, believed every word in this article which quoted pro-Loyalist expressions from the great, cultured, intelligent Catholic leaders, and sent the story to the *Post*.

The *Post* published the story word for word. I know of few such instances of journalistic courage in dealing with a tabooed subject. I stress this fact because of the disastrous *Record* episode.

Sometime in 1937, however, a change seemed to come over the liberal viewpoint of the *New York Post*. It is difficult to say just when and how it happened, just as it is difficult even today to make too general an accusation inasmuch as several writers whose editorials gave the *Post* its reputation for liberalism, are still writing liberal editorials, which now alternate with weaker, straddling and at times reactionary editorials. The *Post* is still in an ambiguous state. There is still hope it will return to the liberal fold.

Whether or not negotiations with the Newspaper Guild were the main cause of the change, or merely touched it off, is not known to me, and may not be known to any man, not even Mr. Stern, but there is a change, and it is not toward liberalism. In fact Heywood Broun * not only puts the *Post* among the reactionary Red-baiting newspapers, but gives the gold cup and blue ribbons to its publisher. "Once," he writes, "there was a liberal paper in New York City and now there is none. . . . In the Red-Baiting Handicap . . . J. David Stern was a slow starter. He was practically left at the post (what a pun, Heywood, what a pun). . . . Hearst was way out in front. . . . Behind him came Ogden Reid and Roy Howard, but they were whipping. Yet when the horses straightened out in the stretch quite a different picture was set for the crowd which watched the Red-Baiting Handicap. J. David Stern had dropped out of the clouds. . . . As they charged across the finish line it was evident that Stern had won by a head. A photograph will have to be taken to determine place and show positions, because they could cover Hearst, Roy Howard and Ogden Reid with a blanket. And not a bad idea at that."

When did the *Post* enter the race? On October 5, 1937, when the President excoriated the aggressor nations which were shedding blood and preparing to rush the world into another general war, the *Post* published the photographs of the heads of the lawless nations, and included that of Stalin with Hitler, Mussolini and the Mikado. No other newspaper, not even the professional Red-baiters which never hesitate to falsify news and pictures, followed the *Post*. Its readers, finding no reference to Russia and no implication in the President's words, probably believed that an error had been made. The *Post* in fact admitted it had erred.

While I was willing to give the *Post* the benefit of a doubt in this episode, I was shocked by an editorial in the issue of December 2, 1937, ON THE RIGHT TO PICKET—AND ITS ABUSE. On that or the following day every newspaper in New York City published an editorial against picketing. That too is a significant fact. In Russia it is said that the press is controlled

---

* *New Republic*, March 9, 1938.

by the government, and in Italy and Germany we know that there are daily orders on every editorial and news item of any importance, but in free America, where not even big business is supposed to have any sinister relationship at all with the free press, here was one instance where every paper spoke as if in echo to a master's voice, a dictator's voice. On this subject the *Post* and the *Sun* ran almost identical editorials. The *Sun,* however, did not try to make out that its attack on picketing was in the interests of labor. The *Sun* makes no pretenses of being liberal or of favoring labor.

The *Post* said it believed, "that the right to picket is one of the fundamental rights of labor," which it is, "but . . ." And from now on it will be noted that there were many "we-believe-in-this-but . . ." editorials appearing in the *Post*. In this case the "but" was followed by the belief, "that, like other rights, it may be abused," and the hope is expressed that labor will be careful. We are living in a time when the Chicago police murder ten unarmed peaceful pickets and the Spanish civil war has become largely a war of the employers against the labor unions and poor peasants, but the *Post* advises caution where a year ago it advised audacity.

"Even more obnoxious," continues the editorial, "is the use of pickets in what the courts have called and often condemned as 'secondary boycotts.' These are cases in which a man is picketed, not because he has a dispute with his employees or with a union, but because he is doing business with some one else who may have a dispute with employees or a union."

The fact behind the entire press campaign against picketing and notably "secondary picketing" is that these methods hurt business. The Newspaper Guild, striking at the *Brooklyn Eagle,* made notable use of this new weapon. It attacked the *Eagle* through its advertisers: it sent its men, reporters and others whom Brooklyn liked and trusted, to the department stores and other large advertisers. These pickets carried placards urging the public not to deal with shops advertising in a newspaper which labor held unfair to its employees. The *Guild Reporter* published a weekly list of stores, cigarette companies, and other advertisers with the recommendation they be boycotted. It is therefore easy to see that labor had discovered an effective weapon which incidentally hit newspaper revenue, the financial support of the press, harder than any weapon used for a century.

The fact that the *Sun, Herald Tribune, Times* and Hearst press threw dignified tantrums when their pocketbooks were touched surprised no one; the fact that the *Times* and *Daily News* also attacked picketing was no great shock; but there was distinctly a journalistic tremor when the *Post* joined the others.

This editorial may mark the change. News stories and editorials in which the Guild and its methods, the war in Spain, unions in general and especially a reactionary demand that they be incorporated so that they can be emasculated, have followed, and have caused the most loyal *Post* readers to squirm.

Among the 260,000 circulation which the paper had added were all shades of liberals and radicals. On February 15, 1938, the *Post* deliberately set out to drive the extreme left wing out of its ranks. Its purge came in the form of an editorial, two columns wide, on page 1, under the heading STALIN TAKES OFF HIS MASK. It was based on a letter in which the Soviet leader urged, "We must also increase and strengthen international proletarian ties of the working class of the U. S. S. R. with the working class of bourgeois countries. We must organize political help of the working class of bourgeois countries to the working class of our country in case of military attack. . . ." There was nothing sensational and certainly nothing new in the statement. But the *Post* said there could be but one interpretation: "American workers MUST, according to Stalin, be prepared to fight for Soviet Russia when he wants them." And on the 18th, defending itself from the attacks of many readers, many of them non-

Communists, the *Post* repeated its view that "the 'united front'—union of liberals with Communists against Fascists—is a greater threat to democracy than the frontal attack of reactionaries." With this view anyone who has been in Spain must disagree. Although the Communists are a minor part of the population of republican Spain, numbering only 50,000 men when the war broke out, they have supplied a great proportion of the best troops and fought better than any other political faction in the country, without claiming credit or attempting to take over the command of the army or the government from the majority liberals and democrats who control both.

The publication of this editorial did more to upset the *Post* editorial and news staff than any event under the Stern regime. So far as I know there are no Communists on this paper—as there are secretly on the *Times* and larger journals —but all the liberals felt that the day of Red-baiting had arrived and some questioned the wisdom of remaining with a paper following the Hearstian line. It was at this time that Broun read Stern out of the liberal ranks. "He was all for trade unionism until it took a bite at his own budget," said Broun. "When the C. I. O. was a bright dream J. David Stern applauded. When it became a successful reality it scared the hell out of him. . . . The soul of Stern was shocked when Stalin suggested that the workers of the world might have a stake in winning out against war. To J. David Stern that was subversive and undemocratic. . . . Stern is the most tired of all the tired liberals. . . . He wants to hit the hay and forget most of the causes he previously espoused. It is not unknown for a paper's policy to vary according to its circulation."

I do not agree about the tiredness, nor about the influence of circulation, because the *Post* has not yet reached *World-Telegram* heights and money. I believe the episode is another illustration of the Stern policy of operating as liberal a newspaper as the money interests will allow. Apparently there had been a clamping down on policy by certain interests, a threat to the financial future of the *Post* which had to be answered by a gesture of Red-baiting, and the compromise had to be made. It was the same sort of necessary surrender which the *Record* had made to the Catholic Church.

The reactionaries on the *Post* staff must have felt victorious because on the 22nd of that February when the *Times*, *World-Telegram* and *Herald Tribune* united in hailing the Soviet arctic expedition, a brilliant, successful exploit which will take a permanent place in heroic traditions, the *Post* said editorially:

"Those Russian scientists who can't be coaxed off the ice floe on which they have drifted for eight months may be smart.

"Having a radio, they may have heard rumors of the wholesale liquidations of big shots in Moscow. Having scientific minds, they may have put two and two together and concluded that the more famous one becomes in Russia the more likely one is to be liquidated. And, having the primitive instinct of self-preservation, maybe they've concluded that an ice floe may be a pretty comfortable spot, after all."

This editorial disappeared in the second edition. It was even too raw for the editors of the *Post*. In the *Daily Worker* it was called a "crime against science, human progress and journalistic decency," never to be forgotten or forgiven by the American people. The American people of course know nothing about this. And most of the readers of the first edition did not give a hoot. But we may be justified in asking whether either the advertisers or the intangible forces which drive newspapers out of the liberal and progressive camp really expect Red-baiting editorials to prove to their financial backers that they are in the money camp.

What this country needs, and has not got, is a newspaper free enough to defy every enemy pressure.

CHAPTER 13

Special Interests in Chicago

ONE of the really great tragedies of American journalism began when the Northcliffe bug, transformed into an American Presidential bee, lit in Colonel Frank Knox's bonnet sometime in 1934 or 1935.

The Colonel, with the help of numerous Chicago bankers, steel masters, and other corporation heads, had gotten ownership of the *Chicago Daily News* in 1931. He was determined "to round out his life with a great achievement. He dreamed of making it the best newspaper in the English-speaking world; best in style, information, opinion and appearance." We have this on the authority of Raymond Gram Swing, who for many years represented the *Daily News* in Europe and who knows the Chicago publisher well. Mr. Swing also learned at the dawn of 1936, that the employees of the paper were enthusiastic supporters of their chief, and they were especially proud of the fact that he never made the *News* a personal organ during the campaign and never perverted it to party uses, as did his rival publishers but political friends Hearst and McCormick. Knox had enough sense of humor to permit one of his star writers, Howard Vincent O'Brien, to criticize his candidacy in his own newspaper. Such things could not happen among the humorless Hearsts and McCormicks.

O'Brien said in his *News* column that if his boss were President he was convinced Knox "would do things that are utterly abhorrent to him now, and perforce leave undone practically all the things he now advocates." And Swing points out that Knox, veteran of two wars, making a strong bid for the Legion vote despite the fact he had in his non-political days sternly opposed the bonus for the veterans, "found as candidate that it might as well be paid, if it could be out of funds already appropriated. Whether he would be as quick to rationalize the suppression of academic freedom and 'the perennial quest for truth' to please the Legion remains to be seen."

Throughout 1936 the change was seen. The Colonel, who had refrained from joining McCormick and Hearst in their Red-baiting hysteria and witch hunt at the University of Chicago, now indulged in those hobbies. In one address he declared that "the most irreligious atmosphere in America today is in the meeting of radical Socialists who would substitute planned economy and socialistic philosophy for our free institutions." When the President said he welcomed the hatred of those American business men who oppose his re-election, Colonel Knox thought this helped class warfare of which "America is tired." Of the President's promise to master the forces of reaction, Colonel Knox said such talk, utterly foreign to the American system, "fits in perfectly with the Fascist or Communist philosophy of Europe." In Pittsfield, Massachusetts, he said his campaign was not a fight against the Democratic party but against "alien and un-American elements" which he said had seized the party. In Toledo, Ohio, he said, "I hate to see union labor entering politics after forty years of making its own way."

The Toledo speech, incidentally, was answered by James L. McDevitt, executive director of Labor's Non-Partisan League, who said: "When Colonel Knox said his *Chicago Daily News* was 100 percent union he was making a deliberate misstatement of fact. He has no contract with the American Newspaper Guild, a union of editorial employees affiliated with the American Federation of Labor.

"He insulted labor's intelligence when he said it has sold its birthright for a mess of pottage. He didn't explain just what he meant by that but if he calls the Wagner Labor Relations Act, the Social Security Act, the Railroad Retirement Act, the Prison Made Goods Act, the National Re-employment Service Act and all the other labor legislation a mess of pottage we'll have another helping."

Again, when the Colonel said in his Connersville, Indiana, speech that labor had not gained by the NRA, that unemployment grew worse, consumption was reduced, etc., General Hugh S. Johnson replied that the candidate had made nine statements in one paragraph which were "false and made with intent to deceive." He accused the Colonel of a "rhinoceros-hided disregard for even the appearance of fairness."

The Colonel continued to call the Roosevelt "measures" "pink pills" and accuse the Democratic party of having "written into law wholly or in part the twelve principal planks of the Socialistic platform." In the eyes of Norman Thomas not a single Socialist measure had been adopted; it was purely another Knoxian attempt at Red-baiting.

And since the Colonel as a political candidate had to make the necessary gesture in favor of labor, which even Fascist leaders make before they come into power and destroy the unions, the Newspaper Guild took advantage of the situation by asking him to recognize the movement for collective bargaining, higher wages, and better journalism. Mr. Broun wrote Mr. Knox saying that the Guild must take in all papers, disregarding the fact some pay wages better than the minimum demanded. Mr. Broun also wrote Knox that to the Guild's surprise "your editorial department employees are afraid to join. . . . They admit they fear reprisals from the management. They fear the announcement of the formation of a unit . . . will bring swift reaction from the management in the way of abrupt dismissals." Colonel Knox was asked to make a public statement of policy.

He replied he did not consider the letter frank. "It has the familiar flavor of innuendo and propaganda. . . . The insinu-

ation that any employee of the *Daily News* has been intimidated . . . is entirely without foundation." He then upbraids
Broun for failing "to recognize 'intimidation' as the standard
alibi for failure to organize" and concludes with a bitter
criticism of the Guild by urging "that you look into the real
reason for the failure of the Guild to click in Chicago. My
guess is that intimidation hasn't anything to do with it, but
rather that the hard-boiled, individualistic and realistic men
who staff the Chicago papers don't see the benefits."

The Guild however insisted it had found *News* men intimidated and a similar situation existing on other Chicago
papers where the owners, arrogant press lords, were in the
habit of referring to their "loyal" employees in much the
same way medieval lords referred to their faithful serfs. The
highly paid employees, it must be admitted, were mostly
"loyal."

As the press swung in behind Landon and Knox, its methods and motives were criticized only in the liberal weeklies,
to which the big politicians paid no attention. But when
Filene, the Boston merchant, philanthropist and heavy advertiser, made a public exposure of the situation it was
Colonel Knox who took it upon himself to defend the press.

"In America," said Filene, "at least theoretically, the people rule. . . . And yet, in a great national crisis in which our
national administration working for better distribution of
wealth, has somehow come into conflict with the great financial and business interests, it turns out that our newspapers—
the very source of the average voter's information and education—are usually owned and controlled by these same special
interests."

Said Colonel Knox, whose entry into metropolitan journalism had come about through the financial backing of Dawes,
Avery, the head of American Foundries, and other corporations: "In his home city of Boston does Mr. Filene allege
that the Taylors of the *Globe*, Mr. Grozier of the *Post* and

Mr. Hearst of the *American* and *Record* are pulling chestnuts out of the fire for special interests?

"In New York does Mr. Filene indict Arthur Sulzberger and Colonel Julius Adler of the *Times,* William Dewart of the *Sun,* Ogden Reid of the *Herald Tribune?*

"Does he think that Bob McLean of the *Philadelphia Bulletin,* Jack Martin of the *Public Ledger,* or Charles Tyler of the *Philadelphia Inquirer,* would accept dictation from the 'interests'?

"Let Mr. Filene but call the roll of the outstanding newspapers the country over—the *Sun* of Baltimore, the *Star* and *Post* of Washington, the *Buffalo News,* the *Detroit News* and *Free Press,* the *Plain-Dealer* of Cleveland, the *Times-Star* and *Enquirer* of Cincinnati, the *Chicago Tribune* and the *Chicago Daily News,* the *Milwaukee Journal* and *Minneapolis Journal* and *Tribune,* the *Pioneer Press* of St. Paul, the *Omaha World,* the *Kansas City Star,* the *Los Angeles Times,* the *San Francisco Chronicle,* the *Seattle Times,* the *Portland Oregonian,* the *Spokesman-Review* of Spokane, to name but a few of them—does Mr. Filene contend that these great newspapers are owned or controlled by the 'special interests'?

"He surely knows that there are no newspapers more completely independent of any form of financial duress than those included in the great Hearst, Scripps-Howard, Block and Gannett chains, and the Booth group here in Michigan."

Mr. Knox claimed that the reason the American press attacked the President was disillusion over the Newspaper Code, the President's violation of his promises, and the fact that "under the dominating influence of a group of radicals" he had "embarked upon a course far away from an American form of government and toward a dictatorial government." (This of course is nonsense, but nonsense is ninety percent of political campaign talk.)

"All these things and many others—lost for Mr. Roosevelt his hold on the majority of men in the Washington press gallery," concludes Knox. (The very opposite is the truth.) "It was their disillusionment in the President, and in his New Deal, that caused the majority of newspapers to become critical."

This last statement was proven absolutely false by the scientific and unquestioned survey which Leo C. Rosten made for the Social Science Research Council and which will be discussed at length later. The truth is that the great majority of Washington correspondents stood by the President then and do so now and moreover that the majority of Roosevelt-baiting newspapers have correspondents in Washington whose views are contrary to editorial policy and who in many proven instances have to write against their convictions.

But this does not answer Knox's main contention. He asks whether the big newspapers are controlled by the "special interests." The answer is that in many cases they are and that in most cases—the exceptions are few—they are part and parcel of the special interests, and that Filene was absolutely right. Or are we to believe that the fact that the social and economic policies—and in many cases the political policies—of the newspapers and the big business interests are identical are just several thousand coincidents? There can be no other general answer.

Colonel Knox has been noted for his courage, sincerity and forthrightness. He became a newspaperman through the letters he wrote back from Tampa and Santiago, Cuba, where he was a Rough Rider with Colonel Roosevelt, and he never got over his admiration of that man.

He made good as a reporter on the *Grand Rapids Herald* and went into the business end. In 1902, with the help of a printer he acquired the *Lake Superior Journal,* borrowing a thousand dollars to make up the fifteen hundred he had to put up as his share. As a publisher he was honest and courageous, fighting vice, gambling and civic corruption. Before he left for his New Hampshire home he had had a fist fight with a drunken saloonkeeper and been the target of a bullet which stopped in an editorial window.

It was the era of crusading and muckraking journalism and Knox made good at it. He sold the paper for $50,000 in 1912.

In the World War he was a major of artillery and returned a lieutenant colonel. He made a success of his Manchester newspaper and soon controlled the press of the town. In 1926 Hearst asked him to pull the *Boston American* and *Boston Advertiser* out of the red, and he did so without ever being tainted by contact with Hearst, as is the fate of the majority of Hearst executives. But he was a very shrewd hard-headed Yankee trader and *Fortune* reports that in 1930 Hearst, who has a more sentimental nature, and whose whole life had been vast and lavish, had secretly restored wage cuts which Knox ordered.

Knox quit. He was ready to retire. He had made half a million dollars working for Hearst and saved almost all of it. He was ready to take it easy. Then came the sudden death of Walter Strong and the chance of a lifetime. Knox came to Chicago fired with the ideal of publishing a great newspaper. I think that every publisher who starts as a reporter has the same dream—the hope of equaling or even outdoing the *Manchester Guardian* in America.

At least that is what many of his employees, associates and friends say. But I have my doubts. I cannot conceive of a great paper without a liberal policy, and the entire history of the owner and publisher of the *Chicago Daily News* ever since the end of the muckraking era and Theodore Roosevelt progressivism, has been made on the road between conservatism and reaction. For example, Colonel Knox opposed Congressional investigations. In the early days they were either caused by newspaper exposés—as for example that of the Armour, Swift and other packing houses after Sinclair published "The Jungle"—or they were approved and headlined by the newspapers. Now Knox says, "I say to you deliberately that most of these investigations are designed by the New

Dealers to draw red herrings across the trail of their real intentions. Their intentions are to discredit private industry so these New Dealers may encounter a minimum resistance and later, it may well be, seize private property on the Marxian philosophy of government ownership."

Can the fact that an Armour Packing Company director is also a *Daily News* director have anything to do with such views? Is it just another coincidence?

Colonel Knox has spoken over an NBC hookup under the auspices of The Crusaders, an anti-labor semi-Fascist organization. *Chicago Daily News* directors are Max Epstein, of American Transportation Company, who had contributed money to Harry Jung's American Vigilant Intelligence Federation; J. E. Otis, of the Central Trust Company of Illinois, director of utilities, banks and the Dawes Pure Oil Company; John Stuart, president of Quaker Oats and director of the union-hating International Harvester; George E. Scott, president of the American Steel Foundries, and Sewell Lee Avery, of U. S. Gypsum, Montgomery Ward and the American Liberty League.

These men are the proof that the *Daily News* is not controlled by business interests; it is merely directed by the men of big business.

Ever since the 1936 campaign ended Colonel Knox has continued to express in daily life and in the *Daily News* the same illiberal abuse of the administration which the labor-fighting industrialists have expressed. In 1938 he attacked the new Farm Act, the Wagner Labor Act, and the Social Security Act. He urged the suspension of social security taxation in order to restore "the American way," and said "The one sure way to bring Fascism to this country is through prolonged government spending of large sums of borrowed money."

Of the *Daily News* of a generation ago Will Irwin said it was "an honest newspaper, first, last and all the time. . . . The *News* is not borrowing money from banks and it does not need support from trust or corporation. . . . In some respects it goes far beyond any contemporary in allegiance to truth. . . . Even should it change hands, should a get-rich-quick policy destroy its character, the *News* would go on paying for a generation by power of its bold honesty."

The *News* has changed hands. It still goes on paying by power of its bold honesty. It still retains considerable of the spirit of the Lawson and Strong regimes, it is still so far superior to the *Tribune* and the *Herald-Examiner* that no comparison is possible. The change has not been, as Irwin feared, followed by a get-rich-quick policy. but merely by a protect-the-status-quo policy. A director of the *Daily News* is a director of U. S. Steel, Peoples Gas, U. S. Gypsum, Armour, Northern Trust, Montgomery Ward, Pullman, Nash-Kelvinator and Pure Oil. I will not underline the House of Morgan in connection with Steel and Montgomery Ward, as Ferdinand Lundberg does in "America's Sixty Families." I would merely like to ask Mr. Knox if he really ever believed he could publish a free newspaper with a board of directors representing what he denies are "special interests" but which are the special interests despite hell and high water and Knoxian denials.

CHAPTER 14

The *Herald Tribune*, Cuba and Fascism

ONE fundamental difference between the *New York Herald Tribune* and the *New York Times* is that the former does not pretend to be a liberal newspaper while the latter not only claims it is but wholeheartedly believes it achieves that end. Both of course are conservative, and the best upholders of the well known status quo.

And since the *Herald Tribune* does not claim to be a liberal newspaper the same yardsticks of criticism which must justly and ethically be applied to the *Times* cannot be used in this investigation.

On the other hand the *Herald Tribune* sponsors annually a public forum in which not only a free press, but an ideal press is one of the chief topics for national discussion. This forum is one of the finest achievements of liberalism in America, if not in the world. To Mr. and Mrs. Ogden Reid, owners of the paper, and especially to Mrs. William Brown Meloney, who has directed the forum for years, the nation owes a gold medal.

The *Herald Tribune* forum is so liberal and fairminded that it permits the severest opponents to air their views. Mrs. Meloney, for example, has asked me to speak my criticism of the American press (including of course the *Times* and the *Herald Tribune*) to her audience and a national hookup over the radio. If I were not such a coward about facing an audience and a microphone I would have been permitted to outline at a meeting sponsored by the *Herald Tribune* the various strictures of the *Herald Tribune* which compose this chapter.

My main contention of course is that the *Herald Tribune* is a class newspaper, that it is the organ of a small, powerful, and rich minority, and therefore hardly a newspaper at all, if by newspaper we take the definitions the newspapers themselves have written from their earliest days to the formulation of the various codes of ethics recently. On the other hand I prefer an honest bias to the pretensions of say the Hearst press which announces "public service" as a newspaper objective when it may mean service to public utility corporations, as the Black Lobbying Commission investigation indicated.

The *Herald Tribune* openly serves money, wealth, power, and the interests Henry George first called "vested" and which Roosevelt I called special privilege. It does not serve the people. It makes no such pretensions. It is the organ of the ruling class, and the ruling class in almost every nation is opposed to the people it rules.

Several years ago I mentioned the will of the late Mrs. Whitelaw Reid leaving the owners of the present *Herald Tribune* more than $16,000,000 in stocks and bonds, and I remarked that "every move the American government made toward intervention in Cuba and Mexico affected Whitelaw Reid's and Mrs. Reid's Mexican and Cuban investments. Every adverse policy of the public utility commissions or President F. D. Roosevelt is a blow to the utility portfolio of the Reid estate." I am now able to illustrate this criticism with rather sensational historical facts. One episode concerns a big business, the other the Cuban government.

The National Biscuit Company strike of 1935 was not much different from other strikes, except in this particular, that it got less mention in the newspapers than any similar event. The National Biscuit Company is a big advertiser, and every publisher and advertising man, and even liberals who contend that advertising no longer suppresses news, should make a survey of what happened when the makers of Uneeda Biscuit locked out 6,000 employees in five of their manufacturing cities.

What happened is simply this: the news was in most instances completely suppressed; in a few instances there were tiny items, half buried; in cases where there was violence, the attack was blamed on labor. Suppression, burial, distortion, falsification, were the rule, so far as the free press was concerned.

One of the acts of violence occurred when scabbing workmen tried to ship some merchandise. Trucks were overturned. Blows were struck. This made an interesting picture which all the services took and distributed. But apparently the National Biscuit Company did not want its name mentioned even in an item which accused its striking employees of vandalism because no newspaper with the exception of the Hearst *Mirror* published a print. The *Mirror* picture had the words "National Biscuit Company" which were on the trucks painted out. And this occurred during the managing editorship of Stanley Walker who had just come over from the *Herald Tribune*.

As for the silence of the latter paper, the strikers and the liberal press explained it by the fact that Ogden L. Mills, director of the biscuit company, was a relative of the Reids and a holder of *Herald Tribune* stock. But apparently no one knew at the time that the $16,000,000 Reid portfolio of stocks and bonds had as its biggest item 84,250 shares of Biscuit common, then worth $5,971,218. In other words, the Reids were probably the largest individual stockholders of the company where the strike was being waged.

The Reid portfolio also contained 11,995 shares of Atchison, Topeka and Santa Fe Railroad shares worth two million dollars, and one may deduce a pro-railroad policy from that fact. Great public utilities, then and now engaged in what is known as a "death grapple" with the Roosevelt administration, are represented by such items as American Power &

Light (897 shares), Commonwealth Edison (2,120 shares), Consolidated Gas of N. Y. (1,000), Pacific Northwest Public Service Co. (2,465). There were 4,448 shares of New York Central then worth half a million dollars and many million dollars' worth in western railroads. Then there were Cuban and Mexican bonds, oil and mining concessions, and 8,300 shares of Cerro de Pasco copper.

The estate had been valued at $34,518,119, but from 1918 to 1929 Mrs. Whitelaw Reid had been giving her son and daughter securities and properties of almost equal value to that left in the will. At any rate it is obvious that the same persons who owned the *Herald Tribune* were also owners of some $20,000,000 to $25,000,000 or more of stocks and bonds in American utilities, railroads and other forms of big business and in Mexican and Cuban properties.

Whether or not the news in the *Herald Tribune* was cut to the bias of every corporation, as in the case of the National Biscuit Company, one cannot tell. But it is as obvious as the multiplication table that the social and economic and political viewpoints of the big corporations in which the Reids have interests and their *Herald Tribune* are one and the same.

Nor can one say with certainty that it was the Reid interest in the reactionary Cuban regime which resulted lately in the biggest ethical scandal in metropolitan journalism.

One of the most familiar—and most specious—defenses of the American press is to compare it to the European press. The French press is notoriously venal; the British press today publishes more and worse fraudulent medical advertising than our papers did before the passage of food and drug legislation; the Fascist press is perverted beyond description. Our press, on the whole, is not as corrupt, venal, or perverted. That's fine.

I sometimes think it better to have a corrupt press, like the French, where book reviews, art criticism, blurbs about merchandise and statesmen are paid for in cash and where *everyone knows that every item has its price,* than the American press where it is impossible to bribe a book reviewer, a theater or movie or opera or art critic, where products and people as a rule cannot buy favorable reading notices at advertising rates, and where nevertheless, *without bribery and corruption an almost similar treatment of people, things and events occurs.* I never tire of quoting Humbert Wolfe's verse about the integrity of the British journalist whom you cannot hope to bribe or twist: "But seeing what the man will do unbribed, there's no occasion to." Ninety percent of the American publishers unbribed support tory and reactionary men and ideas, fight reform and progress, attack liberalism while pretending to be liberal—and this reactionary philosophy permeates every branch of the paper, including even the book review sections and art criticism. Peter Blume, for example, was recently attacked not for his canvas but for his picture of Mussolini as a jack-in-the-box. Reactionary art critics did not like the social significance of a work of art.

Occasionally something occurs openly in American journalism which reminds us of those things we denounce so strongly in the venal European press. The American public of course knows nothing about the *Chicago Tribune* Paris edition whose advertising department wrote probably the most disgraceful chapter in modern American journalistic history. Its agents actually promised the foreign offices of Fascist nations to support their policies in return for advertising. I know very well that Colonel McCormick in faraway Chicago was not aware that solicitors, many of them foreigners, were using the name and credentials of the *Chicago Tribune* when all they were after was $50 for the Paris edition of the same newspaper, but the fact remains that the Paris business office knew of this and encouraged it, and it would not require much search on the part of the publisher and editors in Chicago to establish the reason for Fascist Portuguese, Fascist Spanish and other editions and special Roumanian, Polish and other pages devoted entirely to praise of reactionary regimes and ideas. The motive was money—and not big money at that. In many respects the *Chicago Tribune* Paris edition was a piker compared to the venal French contemporaries, but no less venal.

If one were to ask American reporters, school of journalism professors, advertising men or others who follow journalistic events closely what was the most shocking single episode in recent history, there is no doubt that the answer would be: the publication of the *New York Herald Tribune* Cuban advertising section as news matter on November 21, 1937. It shocked even the *New York Times*.

On that Sunday the *Herald Tribune* carried a Section XII of forty pages of glorification of the Cuban regime. The front page had on it the following legend:

CUBA
TODAY

Land of
Peace and Progress

(This section, devoted to the Government and Industry of Cuba, is written and presented by friends of Cuba)

There was no indication that the whole thing was propaganda, and paid advertising. The purpose was to misinform the American people about a regime which all fair, open-minded, honest reports call harsh, repressive, or dictatorial and even terroristic. The first page of text is a glorification of President Laredo Bru and his "democratic program of peace and reconstruction." The main page is headed

COLONEL BATISTA'S LIFE DEDICATED TO
RELIEVING CUBANS FROM OPPRESSION

Army Chief, True Son of Soil, Rises to Leadership by Assisting
Countrymen; Regarded as Presidential Timber

It is signed by one Lawrence de Besault, who is said to
have been the negotiator of the advertisement. The climax is
a paragraph saying, "Colonel Fulgencio Batista should and
must be the next president of the Republic of Cuba." This is
not an editorial, this is a feature story news item, and it also
comes under freedom of the press.

On page 4 occurs as violent a transgression of ethics as has
been noted by professors and pupils in the history of journalism schools. On the face of it it appears to be an endorsement
of the Batista regime made especially for the *Herald Tribune*
section and the important news that our President plans to
revisit the island. Actually it was nothing of the sort. Some
one had taken news items and statements of the past, pasted
them together, carefully eliminated the old dates, and made
an ambiguous item out of it for the purpose of fooling the
reader.

On the next page there is a message from the Cuban president beginning with these remarkable words: "With the
greatest affection I salute the great American journalist, the
Hon. Lawrence de Besault. . . ." This seems to be carrying an
advertising joke or hoax too far. But this unknown and unheard-of press agent or advertising man or whatever he is,
does not return the salute. He sticks to the paymaster, the
little dictator Batista, with a story (page 13) about the "tower-
ing personality of army chief," the "savior of his country."

Forty pages of praise of sugar, tobacco, the school system,
the heads of the Batista dictatorship, prize fighting, the army
and again the military leaders. Not one word of the true situation in Cuba. Now whether the true situation is that a
virtual Fascist dictatorship exists, with the usual suppression

of freedom of speech, the press, assembly and labor unions, or whether there is merely a semi-dictatorial government with arrest, imprisonment and deportation of the editors, politicians and leaders of the opposition and the jailing of all those who oppose the militaristic regime of Batista, I do not know, but I do know that the *Herald Tribune* supplement story of the Cuban situation was false. Even if marked "paid advertisement" it would have been unethical; it would have proven again the viciousness of the advertising system. But appearing as editorial matter it was a million times as vicious and as reprehensible.

Moreover, thanks to the publication by the *Guild Reporter* of a confidential memorandum sent by Don Bridge, advertising director of the *Times,* to his staff, we have an exposure of one of the finest pieces of hypocrisy which has marked the downward path of the conservative press of America. The *Herald Tribune,* having published the supplement as editorial matter, later insisted that it be credited by the Publishers Association of New York with 40,000 lines of paid advertising in the same instance. In other words the *Herald Tribune,* after having fooled its readers by not labeling a paid advertisement as such, later desired the credit which 40,000 lines makes in its standing as an advertising medium, and therefore admitted the truth to the trade. Mr. Sulzberger of the *Times* was greatly shocked by what he termed the "disloyalty" of a member of his staff in making the Bridge letter public, nevertheless it was a public service which the *Guild Reporter* appreciated. The letter, a real journalistic exposé, told how the Publishers Association held a special meeting "to protest against measuring the Cuba Today section . . . as paid advertising. Every newspaper present except the *Herald Tribune* vigorously opposed the measurement by Media Records of paid-for news matter as bona fide advertising. . . . The feeling was strong among the publishers that advertisers and agencies must not be misled by the inclusion of paid-for propaganda as advertising lineage.

"Cables and letters from Havana report that the section was arranged for directly with Batista and the Cuban Army Propaganda Bureau. . . . The intermediary in the deal was one de Besa (also referred to as de Besault). . . .

"One Havana report states that the price paid to the *Herald Tribune* was 'between $25,000 and $30,000.' . . . The propaganda in the section was destined to promote favorable opinion in the United States for the Batista army regime which is endeavoring to set up a Fascist 'three-year plan.'

"The *Herald Tribune* requested in a letter to Media Records that every line of the forty pages be measured as 'advertising regularly charged and paid for.' There was no display or other advertising in the section—only 'news' articles and pictures. The section did not carry anywhere the word 'advertisement' which according to Paragraph 2, Section 537, of the Postal Regulations, must be printed on every page if the news text is paid for. Washington reports that the *Herald Tribune* has been cited for violation of the law. . . ."

The law provides for a fine of $500. In a twenty-five or thirty thousand dollar deal this sum is trivial. At that price newspapers can afford to defy the postal regulations just as they have defied the National Labor Relations Board and the Wagner Act.

The reader will note that the *Times* advertising department exposed the *Herald Tribune* in a memorandum, and Mr. Sulzberger was angry at both his rival for perpetrating this trick and the Guild for mentioning the memorandum, but the *Times* did not comment editorially. Only liberal publications did so. The *Post,* the *Nation,* the *New Republic, New Masses,* and the Federated Press carried news items and editorials, and even the conservative publishers' organ, *Editor & Publisher,* denounced the episode, saying that "the whole enterprise comes perilously close to the ethical line." It smashes the canons of the code of ethics into scrap iron and *Editor & Publisher* talks about the ethical line! It proves that publishers have no ethics, wrote the *Guild Reporter.* However, *Editor & Publisher* does state its disbelief in the *Herald Tribune's* picture of peaceful democratic Cuba and condemns the "skilful counterfeit of news features."

To the *Nation*, "The incident is fairly typical of current journalistic ethics. It is a sign of the extent to which totalizarian morals and methods have penetrated public life, and indicates the tools that a Fascist regime in this country would find ready to hand. It demands a thorough investigation by the State Department."

It is becoming more and more commonplace—despite the attack of purists and the students of semantics—to use the words conservative and Fascist as synonyms. There are of course considerable differences, although every man who is a Fascist is *ipso facto* a conservative, and the reverse is not necessarily true. It is true, however, that the man who founded Fascism defined it as reactionary and anti-liberal.*

The *Herald Tribune* is not Fascist. But it would not have great difficulties making peace with a future Fascist regime. Such a change in government would come about through the machinations of a demagogue, the march of a veterans' organization such as the American Legion, subventioned by reactionary associations of manufacturers and commerce, institutes such as financed Fascism in Italy and Germany. The *Herald Tribune* can be said to be the voice in America of the National Association of Manufacturers and the United States Chamber of Commerce.

In this newspaper you can read letters saying that "nevertheless, a case can be made out for Fascism" (June 1, 1937) and great stories of Mussolini's accomplishments (December 28, 1937). When a reader protests that two-thirds of the statements made in the latter item are false he receives a

---

* "Force and Consent," by Benito Mussolini, *Gerarchia*, March, 1923.

letter from E. J. Toms, secretary to the editor, saying that the protest is being considered for publication, but no publication follows. In the *Herald Tribune* you can also find a letter prominently headlined "Fascism in Mexico" which begins by saying, "That Mexico has become a Fascist state may have escaped the attention of the casual observer." That same week Mexico had become a "Red Bolshevik state" in the Hearst press and in the *Los Angeles Times*. It so happens that Hearst and Chandler and Reid, all three of them, are interested to the tune of millions in Mexican property. Mexico had become neither Fascist nor Communist: it was carrying out the 1917 constitution. But it was hurting American big business. And big business everywhere is the enemy of progress.

In the Spanish civil war the *New York Herald Tribune* has been as fair as most newspapers, and frequently its strong editorials against the bloody Spanish Fascists have been notable. But in Paris this same organization publishes a newspaper for the half-million or less American tourists who go to Europe every year, and in this sheet the frankest advocacy of Fascism has been published. There are stronger pro-Fascists in America than the *Herald Tribune* editor in Paris but they are of necessity diplomatic. In Paris the stark face of Fascism is apparent.

The matter was called to attention in New York by the publication in Leonard Lyons' gossip column * of the following paragraph:

The editorial staff of the Paris *Herald Tribune* is somewhat disturbed these days. Before the paper goes to press each night proofs of the Spanish revolution stories are sent to a member of the Ogden Reid family who resides at the Hotel George V. . . . There the proofs are checked over carefully and changes made. "Loyalist troops" is altered to "Reds," "Bolsheviks," or "Anarchists." . . . And "Rebel army" always is changed to "Patriots."

---

* Lyons' Den, *New York Post*, September 2, 1937.

Of the millions of Americans who have visited Paris since the Great War not one in a hundred has noted the fact that the three newspapers published there in the English language are generally pro-Fascist, or that they indulge in Red-baiting or that they have faked the news from time to time and published falsely captioned photographs to substantiate the fake news. The public misses these fine points in the everyday battle of freedom of the press, but there is not a newspaperman in Paris who does not know that these things happen.

The Paris edition of the *Chicago Tribune,* now absorbed by the *Herald,* was pro-Fascist for the simple reason that Fascist European regimes advertise, democracies do not. Thus Primo de Rivera, first Fascist dictator of Spain, made a contract with almost all the newspapers published in Paris which was conditioned by active editorial support of his system. The advertisements did not say, "Buy a bottle of Fascism today; it's good for what ails you." What they did say was that Spain was a fine country for tourists, that the new hotels were good, that the mountains were superb. Some people call this "institutional advertising," others call it bribery.

Mussolini and Italy did the same kind of advertising in the Paris *Tribune.* So did Pilsudski and Poland, likewise the Roumanians, and the Portuguese, and other Fascist dictators.

So every time I went on a trip to the Balkans or visited a dictator country, I found that an advertising man from the *Chicago Tribune* had preceded me and sewed up the advertising there, promising that the *Tribune* editorial policy would be directed in favor of the particular brand of Fascism prevalent. I must add, to be absolutely correct, that I do not believe that the editorial department of the *Chicago Tribune* in Chicago knew about these goings on. But I have no doubt that the business office in Paris knew all about it. Did I say I have no doubt? I have in fact the documentary proof. . . .

And when it came to taking money from foreign governments the Paris *Herald* was no more shy than the Paris *Tribune.*

The biggest advertiser among the Fascists is Mussolini. As a result news favorable to Mussolini is published, news unfavorable to Mussolini is suppressed.

However, the *Chicago Tribune* never did endorse Fascism. It suppressed news unfavorable to Fascism, but it did not come out for Fascism. In that way it differed from the Paris edition of the *New York Herald.*

On Sunday, May 22, 1932, the leading editorial of the latter paper caused a sensation. I remember clipping it then because I could not believe my eyes. I have it right here on my typewriter now. I've had photostats made of it because no one in America will believe me when I say there is an actual instance of an American paper endorsing Fascism and recommending Fascism for the United States of America. Well, here is part of the column:

THE NEW YORK HERALD

Laurence Hills, Editor and General Manager

FASCISM FOR AMERICA

The social phenomenon known today as Fascism has existed in many countries. . . . Whatever its special characteristic or name, it has always consisted essentially of a mobilization of moral force. . . . The youth of Germany, ardent to reconstruct the pre-war ascendance and self-confidence of their race, calls itself Fascist. The Youth of Italy, bended to stem Communism among the workers (note: this is an absolute falsehood. G. S.) and sluggishness and ineptitude in the public services call themselves Fascist. . . .

The hour has struck for a Fascist party to be born in the United States. In the face of the most critical financial situation in the history of the country, Washington presents the amazing spectacle of more special groups seeking to get their fingers in the national treasury than ever before. . . .

Someone will give the signal. It may be a mechanic, coming out of his engine-room, wiping his hands upon oily waste, in despair at the insecurity of his home: it may be a veteran teacher—like Peter the Hermit preaching a crusade—shocked to find the holy sepulchre of our national liberty in the hands of vandals. It may be the clean youth and imagination of a Charles Lindbergh calling upon men of good will to join him in a party of law and order. It may be the sagacity and experience of a Henry Ford, summoning men to match the organization of the underworld with a still more potent organization. In every part of the country men are waiting for the call, and when it is heard, there will be a roar of assent from a million throats.

The elements are assembled for the formation of this kind of Fascism in the United States, composed of householders, heads of families and taxpayers. The stage is set.

When in 1933 Hitler established Fascism in Germany and in 1934 purged his party with bloodshed and murder, the Paris *Herald* took the matter in its stride. It retained the official government advertising, including one or two swastikas strewn among the items. I know of no other American publication which publishes the swastika daily.

When Franco began his mutiny, the course of the paper, now amalgamated with the *Chicago Tribune* and inheriting the worst feature of both, was simplicity itself. Primo de Rivera, the first Fascist dictator, had been a liberal advertiser: it was natural to suppose that Franco, the self-admitted Fascist pretender to the dictatorial throne, would also advertise liberally in the Paris *Herald Tribune*. And so he was supported.

From the editorial staff of the Paris *Herald Tribune* I learn that the city editor censors or kills all anti-Fascist letters sent in by readers, and publishes all pro-Franco letters. Just to test out this statement I sent in several letters under many names, but none was used. (It is true that a letter signed by my own name as correspondent of the *New York Post* protesting numerous lies in the letter department was used by this paper, but equally important letters sent by prominent persons, as for example, Robert Briffault, author of "Europa," were suppressed.) I know that the "letters to the editor" department is not very important: the important fact is that orders on what to use and what to suppress have been given by those in authority. The editorial staff further informs me that in case the city editor overlooks an anti-Fascist letter, it is killed in proof by managing editor Hawkins, and should he fail, the final stabbing is done by the editor and general manager, Mr. Hills himself. He has given the orders to one Louis Harl, an Irish Catholic philo-Fascist journalist who is permitted to edit and censor the news on Spain.

A curious sideline on this dirty business of coloring the news to suit the Fascists was furnished to me by Minifie, the correspondent of the *New York Herald Tribune* in Spain. James M. Minifie is one of the best, a truly objective journalist who writes without bias and color and who tells the truth, let the chips fall where they may. Mr. Minifie noticed the coloring of the news on Spain, wondered about the U. P. dispatches being biased in his own paper, but said nothing until one day he began to notice that someone, presumably Harl, was writing in "Reds" for "Loyalists" in his own cables. But that was not all. He tells me that whole items were changed, that parts were suppressed, that sometimes the exact opposite was printed of what he had written *in the Paris, never in the New York edition.*

At first Minifie tried to fight it out. He demanded that his stuff be published as written, but somehow this didn't work. It might have been stupidity, it might have been sabotage. Probably the latter. At any rate here we have the astounding spectacle of a well-known journalist giving instructions to one of the two newspapers published by his own organization never under any circumstances to use his material because he could not trust it to use it honestly.

"What do you think caused the manhandling of your stuff in the Paris office?" I asked Minifie when I first met him in Valencia, one night just after the sirens had stopped calling alarm for an air raid.

"Pressure groups," he replied. "There are plenty of American legionnaires in Paris on the Fascist side, also pro-Fascist church organizations. I have seen letters they have sent to Hills saying I am a Red just because I was sending news from Madrid. In fact a certain Sister R—— demanded that the Paris H. T. stop publishing any news from the government side, her idea of objectivity being news exclusively from the Fascist side."

It is a fact that the Paris *Herald Tribune* stopped publishing even the official Madrid-Valencia government communique on the progress of the war. I make this statement from an examination of the paper from January to May, 1937, when I saw it every day.

On the other hand the Paris edition publishes fake news about republican Spain. I make this statement because I have clipped some of these fakes. Here is one for example which is the story of how Companys, the president of Catalonia, has fled from Barcelona to a haven in France. It is true that the first place this fake appeared was in the *London Daily Mail,* but that does not alter the fact it was still a fake when the *Herald Tribune* republished it.

The Paris edition suppressed the most important parts of the sensational speech on Spain which Taylor, the *Chicago Tribune* correspondent with Franco, made before the American Chamber of Commerce, of which editor Laurence Hills is a shining light. It is true that the chamber and the reporters who covered the speechmaking expected a bitter attack on the Spanish republic from the man who had been with the Fascists; they were not prepared to hear someone on that side and a Catholic too, call Franco a mad dog and refer to his soldiers as murderers. It is also a fact that Mr. Hills' newspaper published only a few paragraphs leaving out the most damning anti-Franco statements.

The Paris edition, furthermore, gets a lot of its information on Spain from Quinenos de Leon, the dismissed ambassador of the Spanish republic. It is also a fact that the Paris Popular Front newspapers exposed the chief Franco espionage bureau as being situated at 21 Rue du Berri and alleged that Quinenos de Leon was the chief Franco spy in continental Europe. 21 Rue du Berri is the office building constructed by the old *New York Herald*. In this building there is a Franco agency which occupies the best part of an entire floor. It is a fact therefore that one of the largest rent payers of the Paris *Herald Tribune* is the Franco Fascist agency. I do not believe that the dollars of rental paid would amount to one-hundredth of one percent in the budget of the Reid family which owns the *New York Herald Tribune,* but I do know that the Paris edition budget depends largely on building rental, and that the Franco payments to the newspaper are very important.

CHAPTER 15

Gannett: Chain Lord

THROUGHOUT the world journalists have risen to power. Lenin and Trotsky published their small revolutionary papers in Russia and abroad; Stalin edited *Pravda* in Petrograd during the Kerensky regime which it helped overthrow; Mussolini was the big shot in Socialist journalism in Italy until the French government paid him to establish and edit a pro-Ally paper, and on its presses Fascism began its advance. Kemal Ataturk once ran a rebel sheet. Hitler had his *Beobachter*. Every French premier has a personal organ. In Europe the press is an open weapon with which men and parties fight for power.

In America the ruling powers prefer to let the press maintain the aspect of impartiality and independence, so long as wealth, the profit motive, and the status quo are never endangered. There is, however, very little difference between the European and American press, in fundamentals. But one striking feature is obvious: in Europe the editors and publishers themselves become part of the political machinery, whereas in America they have not yet stepped into the public light.

The only American editor and publisher who ever became President was the most tragic incompetent the White House had ever seen. In his reign the building became merely an office for the greatest bunch of crooks that ever looted the country. The cabinet itself was distinguished for the fact that it supplied the only member of a Presidential family ever to enter a Federal penitentiary. Unfortunately scores of even greater crooks remained unjailed.

In the great Ohio gang scandal newspaper editors played various rôles: Carl C. Magee, editor of the *Albuquerque Morning Journal;* Paul Y. Anderson, of the *St. Louis Post-Dispatch,* and the *Kansas City Star,* were the heroes, but others, notably Alexander P. Moore, of the *Pittsburgh Leader* (who was never exposed); Tannen and Bonfils, of the *Denver Post* (who used journalistic blackmail trying to get a million dollars and actually got $250,000), were the villains. There were also great newspapers, including the *New York Times,* which did everything to prevent a Congressional investigation.

Certainly the first occupancy of the White House by a publisher was a tragic fiasco.

Better men than Harding have tried before and after him. Horace Greeley, if one judges his character from his biographies, would probably have been the Theodore Roosevelt of his time, a pugnacious, single-tracked but powerful, dynamic, President who would have left colorful rather than disgraceful pages in history.

Of Alf M. Landon and his journalistic mate, Frank Knox, their backers in 1936 expected nothing but a safe and sane, quiet and honest administration, with big business legally flourishing—at the expense of the people—as it did under Coolidge and Hoover and Mellon for a while.

The nomination of Frank Knox, it has been said in public political speeches, caused abysmal chagrin to his Chicago colleague, Colonel McCormick. I do not know whether this is so. But Frank Knox's candidacy, despite its failure, has caused a great buzzing of hornets in all the bonnets of big and little publishers, and chiefly in the dovecote of the country chain owner, Frank E. Gannett.

He too has been afflicted with the Northcliffe complex. The list of American publishers who either want to rule or to manipulate the strings of the stooges who rule, is an imposing one and keeps growing. In fact the situation poses the question whether or not most publishers, realizing the power of the press, do not at some time in their lives succumb to the desire to exercise it for their own advancement or satisfactions.

Curiously enough in years gone by Frank Gannett used to deliver a pronunciamento against publishers in politics.

Frank Ernest Gannett is sincere, humanitarian, a man of good intentions, and one of the most confused persons in public life today. As millionaire owners of the press go, he is one of the minor lords, his fortune being valued at a mere $12,500,000. He has great plans for devoting it to the welfare of his fellow men.

He has announced that public service rather than private profits would be the program of his papers. His chain, which once reached a maximum of nineteen, is concentrated mostly in New York State, and the best known papers are the *Knickerbocker Press* in Albany and the *Rochester Times-Union* and *Rochester Democrat & Chronicle*. Gannett has provided for a foundation which will control the ownership of the common stock in all his papers. After dividends on preferred, which will be held largely by employees and executives, have been paid, the remaining profits will be available for "public charitable, educational and general philanthropic causes and purposes." The board of directors, self-perpetuating, will consist of eleven persons of whom at least eight must be newspapermen, and each director must hold at least 100 shares of stock. The consolidated net profit of the Gannett company in 1937 was $1,123,085 and in 1936, $1,026,150.

In 1935 Gannett also announced that *The Agriculturist,* his farm paper, would be directed by a man chosen by the readers, profits to be turned into a fellowship fund for research.

When he went to high school in Bristol, New York, where he was born on September 15, 1876, young Gannett made some money as a bartender's helper in the local hotel and the result was his almost fanatical prohibitionist attitude. "After watching booze ruin men," he says, "I made up my mind that if I ever got a chance I would fight it." He fought. The prohibition amendment was a great personal triumph, the repeal a sad day, but when beer returned and the question of alcohol advertising agitated many publishers, he said, "I must recognize . . . that a newspaper is a semi-public institution. No matter what my personal views may be I have come to appreciate that it may be dangerous to exclude advertising not in conflict with the law. . . . It threatens . . . free speech and a free press, which are precious liberties."

So it looked for a while as if private profits would triumph over idealism, but it turned out differently. The childhood conviction did triumph. Gannett again barred liquor advertising in his papers.

The war also taught Mr. Gannett something. He has been militantly anti-militarist. He is a member of the executive board of the National Council for the Prevention of War.

In 1935 Gannett was elected a director of the Associated Press to succeed Adolph Ochs. At that time he held seventeen franchises for that many journals and it was generally agreed that he would be the spokesman of the small newspaper in the great organization. In the press associations Gannett is said to be the best versed economist in the profession. *Editor & Publisher* reports that "book upon book in the elaborate office-library in his Rochester home testify to the thorough study of economic problems Mr. Gannett has made in recent years." Apparently this economist believes in cyclical recovery. "Believing that the depression was due largely to a collapse in prices caused by the increasing value of gold, Mr. Gannett is vitally concerned with the effect of a managed dollar." The economist is quoted as saying: "America is practically the same as it was in 1929. We have the same resources, the same (etc., etc.). . . . Readjust prices and we will go forward rapidly toward prosperity. Prices affect our lives profoundly. . . . Depression and booms are just great fluctuations in prices. . . ."

Years ago Gannett announced that it was his policy "never to buy a paper where the policy has to be changed." It was not until midsummer in 1936 that this publisher joined the vast majority of his colleagues who for diverse reasons, chiefly financial (as the *New York Daily News* showed), indulged in one of the most prejudiced, unfair, and unethical campaigns in our history. "I am personally very fond of President Roosevelt," said Gannett. "We have been friends for thirty years but I can't go along with him on his ideas of government. . . . I can't stand for his planned economy, centralization of power and extravagant use of public moneys."

From now on Gannett was launched on the dubious waters of party politics. He still continued to publish the statement that "the Gannett newspapers are dedicated to the welfare of all the people. Theirs is the pledge to publish each day clean, wholesome, educational and entertaining newspapers. Knowing no selfish interests, no entangling obligations, each newspaper within this group can be, and is, fair, just and tolerant, ever sympathetic with the unfortunate and eager to present all sides of any question. Each of these newspapers has ever before it the ideal of Lincoln, to be for and *of the People*." And the *Knickerbocker Press* still announced its purpose was "Fully, honestly, accurately and intelligently to inform the public." The slogan of the group still was "The integrity of a Gannett newspaper must never be questioned." But questioned it was.

The altruist and humanitarian Gannett came into conflict with the employer Gannett, and the newspapermen who were organizing soon found out which of the two they were dealing with. There were problems of journalistic ethics and problems of hiring, firing and paying of wages. Gannett was anti-Roosevelt on the Supreme Court issue. The reporters may have been pro-Roosevelt but they at least were ethical: they wrote the news as news. Albany Central Federation of

Labor unanimously endorsed the President. This of course was fairly big local news and Albany newspapers were expected to play it up. At the same time two small items came in over the telegraph desk from Schenectady and from Little Falls. They were reports that lawyers' associations had disapproved of the President.

On February 18, 1937, the *Knickerbocker Press* ran its story with the following head:

TWO BAR GROUPS
RAP COURT MOVE
Mohawk Valley Lawyers Express Disapproval
of Proposal.

Tacked on to out-of-town items was the vastly more important local story in favor of the Roosevelt plan. The reporters were angry. They declared that the labor council story had been written separately but the editors had buried it. That whole morning the telephone calls to the evening Gannett paper, the *Albany News,* brought protests from labor unions. And so, despite the fact that the news was already stale, having appeared in a morning paper, the *News* played it up first on page 4, then page 2, with an eight-column banner heading.

And when the newspaper writers suggested that a clause in the new contract should permit them to write "a full, accurate, truthful and fair presentation of the facts," the management said such a proposal would be virtually an insult to Frank Gannett and the integrity of his newspapers.

In January, 1938, the Tri-City Newspaper Guild at a labor board hearing charged the Gannett firm with using stoolpigeons, strike breakers, and finks during a printers' strike, and with the discriminatory discharge of Guild members, no less than twenty-seven of the twenty-nine persons fired when the *Press* and *News* were amalgamated being members of the organization. The Guild accused the editors and publishers of a three-year campaign aimed at breaking one of the strong--

est newspaper groups in the country. The Gannett firm of course denied that unfair labor practices had been employed, but it could not deny the firing of twenty-nine men. Nor the fact that Mr. Gannett was planning to devote his millions for charitable purposes—after he died.

Also, shortly after this wholesale discharge of employees, Gannett went deep into political waters with a recovery plan in which profit sharing of capital and labor was one of the main points. It would, he said, "establish confidence between labor and capital and promote friendly relations and bring about real co-operation for the production of more wealth." One can justly ask whether this was mere mental confusion or Machiavellianism. At home Mr. Gannett was fighting labor, firing his men, but at the Union League Club of Chicago he was speaking for sharing the wealth of production with labor.

The rest of Gannett's political credo was mostly pro-big business. It consists of the following points: 1. Abolish surplus profit tax and capital gains tax. 2. Abandon economy of scarcity. 3. Encourage business and help make business profitable. 4. Encourage distribution of profits among workers. 5. Cut down government expenses. 6. Lessen taxation because it burdens all. 7. Study English system of labor relations and adopt English system of compulsory arbitration. 8. Establish honest monetary system. 9. Set up long-term planning board to handle public works, high-speed toll roads. 10. Set up central information bureau on production and consumption in order to help business stabilize production. 11. End restrictions on farm production, arrange for distribution of surpluses. 12. Promote economy of abundance, more production, lower prices, put idle millions back to work.

Shades of Adam Smith, Ricardo, Karl Marx and Thorsten Veblen! Can this be the result of white nights among those books in the elaborate home study? Or is this purely Republican party economics?

With the announcements of principles and platform Frank Gannett began organizing his plan to defeat practically all liberal and progressive measures in Washington. His first move was to write 35,000 prominent men to help his drive against the reform of the Supreme Court, his second was to fight the Reorganization Bill. This fight, as is now generally known, was directed not so much against a necessary measure as against the Roosevelt idea of government by reform. Gannett sent every editor in the country an appeal to help the National Committee to Uphold Constitutional Government, as he called his organization. Most editors who replied were favorable. An exception was William T. Evjue of the *Progressive* who wrote Gannett that "he and the crowd surrounding him are actuated by special interest in fighting Roosevelt. . . . The reference to the freedom of the press in the voluminous literature . . . is becoming more and more nauseating. You big moguls in the American publishers' association are hypocritically using the freedom of the press to promote your own selfish special interests. . . . I am not going to help you play the game of the selfish big newspaper publishers who hate the Roosevelt administration because the Roosevelt administration hasn't been willing to follow the traditional policy of treating big newspapers as a privileged class."

When the Supreme Court plan was defeated *Editor & Publisher* said history would record that the name of Frank E. Gannett "perhaps will stand out as the individual outside official life who contributed most to its rejection." It described the way in which Gannett used all the power of his newspapers and "personal efforts." The general round-up of legislation defeated in the session was headlined "Journalists had stellar rôles in current Congress session."

In his second attack, on the Reorganization measure, Gannett ran into great Senatorial opposition. An investigation was proposed of his organization, administration leaders demanding to know who besides Gannett were investing their money "in defeating all legislation" and what men were really back of it. This information Gannett, a newspaper publisher whose business it is to inform the public of such matters "for the general welfare," refused to divulge. He yelled freedom of the press. . . .

Among those who denied the Senate's power to issue subpoenas *duces tecum* and to ask indiscreet questions was Gannett's manager of the committee, a certain Dr. Edward A. Rumely, a wartime pro-German propagandist who with the aid of pro-Germans bought the *New York Evening Mail* for the purpose of presenting the Kaiser's cause. Mussolini had sold out to the French foreign office and thousands of editors and publishers everywhere were being bought by either the Kaiser or the Northcliffe commission, but it was unfortunate for Doctor Rumely that he was on the wrong side because he was convicted of trading with the enemy and sentenced to serve a year and a day in the Federal penitentiary in Atlanta.

Among the measures Rumely admitted his committee fought against was the first wages and hours bill.

Senator Minton in a radio address said, "Don't be misled by Mr. Gannett as he directs his propaganda machine from sunny Florida. He has no more idea of saving you and your Constitution than the Liberty League did. If you are gullible you might be persuaded by the flood of misleading propaganda being sent out by Gannett's committee. . . . Mr. Gannett's speech the other night that our procedure was unheard of was deliberately falsifying the record. . . . Mr. Gannett . . . being a newspaperman, saw the metropolitan newspapers losing their influence with the people. With radios in as many homes as take newspapers, the people began to catch on that the metropolitan newspapers were propaganda sheets that didn't hesitate to misrepresent the facts in their news columns. So Mr. Gannett, seeing the newspapers slipping, set up a propaganda organization on a direct-by-mail basis. . . .

Let me nail another falsehood of Mr. Gannett's. . . ." (The rest of this speech may be found in the *Congressional Record* of March 28, 1938.)

Minton and fellow Senators demanded the facts about the men and money behind Gannett, but the humanitarian replied by shouting "Fascist dictatorship" and "Stalin OGPU" at the inquisitors. The truth never came out. It is known that a huge sum was spent and that the Reorganization Bill, which conservative weekly *Time* admitted was "a straightforward attempt to increase efficiency," and could not be presented as "an effort on the part of Franklin Roosevelt to make himself dictator" was defeated by a combination of publishers and politicians, notably Gannett, Roy Howard, William Randolph Hearst, Paul Block, Dorothy Thompson, Father Coughlin, and other reactionary forces whose claim was exactly that which *Time* had denied.

Gannett accepted his laurels like a modest hero. He made a radio speech in which he fixed the responsibility for the depression on the Roosevelt administration and called the Wagner Act (the Magna Carta of labor in America) "a potent factor in promoting strife" which had discouraged production.

This short history of Frank E. Gannett shows that he has fought his own employees, used his newspapers to present his personal views, made use of all the usual typographical devices of playing news up or down, that he has made his chain the expression of a narrow and prejudiced policy, that he has never supported liberal measures, and that he has on the other hand advocated ideas inimical to labor.

Years earlier he had been in debt heavily to the power and paper trust but within forty-eight hours after an exposure by Federal authorities he switched the loans to a bank.

In the Tugwell Pure Food and Drug Bill fight he offered the chain of newspapers to the drugmakers and advertising men for the free expression of their opinion.

Altogether it may be said that Gannett is the typical small-

town publisher. The difference is that he has humanitarian
ideas as well as Presidential ambitions.* And with his devotion to the latter motivation in the past two or three years
it is becoming more and more apparent that the humanitarian headlines will not be written in his lifetime. Post mor-
tem Gannett may become known as a social instead of an
anti-social personality.

* Asked, on August 8, 1938, at the home of his host, Lord Beaverbrook,
in London, if he would accept nomination for Governor of New York or
President of the United States, he declined the Governorship, and said of the
Presidential offer: "No one could sincerely refuse the nomination. The
honor and opportunity for service are too great."

CHAPTER 16

Boston: Brahmins, Bourgeoisie, and Boobs

IF IT is true that cities get the newspapers they deserve—and I doubt it because I believe many benighted cities in America deserve at least one good paper—Boston would be the place to prove the aphorism. It gets its *Christian Science Monitor* for its 2,817 (latest *World Almanac* figures) Christian Scientists, its *Transcript* for its Brahmins, its *Globe, Post, Herald* and *Traveler* for its bourgeoisie, and its *Record* and *American* for those whose mentality hardly rises above the Hearst or comic strip level.

Of all the great cities in America, Boston, which once had the reputation of being intelligent, has the lowest ranking, judged by journalistic standards. In fact it is the only city which had—until such time as they could not stomach association with a vital and progressive force—Newspaper Guild units which themselves were Red-baiting and reactionary.

Boston, like New York, has two Hearst newspapers. But unlike New York, Boston has no liberal or even semi-liberal newspapers, and it is therefore easier to resort to the crudest methods without fear of *colleagual* criticism or exposure.

Hearst papers in Boston are notorious for "making" of the news. Public opinion frequently is influenced by stories which originate not in events but in the minds of editors. On the Hearst papers, says the Institute for Propaganda Analysis, it is the incompetent reporter, indeed, "who cannot arouse public opinion to fever pitch at twenty minutes' notice, and with only the help of the nearest telephone book." The system is simple. The reporter calls ten or twelve notable people, men and women he knows and who may owe him a favor, or who are dogs for personal publicity, or who happen to have such perverted political minds that they agree with Hearstian policies, and each person makes a statement suggested by the reporter. The statements are then collected under a general "lead," and the story appears on page 1 of the Hearst papers under headlines which begin

PUBLIC DECRIES . . .

or

PATRIOTIC LEADERS ENDORSE . . .

Of course the other newspapers do the same thing when they ride their pet hobby horses into the political arena.

In the Hearst press the same trickery is used in the general Red-baiting campaign in every town. It is very easy to call up the head of the American Legion, the leading Daughter of the American Revolution, the loudest Knight of Columbus or other Catholic organization with which Hearst has worked ever since he married a Catholic, and start a Red scare. The fact that most of the endorsers of Hearst scares made fools of themselves when the campaigns against colleges, college professors, labor organizations and individuals have been exposed, and Hearst-sponsored legislation has been found to be as stupid as it was sinister, has never deterred the "patriots" from endorsing.

In Boston the old-style venality, so usually denied by publishers, still flourishes in the old-style way, with the public utilities, the department stores, the beer manufacturers, and other interests suppressing news right and left—chiefly right. Most of the papers do a little Red-baiting now and then, but the Hearst *Boston American* leads the pack. Since there is no real liberal paper to criticize it, as there is in other cities, the Hearst sheet is more reckless and vicious in its methods.

One of its tricks is to manufacture the news. Just as its reporters make what they call public opinion by getting their friends or Hearst's friends to endorse a Hearst idiosyncrasy, so they also *make* stories by their own actions. The appointment of Granville Hicks to a fellowship at Harvard University was an example. Hicks is one of the leading literary critics in America. He happens to belong to the Communist party, just as other literary figures and Harvard professors happen to belong to the Republican and Democratic parties. Under the law of the land these three parties are equal in everything, and membership in one or the other cannot be a bar to the enjoyment of everything the Constitution guarantees citizens. This fact, however, is either unknown to or ignored by Hearst editors. And Hearst reporters, who are forever apologizing for the "dirty" things they have to do in the Hearst service—the hounding of Lindbergh is the best example—instigated actions in Boston in an effort to drive Hicks out of Harvard. *Boston American* reporters got twenty members of the Grand Army of the Republic to protest, and then reported the protest as "spontaneous." They also influenced the Watertown Lodge of Elks to take similar action. The national commander of the American Legion, Daniel J. Doherty, whom decent and intelligent well-wishers of the Legion expected to put an end to its long records of Red-baiting, joined the Hearst movement. But even that was not enough for Hearst.

Someone on the *American* got the brilliant idea that there should be a student revolt. Accordingly the reporters were sent out to stir one up. They circulated in Harvard Yard with petitions, asking all and sundry to attach their names. But even the conservative lads who people Harvard nowadays are getting too wise to play the stooges for Hearst newspapers, and very few lent their rich and aristocratic names to the *American's* representative. This fact, however, did not deter the editors from using the previously prepared headline, '

STUDENTS REVOLT ON RED PROFESSOR

which led one day's paper. The next day, to Hearst's consternation, the Harvard Young Conservatives, the most reactionary student group in a university not well known any longer as the leading institution for fostering liberal, enlightened and progressive thought, actually announced its approval of Granville Hicks to a fellowship. And that was the end of Hearst trickery in that affair.

However, on the second of May the Hearst press in Boston notably and in New York and elsewhere to some extent, had another chance for sensational Red-baiting. The news fact concerned an attack on three nuns near Sts. Peter and Paul Cathedral in Providence. It is a fact that Bishop Francis P. Keough told the press he "suspected" the attack to be due to a campaign by Communists, a charge for which he had no ground whatsoever except his own hatred of Communists. However, the slanderous charge made by a high clergyman gave that section of the press which also engages in Red-baiting an opportunity to do so and lay the blame on a person of some standing in the community. The Hearst headlines were disgraceful. The story was proven false. And the next day when Phil Frankfeld, secretary of the Massachusetts Communist party, protested the "false, deliberately misleading and slanderous charge," there was no mention of that in most Hearst papers.

The *Boston Transcript*

For many years the *Boston Transcript* has had the reputation of being the journal of the Brahmins; in more recent times it has become a little more popular in its headlines and makeup, but it is still the only newspaper which one can pick up and read a head such as the following:

INERTES, IGNAVE FUIMUS: OPERAE PRETIUM FUIT

De Praeteritorum Memoria per Annos Quator in
Collegio Harvardiensi

Underneath, in the issue of June 24, 1937, followed the Harvard Commencement Latin oration by Laird McK. Ogle, but the "little old lady in black bombazine" never felt it necessary to tell its readers that its headline meant, "we have been lazy and ignorant, but it was worth it"—"Memories concerning happenings of the past through four years in Harvard College." Moreover, this story made page 1.

This same aristocratic newspaper, however, will defend child labor and even publish a pamphlet on "The Newspaper Boy."

The *Transcript* also refused to publish the news about one of its advertisers who refused to obey a minimum wage law board's decision, and an advertisement naming the firm, despite the fact the state law provides a fine of $100 upon newspapers refusing or neglecting to publish the findings of the commission.

Some years ago when Dr. Charles Harrington, health officer, investigated the breweries and found that beer was being adulterated with salicylic and fluoric acids, he succeeded in getting jury indictments. Hearst published the facts because he was starting a campaign for circulation. But the *Boston Transcript* did not mention Red Fox Ale being indicted; neither did the *Globe* or *Post* mention the matter.

Later, Harvard Beer was indicted.

In both instances the Boston papers and notably the *Transcript* carried beer advertisements of these concerns. In the first instance the *Transcript* published a list of indictments, cutting out the name of the advertiser.

Three days after the Harvard Beer indictment, moreover, the good old *Transcript* carried the first of a series of larger-than-usual advertisements which proclaimed "Harvard Beer, 1,000 per cent Pure."

Today I doubt the possibility of Harvard Beer or any other advertiser being able to suppress an important news item in the *Transcript*. I do not believe that the *Transcript* is venal. I am sure that if an advertiser came into the office and attempted to bribe an editor or publisher he would not only be thrown out on his ear but the paper would publish the facts in the case and an added exposure of the attempted corruption. But I am just as certain that the *Transcript* would never endanger either a dollar's worth of legitimate advertising or a cent's worth of the status quo by publishing news or editorials harmful to either. However, there is some hope that the reorganization (September 1938) will be followed by a more liberal policy.

The *Christian Science Monitor*

The *Christian Science Monitor* is unique. It is the only national newspaper we have—the *New York Times* has a national influence and can be called a national newspaper on that account, but it is not published for national circulation as is the *Monitor*. The latter is also a non-commercial enterprise. It is therefore one of the few papers which can call itself free. The only chains it wears is that of the church which subsidizes it.

A circulation of about 125,000 is nothing compared to any of the mob newspapers, but nevertheless the *Monitor* is probably as powerful an organ as a combination of papers serving many millions. Every subscriber to the Christian Science journal can be put down as a man or woman belonging to the upper brackets in the income tax returns, of considerable culture and intelligence, and an influence in local or national affairs. There are practically no poor Christian Scientists in America, and none with the low I. Q. which make up the readership of the yellow press. Oswald Garrison Villard who wrote an essay on the *Monitor* many years ago said he was "hopeful that in the future struggle between the two great groups of thought in America, between the powers of privilege and the masses of the people," this paper's voice "will be heard on the side of the masses rather than of the privileged," but that day has not yet arrived. On the other hand it must be said that the *Monitor* is fairer to the masses than the *New York Times* and a vast majority of the hypocritical press which proclaims itself the organ of the millions.

The *Monitor* is the property of the trustees of the Christian Science Publishing Committee, its directors being the directors of the First Church of Christ Scientist, in Boston, the mother church. The paper was established "to publish the real news of the world in clean, wholesome manner, devoid of the sensation methods. . . . No exploitation or illustration of vice or crime, but the aim of the editors will be to issue a paper which will be welcomed in every home where purity and refinement are cherished ideals."

Christian Science itself is expounded in only a few columns on one page. The rest of the paper is a newspaper. There are of course tremendous censorships at work, not the least of which are against fraudulent advertising. There is no drug advertising whatever of course, and none of the phony sales by department and other stores which contribute so much of the revenue of the commercial newspaper. The *Monitor* would probably be the only newspaper whose advertising columns could pass a Consumers Union test or any ethical test.

The *Monitor* is not anti-advertising. Its advertising manager Norman S. Rose believes there are three reasons for bad advertising—greed, selfishness, and fear. He explains:

"Greed: Get the results, get the business, get the money. No matter how you advertise in order to get it, but get it.

"Selfishness: Don't pay any attention to the effect that what you are doing may have on the interests of others . . . just look out for yourself.

"Fear: Fear that sane, decent advertising won't work and that you've got to drag your copy through the gutter to make it outsmell and outsell your competitor's. Fear on the part of such advertisers, that a day of reckoning is not far off, when either the advertising profession itself or outside forces will clean up advertising practices—and that they'd better hurry up and sell as much of their wretched stuff as they can, before somebody stops them."

Mr. Rose closes his criticism with an apostrophe. He exclaims: "If these three things could be eliminated from the thoughts and motives of mankind . . . !" It is impossible to imagine any advertising man except the *Monitor's* expressing such an ideal thought.

In its news columns the *Monitor* has always given space to peace in the midst of all wars. In 1935 it covered the Italian attack on Ethiopia thoroughly and fairly. It published an editorial the first day saying: "In reporting as a newspaper the story of warlike measures or war, the *Monitor* as a Christian Science publication, also bespeaks its readers' attention to the fact of peace." More analytically than most papers it published the basic causes of the war and showed the part the munitions trade is playing throughout the world.

In national and local politics the *Monitor* is independent. This means independent in the dictionary sense, not in the sense of a great number of our newspapers which so style themselves despite an unbroken record of subservience to the political machines, both Democratic and Republican.

The *Monitor* is sold on its merits. The church does not ask anyone to buy it. Many non-Scientists also believe it is the ideal newspaper of our time and of all times.

Hearst

The stupidities and crudities of the Hearst Boston newspapers in the 1936 election campaign may seem ridiculous today, but the reader must remember that despite the general disgust with Hearst throughout the nation, he still has numerous followers in the former hub of American civilization. The city teems with the *Lumpenproletariat,* the ignorant and betrayed workingmen who in foreign countries form the vanguard of a Fascist dictator's labor army, and who in

America blindly follow Huey Longs and Father Coughlins rather than those who teach them their own self-interests.

The *Lumpenproletariat* makes up the Hearst readership everywhere. In Boston the *American* claims it has more than 261,000 circulation, the largest of any evening newspaper. In the 1936 campaign it ran a heading SHALL IT BE FREEDOM OR DICTATORSHIP? suggesting that Roosevelt meant the latter; it called the security law a wage cut and said Landon would end it; it published the most absurd story by Harold Lord Varney headed TUGWELL PROMPTER OF ROOSEVELT, and for weeks it republished its buncombe under such headings as BOSTON COMMUNISTS DROP MASK, OPEN DRIVE TO DEFEAT LANDON and REDS UNMASKED IN MOVE TO ELECT ROOSEVELT. In the issue of October 28, 1936, the *American* gives special emphasis to Catholics urging them to beware the Communist party, then proceeds to link the latter with the Roosevelt elector who favored the Spanish republic. The falsehood concerning "the suppression of all religion" in Spain is repeated.

As a rule newspapermen do not believe what they read in the papers or have faith in the papers themselves. At least the intelligent ones do not. (There are of course the exceptions, when the paper happens to be a great newspaper, but such instances are few.) The average reporter has been pictured as a cynic, a wise-cracker, a souse, three angles on the behavior pattern which perhaps betray a road of escape, or a valid reaction to the ancient and by now almost forgotten accusation that there was a relationship between the words "journalism" and "prostitution."

In the history of the American Newspaper Guild there have been instances of disputes among newspapermen themselves. The supposition that reporters are at least intelligent enough to know the fundamental facts about their own interests and the strength that comes with organization, was proven false in some cases, and in others the love of the bordellos was found stronger than the new freedom which beckoned.

In Boston the Guild had the strange experience of meeting a group of Hearst men who believed in the Hearst propaganda. They also have swallowed Hearst bunk against Loyalist Spain. Among the twenty or thirty thousand volunteers who came to the republic's aid was Ben Leider, an aviator and Guildsman, who was shot down after a heroic fight with the Fascists. A Ben Leider Memorial Fund had been organized and President Broun of the Guild asked units to contribute. The *Boston Daily Record* Guild thereupon countersigned a letter from Harry Benwell in which he said: "I am going to mind my own damn business. . . . The late Mr. Leider may have been a hero but the fact he gave his life fighting for Spanish Communists is nothing for American newspapermen to get excited about. . . . It seems to me it is going to be difficult to put ourselves over with publishers if we openly align ourselves with Reds whose avowed purpose it is to overturn capitalism. . . ."

In December, 1937, the *Daily Record* and the *American* Guilds quit the national organization and joined the American Federation of Labor. Telegrams from the Hearst *Mirror* and *Journal-American* units in New York asking Boston to remain in the C. I. O. were left unanswered. Representatives of Boston Guild headquarters who tried to address the Hearst meeting were not allowed to speak. (The Hearst men's idea of a free press is apparently a denial of free speech.)

The bourgeois as well as the boob papers go in for Red-baiting in Boston: it is a Catholic town and the Catholic hierarchy press has gone in for unadulterated Red-baiting itself and apparently the word has been passed on from the various "power houses" that this "party line" shall be pursued everywhere.

When the Spanish republic's ambassador visits Boston he receives no police escort, no public acclaim, and certainly no press headlines. When Fulvio Suvich, the Italian ambassador, arrives, Governor Hurley, Mayor Tobin and ex-Governor Curley (Commendatore of the Order of Italy) and press and public reply to his Fascist salute with an ovation and delirious newspaper columns. When a bill is introduced to end child labor the Catholic reactionaries get the publicity, the Catholic liberal view gets none. The *Traveler* calls the proposed Constitutional amendment "a carefully worded piece of radical legislation designed to rob parents of their rights over children and transfer control of every child up to eighteen years of age to a bureaucratic group in Washington." Apparently there are Bostonians benighted enough to believe such nonsense. When the WPA guidebook published the mildest sort of factual statement about the Sacco-Vanzetti case—the judicial murder of two radicals whose innocence has been proven beyond the shadow of question—the Boston press, excepting of course the intelligent *Monitor,* grew hysterical at what it considered an insult to the great commonwealth of Massachusetts.

With Red-baiting come the usual corollaries: anti-labor, pro-corporation, anti-Guild, pro-utilities, anti-liberal and pro-department store policies. These can be seen at work more clearly in Boston newspapers than elsewhere.

Herald and *Traveler*

In 1929 the *Boston Herald* and the *Boston Traveler* were exposed as being part of that vast newspaper empire which the International Paper and Power Company had built. Its defense that it was merely assuring an outlet for print paper, was disproved by the fact that it was largely a power corporation, and immediately afterward Frank Gannett of the *Brooklyn Eagle* and likewise the two Boston papers rushed out of the poison gas clouds the Federal investigation had spread over press ownership. This action was applauded generally. And so today we have the Boston newspapers controlled by the United Shoe Machinery Corporation directors instead of the I. P. and P. corporation.

In fact the *Traveler* and *Herald* are connected with many of the major banking interests of New England. Their president is S. W. Winslow, Jr., who in addition to the shoe directorship is director of the Morgan-affiliated First National Bank of Boston and the John Hancock Mutual Life, and U. S. Smelting. G. R. Brown, another director, also directs Shoe and banks. J. L. Hall, vice-president, directs Westinghouse, N. Y., N. H. and Hartford. Channing H. Cox is president of Old Colony Trust and director in United Fruit. The Boston Herald-Traveler Corporation is known as the wealthiest newspaper outfit in New England.

When the Guild asked for an increase in wages in 1938 the management replied that business conditions made it impossible. The Guild discovered that the corporation had a surplus of $5,035,401 in 1936 and paid $1,000,000 in dividends in 1937. Its net profits had been running from $600,000 to $900,000 in depression years. The Guild vote of 105 to 19 to strike won them a contract which meant the corporation would have to pay its employees $100,000 a year more.

The editorial pages of the *Herald* and the *Traveler* are violently anti-C. I. O.; they deplore strikes, they denounce picketing, they believe the 1936 sit-down strikes were criminal actions and they mask their big-business special pleading by pretending that all they say is in the interests of the general public—whatever that may be. I also have a collection of *Boston Herald* front-page news stories dealing with strikes and violence signed by Russell B. Porter. These dispatches are about ninety-five percent the same as the Porter stories in the *New York Times*. The five percent differences, however, are significant. In the Boston paper labor is reviled, vigilantes are approved, strikers are charged with violence, the police and legionnaires are praised. All this is done by changing a few words or purposeful editing. In the New York paper labor is not treated in too friendly a way but in Boston it actually gets a raw deal.

But what is one to expect in a press largely owned by the United Shoe Machinery Corporation and the leading banks of New England? A social conscience?

CHAPTER 17

Farewell: Lord of San Simeon

THE reader, if he is a layman to whom American journalism is a closed field, or the reviewer trained to ask for a presentation of "the other side" in every book he reads, may by now be somewhat shocked by the tragic pictures of our great publishers. Is there no good news at all, they may ask. Is there no hope for a better day and a better press?

The answer is that there is really cause for optimism. It is the answer based on the case history of William Randolph Hearst, the first of the great press lords, ruler of a $220,-000,000 domain, against whom an enlightened people has at last voiced its anger and disgust. From California to New York, labor and liberals, the unions and the universities, notable men including the President and Senators and the head of the Society of Newspaper Editors, hundreds of organizations and thousands of men and women who are the leaders of the intelligent minority, have taken a forthright stand against Hearst. There has been a great boycott of his newspapers, his magazines, his newsreels and his radio stations. There has been repudiation in Congress, in the press, on the platform and from the pulpit. The episode is one of the most heartening in the history of American journalism.

For more than a generation Hearst posed as "the friend of the people" and many believed him. The Hearst communication system reached at least 30,000,000 people—he claimed that many readers for his newspapers, and many more millions for his magazines, newsreels and radio broadcasts. His power was supposedly tremendous. But less than five years ago certain leaders made the charge that Hearst actually is the enemy of the people. In recent days he has been called the nation's No. 1 enemy, a place previously held by Al Capone and Dillinger. The latter two, the reader need not be reminded, were connected with bootlegging and murder, whereas Mr. Hearst has been connected merely with influencing the minds of the common people.

It is of course difficult to say just when the counter-attack began. It must not be forgotten that Hearst has been repudiated before; he was twice hanged in effigy by angry mobs, once when a demented person shot President McKinley after the Hearst papers had published vicious editorials against the President, and a verse about the bullet which had shot a governor speeding its way to Washington; the second time when he espoused the German cause before Wilson led his pacifist nation into the useless World War. These popular uprisings against Hearst did not affect his empire. Nothing is as fickle as the public, nothing as forgetful, nothing as easily misled. But the third, or present attack on Hearst, is made up of something more than emotion and hysteria.

It is first and most important of all, a labor union attack, in which American Federation of Labor, C. I. O., and independent labor organizations are united. It is also an attack from the schools and colleges of the country. It was in 1936 an attack from political leaders also, but that is the sort of reaction which may mean absolutely nothing in the end. The strength of the war against Hearst is the labor and intellectual union against him.

The most important individual blow was that struck by two private citizens, Bernard J. Reis, the certified public accountant and author of an enlightening book on crooked finances called "False Security," and Paul Kern, civil service commissioner of New York City. Mr. Hearst had applied to the Securities and Exchange Commission for permission to float $22,500,000 in bonds for Hearst Publications and $13,-000,000 for Hearst Magazines. Mr. Reis, who can read financial statements between the lines better than most men, objected to a lot of things. He did not like Hearst Publications listing as assets $38,000,000 for good will, franchises, reference libraries; he did not like the fact that four Hearst magazines lose money and six dailies made less in 1936 than ten years earlier; he particularly questioned the financial record of the *Seattle Post-Intelligencer* and *Chicago Evening Examiner;* he did not like circulation losses on six newspapers which he suspected were due to the growing boycott.

Reis and Kern, two public-spirited citizens, filed a brief. They claimed in it that if the money were raised by S. E. C. permission most of it was to be used to purchase a castle in Wales, at a half million more than its assessed valuation, and the good will of a magazine they claimed was losing money; they also charged that the registration statement failed to disclose the fact almost four million dollars were intended to repay loans which Hearst personally guaranteed. They were joined by Labor Research Association in a protest which alleged that profits of Hearst Magazines, Inc., were diverted to holding companies and through them to Mr. Hearst.

No public hearings were held. The application for the bond issues was withdrawn. And so in 1937 Hearst began a series of consolidations of newspapers in which many were killed off, and a general retrenchment in which thousands of employees were fired. On December 31, 1937, most of the newspapers of the country suppressed the fact that there was a trial in United States District Court in New York in which a receiver for Hearst Consolidated Publications, Inc., was asked and also an accounting. The plaintiff was a stockholder named Rudolph Kohlroser.

Another turning point in Hearst history was his victory in 1934 when the San Francisco general strike was defeated. It will be remembered that the press—with the exception of the Scripps-Howard *News*—conspired to smash labor as well as the strike, and that the news columns of the California papers generally lied and perverted the news, and that false issues were created, and the public fooled into believing that a Red revolution was under way when what really mattered was an attempt of working people to better themselves.

The San Francisco publishers won. They were led by James Francis Neylan, the Hearst attorney, acting directly on instructions received by cable from Mr. Hearst. The press announced it was a victory for public opinion, for the people, as against the Reds, but the labor unions passed resolutions for a boycott. Hearst was singled out for marked attention. The "I Don't Read Hearst" sticker was ruled off letters by order of Postmaster General Farley but it could not be ruled out of people's minds.

In Bridges' seamen's union it is a crime to be caught dead or alive with a Hearst paper in one's possession. As a result you will find Bridges called a Moscow agent in the Hearst newspapers.

By 1936 there was a Peoples Committee Against Hearst functioning and Oswald Garrison Villard reported 112 American Federation of Labor unions were members of the trades-union committee fighting the publisher. The Farmer Labor Progressive Federation, meeting in Oshkosh, Wisconsin, passed a resolution to boycott Hearst in which he was called "Labor's Enemy No. 1." In numerous meetings in Seattle pending the *Post-Intelligencer* strike Hearst was known as American Menace No. 1. On May 7, 1936, the officers of the United Automobile Workers of America placed all Hearst papers on the "unfair to labor list." Typical of all resolutions was the Detroit one accusing Hearst papers of having "consistently used every unfair and slanderous method of undermining the organized labor movement."

The year 1935 marked the height of the Hearst Red-baiting campaign in the universities. It must be remarked here and now that there is no Red teaching in the schools and colleges of the United States, but the institutions of learning of our country still attempt to give their students a liberal education. It is inconceivable that they should do anything else.

No school can supply an anti-liberal education, or a Fascist education, as these terms are contradictory. Liberalism and education are one, and all Hearst did was to call liberal education "Red" education.

To this day the Hearst press is filled with Red-baiting articles and attacks upon such notable Americans as Prof. Charles A. Beard, Prof. George S. Counts, of Teachers College; Prof. E. A. Ross, of the University of Wisconsin; Prof. Frederick L. Schuman, of Chicago. Hearst reporters in numerous instances have been sent as students to interview professors or to take courses for the purpose of writing Red-baiting articles. When these reporters found nothing to write about they falsified. In several cases they later confessed.

In the case of Professor Schuman he protested misrepresentation in a report in the *Chicago Herald-Examiner* and incidentally informed the editor that some quotations on dictatorship which all the Hearst papers attributed to Lenin were probably false as there was no trace of them in the collected works of the Russian leader. Hearst ordered an investigation. Charles Wheeler was sent. He conceded misquoting the Chicago professor and admitted the invention of the Lenin quotation. Professor Schuman asked him how such things could be and quotes Wheeler's reply: "We just do what the Old Man orders. One week he orders a campaign against rats. The next week he orders a campaign against dope peddlers. Pretty soon he's going to campaign against college professors. It's all the bunk but orders are orders."

Charles Wheeler, Hearst reporter, appeared to be a decent fellow. But shortly afterward Professor Schuman delivered a lecture which Wheeler covered for the Hearst press. This item is described by Professor Schuman as containing statements which were purely products of Mr. Wheeler's imagination.

"On March 16, 1935," continues the professor, "the *Herald-Examiner*—with Hearst papers elsewhere copying—published an editorial, 'Schuman of Chicago,' which took out of their context two of Mr. Wheeler's misquotations and presented them as evidence that I am making a 'direct challenge to American institutions in the name of Communism.' . . . The editorial described me as one of 'these American panderers and trap-baiters for the Moscow mafia' who should be investigated by Congress and 'gotten rid of' as a 'Red.'

"This is but one of numerous instances of slanderous and libelous attacks upon American educators in the Hearst press. This strategy is exactly comparable to that of the Nazi press in Germany between 1920 and 1933. Mr. Hearst has evidently been taking lessons from Göring, Goebbels, Rosenberg, and Hitler. No individual can defend himself effectively from these assaults. If American universities and colleges are to be spared the fate which has befallen such institutions in Germany, if American scholars and educators are to be protected from Fascist bludgeoning of this type, if American traditions of freedom are to survive, Mr. Hearst must be recognized as the propagandist and forerunner of American Hitlerism and must be met with a united counterattack by all Americans who still value their liberties."

In 1936 the American Federation of Teachers passed a resolution demanding a boycott of Hearst as "the outstanding jingoist of the country" and a "constant enemy of academic freedom," and finally and more important, as the "chief exponent of Fascism in the United States."

The 1936 political campaign also had something to do with the universal discredit in which Hearst found himself in November of that year. However, politics make strange bedfellows, and politicians pass from bed to bed without public disapproval. There is for example a certain Alfred Emanuel Smith, a reactionary, a member of the American Liberty League, a millionaire, a Red-baiter, a discredited liberal. In his youth he was on the other side of the fence. He was not rich, he was liberal, he was one of the courageous politicians who denounced the Red-baiting of the Lusk committee and the expulsion of the five Socialists from the New York state

legislature. And, on the night of October 29, 1929, in
Carnegie Hall, Manhattan, he said of Publisher Hearst:
"I know he has not got a drop of good, clean, pure red
blood in his whole body. And I know the color of his liver
and it is whiter, if that could be, than the driven snow." He
continued to denounce the Hearst newspapers for publishing "deliberate lies," and for "the gravest abuse of the power
of the press in the history of this country." For thirty minutes
Governor Smith of the State of New York denounced the
publisher who was such a power in Tammany Hall, and
concluded by asking the people of "this city, this state, and
this country . . . to get rid of this pestilence that walks in the
darkness."

Today Millionaire Smith and Millionaire Hearst have
everything in common and each other's endorsement.

Perhaps another of the little group of leading Democratic
politicians of that era will not emulate Smith the renegade.
Franklin Delano Roosevelt who once had the support of
Hearst, was forced in the 1936 campaign to issue a statement against "a certain notorious newspaper owner" who
tried to "make it appear that the President accepts the support of alien organizations hostile to the American form of
government. These articles are conceived in malice and
born of political spite. They are deliberately framed to give
a false impression—in other words to 'frame' the American
people. . . ."

F. D. Roosevelt thus added his damnation of Hearst to
that of Woodrow Wilson and Theodore Roosevelt, among
Presidents.

In Congress there were field days when Senator (now
Justice) Black was conducting his lobby investigation into
Hearst and Associated Gas affairs. Black himself did not get
very angry but he did point out the incongruity of Hearst's
action in trying to prevent the investigation. "Year after
year," he said, "this man has sponsored the most ruthless invasion of the privacy of people's lives, yet now he stands on

his 'Constitutional' rights to keep the Senate from looking at his telegrams. He can own property in Mexico and try to start a war between that country and the United States—but he can't be investigated."

Senator Minton,* answering Hearst editorial attacks upon the investigation, accused the publisher of prostituting the press; he said that to Hearst the words freedom of the press meant "license to traduce and vilify public officers as swine and traitors to their country"; and as for the Hearst charge that a subversive Congress was being led by Roosevelt administration officials into a dictatorship, Senator Minton asserted that "the dictatorship we have to fear in this country is that of a purse-proud, insolent, arrogant, bull-dozing newspaper publisher like William Randolph Hearst.

"He is the greatest menace to the freedom of the press that exists in this country, because instead of using the great chain of newspapers that he owns, and the magazines, and the news-disseminating agencies of the country that he controls to disseminate the truth to the people, he prostitutes them to the propaganda that pursues the policy he dictates.

"The question was raised by Mr. Hearst in the name of the Constitution, in the name of our ancient liberties, in the name of the freedom of the press. He would not know the Goddess of Liberty if she came down off her pedestal in New York harbor and bowed to him. He would probably try to get her telephone number. He would not know the freedom of the press if it sprang full panoplied from the constitution in front of him."

Spokesman for the administration, and opening gunner of the Roosevelt defense against the publishers' coalition, was Senator Schwellenbach, who told the Senate that from 1895 on, the decent editors and publishers in America had criticized and fought Hearst. But nowadays, "Mr. Hearst and his stooge, Elisha Hanson, rush behind the Constitution, and

---

* *Congressional Record,* March 26, 1936.

use the Constitution and the freedom of the press to protect them in their right to reduce wages. . . .

"The securing of news by larceny and bribery was the
charge which the Associated Press made and sustained
against William Randolph Hearst, this man who talks about
the sacredness of the press and the sacredness of telegraph
wires. He bribed a telegraph operator and stole the news.
And let it be said to the eternal disgrace of the American
newspaper profession that the Associated Press did not have
the courage to remove Mr. Hearst from membership in that
organization."

Resuming his speech a few days later the Senator quoted
Elihu Root's account of a talk with Theodore Roosevelt regarding the assassination of McKinley, and added: "Can
there be a more clear delineation of the fact that the then
President of the United States, Theodore Roosevelt, directly
charged William Randolph Hearst with the murder by assassination of President William McKinley?" (Mr. Hearst
replied by calling the Senator a "prize pole cat.")

While he was building his Bavarian castle in California,
Hearst three times cut the pay of his employees, the Senator
charged. And in conclusion, he fired this blast:

"It is a peculiar thing that the leader of the movement in
this country today toward Fascism, the man who when he
returned after a visit with Mr. Hitler in Germany editorially
praised Mr. Hitler, the man who more than anybody else
is advocating Fascism in this country—and under Fascism
Senators know what remains of personal liberty or freedom
of the press—this man is the same William Randolph Hearst
who today is so ardent in his protection of the rights of the
people under the Constitution."

Protestant church organizations have denounced Hearst.
Several noted leading Catholics, clergy and laymen, have
also done so but inasmuch as the Hearst press has been the
most pro-Catholic press in America, that Church has refrained from criticism. In fact, when Hearst joined Cardinal

Hayes in supporting the Fascists in their campaigns in Spain, which included the slaughter of women and children in non-military zones, the Catholic press sang the praises of Hearst louder than ever.

The Ministers' Council for Social Action of New York, which includes ministers of Methodist, Baptist, Congregational and Jewish churches, joined in a plan to preach an anti-Hearst sermon the week-end of Sunday, June 28, 1936. Said their official statement: "No single man has exercised so destructive and immoral an influence in dragging into the gutter those very ideals for which all religious institutions stand" . . . as W. R. Hearst. *Metropolitan Church Life,* organ of the Greater New York Federation of Churches, asking preachers to quit supplying Hearst with editorial page texts, said, "We can ill afford to believe that the Protestant Christian Church will make common cause with Hearst." The *Christian Century* seconded the motion.

The Artists' and Writers' Union has picketed the *New York Daily Mirror.* The League Against Yellow Journalism has been organized in Berkeley, California, to boycott Hearst. In the motion picture "Gold Is Where You Find It," the gold-rush figure of Senator Hearst is introduced. He remarks jokingly he does not know what to do with his son. "Willie wants to be a journalist." Instead of a laugh the line got many boos in many cities.

It may indeed be a great satisfaction to William Randolph Hearst to know that his name was powerful enough to bring 6,000 persons to the Hippodrome, in New York, where they paid for the privilege of being a mass jury in the trial of the publisher. The indictment accused Hearst of:

1. Distorting the news in his papers.
2. Using his press for strike-breaking purposes.
3. Supporting Fascism in America and Europe, and notably Hitler.
4. Using his jingoistic press to foment wars.
5. Being anti-libertarian.

The most serious charge of all was that made by the Governor of Minnesota, Hjalmar Peterson, who concluded the opening speech of the prosecution with the following words: "William Randolph Hearst is being judged tonight by the jury of public opinion. I submit he is guilty in the first degree of attempting to destroy democracy."

The witnesses who gave their testimony included: Oswald Garrison Villard, editor of *The Nation;* Robert K. Speer, Professor of Sociology at New York University; Charles J. Hendley, president of the American Federation of Teachers of Greater New York; Rabbi Israel Goldstein, National Conference of Jews and Christians; the Rev. William Lloyd Imes, St. James Presbyterian Church; Representative Vito Marcantonio, Osmond K. Fraenkel, constitutional attorney. Arthur Garfield Hays, counsel for the American Civil Liberties Union, was prosecuting attorney. Hearst was found guilty of "betraying the United States" and the court sentenced the audience to boycott the Hearst newspapers and other enterprises.

If the reader thinks mock trials are somewhat naïve and stickers with "Don't Read Hearst" ineffective, the proof that he is wrong has now been furnished by a survey made by *Fortune* magazine and published in its July, 1936, issue. It does not tell us what has caused the American people to lose all faith in the Hearst propaganda machine, but it proves that those who are intelligent enough to think about the matter disapprove of Hearst in about a three to one ratio.

Throughout the country 27.3 percent of the people asked, replied they considered Hearst influence bad for America, 10.7 percent thought it good, but what is more interesting, the figures against Hearst were bigger in the cities where he has newspapers. Forty-three and three-tenths percent said Hearst influence was bad, 10.5 percent thought it good, and 46.2 percent didn't know anything about it.

Still more significant is the fact that the survey was made during the 1936 Presidential campaign when almost the entire press was for Landon and where Hearst had joined in the popular journalistic yapping.

The *Fortune* survey also proves that after forty-five years of instructing the American people to follow his principles and candidates the American people are overwhelmingly against Hearst. There is perhaps no happier sign in either the journalistic or political heavens at present.

There is but one unfortunate situation to report. The people are growing aware of Hearst and are repudiating Hearst, but the newspapers, including many which fought Hearst for two generations, generally stood by his side when he turned Republican. Most of them had the good sense to keep quiet. But the same hypocrisy prevailed as many years ago when the courts found a Hearst news service guilty of the theft of news from the Associated Press and neither the A. P. nor the American Newspaper Publishers Association had the courage to expel Hearst.

Among the small minority which exercised the freedom of the press to expose their fellow publisher were the *St. Louis Post-Dispatch*, the *Seattle Star*, the *New York Post*, and the *New York Herald Tribune* which published an interview with William Allen White who said prophetically that "I believe that Hearst as an ally of any politician is a form of political suicide."

In Seattle the *Star* answered the *Post-Intelligencer*'s charge that the Federal Council of the Churches of Christ in America was Communistic because it co-operated with the American Civil Liberties Union by saying, "It is a deliberate, gratuitous, malicious, insulting, damnable lie. And W. R. Hearst knows it is a lie. In his campaign of frightfulness with which he has undertaken to browbeat and stifle all Americans who won't accept his brand of politics this mad hatter of yellow journalism has at last gone too far. It is high time for the pendulum of public opinion to swing back the other way and to bump this bullying, would-be dictator off his paper throne."

In the *Post* Ernest L. Meyer wrote: "Mr. Hearst in his long and not laudable career has inflamed Americans against Spaniards, Americans against Japanese, Americans against Filipinos, Americans against Russians, and in the pursuit of his incendiary campaign he has printed downright lies, forged documents, faked atrocity stories, inflammatory editorials, sensational cartoons and photographs and other devices by which he abetted his jingoistic ends."

It has taken forty-five years for the intelligent minority of the American people to turn against Hearst. But the turn has come. Despite the fact that he controls the channels of communications which reach 30,000,000 readers and more movie goers and radio listeners it has been possible through a few newspapers, a few liberal organizations, the small liberal press, some books, some speeches in Congress, to arouse public opinion sufficiently to boycott the man generally admitted No. 1 enemy of the American people.

The history of Hearst should be a lesson to the other reactionary publishers of America, but it probably will not be. The American people will have to exercise eternal vigilance against the other smaller Hearsts in the House of Press Lords.

CHAPTER 18

Annenberg

MOSES L. ANNENBERG made millions of dollars from the *New York Morning Telegraph*, the *Daily Racing Form*, *Running Horse*, *Miami Beach Tribune*, *Radio Guide*, *Teleflash* and the Nationwide News Service, Inc. Through the Cecelia Company he earned considerable sums from the publication of *Screen Guide* and *Official Detective Stories* and other pulp literature. When Moe Annenberg bought the *Philadelphia Inquirer* for $15,000,000, *Editor & Publisher* said "his fabulous career as circulation expert and publisher has created an aura of legend about him."

Moe got his start as a newsdealer. One day he asked Mrs. Moe what were the things needed most about a house, and Mrs. Moe replied, "Teaspoons are the things I need most around the house," whereupon Moe Annenberg became the greatest exploiter of the humble teaspoon in history. Send fifteen cents with this coupon and get a genuine silver-plated teaspoon. That was the trick that started him on the way to millions. Women never have enough teaspoons. He is also the inventor of the state seal teaspoon and many newer spoon ideas.

It was the teaspoon that brought him to Hearst in Chicago in 1900; within four years he was circulation manager of the *Examiner;* in 1907 he had the exclusive distribution rights for all Chicago papers in Milwaukee. In 1917 he was publisher for Arthur Brisbane's *Wisconsin News* and in 1920 circulation director of all Hearst publications. He was a member of the Hearst executive council until 1926 when he resigned owing to pressure of his own activities, chiefly in the horse-racing publication field. Regarding many rumors he says:

"Contrary to the opinion expressed maliciously by some persons from time to time, I have never in all my life had any interest in any gambling device or business. I have never owned a share of stock directly or indirectly in a horse track, and I do not own any race horses and have no desire to own any."

The first thing Annenberg did on getting control of the *Inquirer* was to start a comic strip war with the *Record*. In 1936 he announced he would give anxious Philadelphians no less than 50 comics, and today he is supplying no less than 60 in a special section of thirty pages.

The *Inquirer* was the first newspaper in America which the National Labor Relations Board cited for unfair labor practices. It had refused to obey the law which requires corporations to deal collectively with its employees, in this instance the Philadelphia branch of the Newspaper Guild.

Within a year after Annenberg took over he completed arrangements with the Guild, and although a new wage scale was granted, Annenberg announced he would not recognize the union. A fifteen percent raise in wages, the five-day forty-hour week and other concessions were granted.

Shortly after Christmas, 1937, after he had disposed of his *Miami Tribune* and its plants, Annenberg brought out *Click,* a picture weekly. *Space & Time* reported early in 1938 that this publication which added sex to news pictures, led the field with print orders of between 2,500,000 and 3,000,-000 copies. It reported Moe Annenberg keeping huge sums of cash on hand for quick deals—some ten million dollars ready to rush in and buy should Hearst die or retire.

CHAPTER 19

Northwest: Liberal Despite the Press*

IT IS a fact that the liberal American tradition rolled westward with the covered wagons; it is also unfortunately true that to a certain extent the movement which drained the East of so much of its daring blood also drained it considerably of its progressive spirit. It is not so much the fact that Maine and Vermont voted against the Roosevelt Deal, as the New England attitude against any sort of new deal. The cities and states which produced the great libertarians now sound the alarm when their descendants repeat their great ideas further West.

One would naturally expect that the press would reflect the character of the region. Boston with its cheap politicians, its narrow-minded masses, its prejudices against art and literature, and its domination by a few banks and corporations, can no longer be expected to produce magnificent enlightened mass-circulation newspapers, but the Northwest—Oregon, Washington, Idaho and Montana—where the liberal spirit finds most favorable soil, ought as a corollary, to produce newspapers at least as liberal as its politics.

The spirit of equality and democracy lingers over from covered wagon days and is reflected in much of the liberal legislation of those states. The right of the people to vote directly on issues—the initiative and referendum—had its baptism in the Pacific Northwest, where it soon became

---

* Facts for many preceding chapters have come to me in *letters* from well-known persons; a large part of this chapter, however, was written as it here appears, by an authority who desires no credit line.

known as the "Oregon System" and spread to half the states of the nation. Similarly, Oregon instituted the direct election of United States Senators before that principle was embodied in the Federal Constitution. The recall of public officials, minimum wage laws, maximum hours of labor, public ownership of hydroelectric power, old-age pensions: all of these found fertile soil in the vast Northwest.

From the Northwest have come such enlightened Senators as the late Harry Lane, who with five others voted against America's declaration of war. Thomas J. Walsh and William E. Borah carried the liberal traditions of the Oregon country into the Senatorial chambers, and today Lewis B. Schwellenbach, junior Senator from Washington, is among the staunchest supporters of the New Deal. By and large, the Congressional delegations of these states are far more liberal than the national average, and nowhere—except perhaps in the Solid South—has the President stronger backing than in the states surrounding Puget Sound.

Everyone in the Northwest will admit that it is a progressive region. Even Oregon's "nine-foot-hotel-bed-sheet law" is sheepishly hailed as a forward step in sanitation. But none of the residents attribute the liberal policies of the Pacific Northwest to the influence of the press. Progress has been made in spite of the newspapers, not because of them. Today few newspapers in the four states have any vestige of the pioneering spirit that marked the old independent editors who set up handpresses and typecases alongside the stage relay station or land office. The papers of the Northwest, with pathetically few exceptions, fight all reforms as tenaciously as the chain-ridden press of New England. In common with the newspapers of the rest of the nation, the Northwest dailies ridicule the New Deal, malign the President, and belittle and besmirch all attempts at progressive and reform legislation.

Repeatedly the people have repudiated the concerted efforts of the press to preserve the status quo. It is a byword, for instance, that whatever candidate the newspapers unite for, will be soundly trounced. Three times the press of Oregon tried to saddle the people with a sales tax. Once it was under the guise of relieving property owners, the next time to keep the schools from closing, and finally, social security growing popular, to provide funds for old-age pensions. Each time the sales tax was licked, and each time by a bigger margin. The influence of the editorial page— pride of the elders of the fourth estate—has waned in the Northwest.

A flickering bright spot in the fog of journalistic commercialization is the few weeklies that maintain the tradition of old when editors set their own type and wrote their own editorials. Most of the country sheets, it is true, are splotchy conglomerations of boiler plate and canned editorials with a few columns of "locals" as an excuse for publication. But around the four states a number of editors still believe in trying to print what they believe. C. I. O. and Commonwealth Federation papers once a week tell the stories the press associations ignore. No more refreshing oasis in the newspaper desert can be found than the *Salem Capital-Press,* edited by a picturesque old man named A. M. Church who wears a battered eyeshade and slashes away at his fellow newspapermen with relish. No one has more contempt for the "venal press" than this old Non-Partisan Leaguer from North Dakota, who delights in rattling the political skeletons so carefully preserved among the "sacred cows" of his conservative colleagues. The Colonel has the largest weekly in the Northwest and insults potential power company and bank advertisers and manages to keep up the payments on his linotype machine. Two full pages of classified ads from the farmers of the valley are the backbone of his independence. A jugful of quarters under the counter, collected from farmers and swappers for their livestock ads, kept him going through the depression. Colonel Church is the burr under the Oregon editors' saddle. Progressives look to his new rotary press to make his paper the liberal voice of the state, just as La Follette's *Progressive* is in Wisconsin.

The slightest offense by any liberal or progressive is seized upon greedily by the majority of the newspapers of this great, progressive part of the country. When an automobile driven by Harry Bridges killed a boy in an accident, the mishap was blazoned in screaming headlines. Bridges was later cleared of blame. But when the young scion of Portland's wealthiest department store family was convicted of a felony in a California court, the people of the city did not learn about it through their newspapers. The vigilant defenders of the freedom of the press were too busy to print *that* news. It was published in other cities, where that particular department store, the largest in Portland, did not buy advertising.

The most active of Oregon's newspapers politically is the *Oregon Journal*. Its principal owner is Philip L. Jackson, known about town as "Phil." He inherited the paper from his father, who built it into a powerful publication by being for "Battling Bob" La Follette and Harry Lane and Tom Walsh and other progressives in public life. But "Phil" inherited only the paper and not these enlightened tendencies. He is a playboy sort of fellow who loves to play at being "admiral" at various regattas held to publicize commercialized beach and lake resorts. The *Journal* could not find space to tell its readers what happened to the son of the great department-store family, but it always manages to devote plenty of space to a picture of "Admiral Phil" surrounded by the toothsome beauties who comprise his lovely crew. Various other of "Phil's" enlightened deeds, such as giving a water cart to the University football team, a professional outfit largely recruited from other states, are amply publicized in the newspaper he inherited. Where once the stern, socially useful views of the elder La Follette were heralded in the *Journal*, the paper's readers now learn about Fleet Week and the gay party "Phil" has given for the visiting naval officers.

For a time the *Journal,* being a Democratic newspaper, pretended to be for the New Deal. But as the President steadily adopted liberal policies, the sham ended. "Phil" made the paper's real hero Governor Charles H. Martin, probably the most reactionary man ever to hold public office in the Far West. After being elected by posing as a friend of President Roosevelt, Martin, a retired major-general, turned into a virtual autocrat. He inferentially commended the handling of labor problems by Hitler and Mussolini; he advised the state police to move against labor pickets and "beat hell out of 'em" and "crack their damn heads" and he assailed the New Deal with such temperate language as remarking he would like "to kick the pants off the National Labor Relations Board." The *Journal* made this hero its own, and conveniently neglected to print Martin's advice to a sheriffs' convention:

"The Italians wouldn't submit; they organized their Blackshirts. The Germans wouldn't submit; so they had their Brownshirts and Hitler. I don't think the Americans will submit."

When Martin ran for renomination in the Democratic primaries recently, the *Journal* descended to new depths of journalistic indecency. The rumor spread around the state that President Roosevelt was about to thrust at the militaristic Governor who had run out on the New Deal. Martin's furious denial was smeared at the top of page 1. The President's thrust at Martin a few days later was shoved into an inconspicuous head. Ralph Watson, "Phil's" slavishly reactionary political writer, was turned loose to smear Henry Hess, the progressive nominee. A Hess meeting attended by 2,500 people was ridiculed as a washout in the *Journal.* A Martin gathering attended by 400 was an enthusiastic success. The whole paper became a house organ for this Fascist-minded militarist. Martin's victory was confidently predicted by the willing Watson. The Governor's tour through crucial Clackamas County was heralded in the *Journal* as a trip of triumph and success; Hess's reception was contrasted for its bleakness.

On election day Hess won decisively.

Newspapers are always looking for scoops. But not when the scoop augurs well for liberalism. The *Portland News-Telegram,* of the Scripps-Canfield chain, buys the "Washington Merry-Go-Round" column by the widely known liberal writers, Drew Pearson and Robert S. Allen. Shortly before the Martin-Hess election, their column predicted that the New Deal was washed up with Martin's reactionary policies. It was a clean beat, and preceded by nearly a week a direct attack on Martin led by the President, Secretary Ickes and Senator Norris. It was a national scoop. The *News-Telegram* killed it in Portland. The people of Oregon would never have known about the column had not the *Oregonian,* a rival newspaper, seen it elsewhere and reprinted it. The *News-Telegram* is one of the Northwest's most militant defenders of the freedom of the press; its editor, Tom Shea, is a former football game official.

The *Oregonian,* at Portland, is one of the strange newspapers on America's last frontier. It is extremely unobjective and biased in its attitude toward the New Deal. But it also is one of the few papers in the country that sincerely champions the liberties of the underdog. It led a campaign which resulted finally in the Supreme Court decision outlawing Oregon's abortive Criminal Syndicalism law. It also has been more outspoken than any other paper on the Pacific Coast in its defense of the Spanish Loyalists. The *Oregonian* sponsored a crusade in Portland which resulted in the curtailment and abolition of that city's vicious police Red-squad. In both editorials and feature stories the paper showed that the Red-squad was financed by leading lumber barons and anti-union employers who wanted to prevent the organization of their employees. The editor of the *Oregonian* is a liberal of the old school named Paul Kelty. He fears that the New Deal has taken away liberty, and he looks back to the day that is gone—the day when a merchant owning a corner store could thrive and succeed and prosper and become a successful man. Kelty works with the Civil Liberties Union in Portland, and vigilante activities always draw his fire. His editorials lambasting the Dies Committee were the best in the Far West along that line. The *Oregonian* also conducts its news columns objectively and refuses to make them propaganda for special interests.

For the past decade or so the *Oregonian* has been held under a trust. Now the trust is coming to an end, and the ownership of the paper will revert to a group of wealthy families. They seem to have their eyes on the main chance, and already have enlisted the services of the eminent ex-Hearst efficiency expert, Guy T. Visknisski, who is expected to make a lot of recommendations which may improve the paper as a commercial venture but certainly not as a purveyor of information.

The high hopes for a liberal journalistic force in the Northwest which were occasioned by the appointment of the President's son-in-law as editor of the *Seattle Post-Intelligencer,* have given way to pessimism and sour laughter. Incidentally, the first persons who expressed their doubts about John Boettiger were his employees. The newspaper writers have had difficulties with their new boss, and it is their opinion that any employer who cannot make a satisfactory deal with his men and win their friendship is no friend of labor, and therefore his position as a progressive and a liberal must be ambiguous.

Hearst chose Boettiger after the 1936 election. Boettiger had been one of the *Chicago Tribune's* Washington New Deal baiting crew; apparently he was fighting Franklin D. Roosevelt while courting Anna Roosevelt Dahl, but once given the editorship of the *Post-Intelligencer,* it was expected that there would be a change in Boettiger's political view-point. Unfortunately, however, Boettiger made his first alliances with Dave Beck, the American Federation of Labor Boss, and Mayor Dore, two of the most powerful enemies of the progressive labor movement in America.

In his new book, "Our Promised Land," which magnificently tells the story of the Northwest, Richard L. Neuberger explains the failure of the new editor to live up to liberal expectations. Boettiger, writes Neuberger, "has been in frequent skirmishes with the National Labor Relations Board because of his refusals to bargain with the American Newspaper Guild. Each time he appears before the board some of Seattle's citizens muse on the curious fact that he is the son-in-law of the most important advocate of collective bargaining in the nation's history." A lumberjack wrote in the *Timber Worker* that he had encountered hard-boiled bosses in the woods but none tougher than the President's son-in-law. Whether Dave Beck took Boettiger into camp or vice versa, is unimportant, but "the two are now boon companions and apparently it pays," reported the Washington Merry-Go-Round, and the *Guild Reporter* noted that when Pegler wrote some columns attacking Beck's kind of labor movement they were "omitted and distorted in Boettiger's paper."

Neuberger gives most amusing details of how both Boettiger and his wife, writing her "Homemakers" section under the name Anna Roosevelt, exploit both the President and Mrs. Eleanor Roosevelt in their news and feature columns, but when it comes to real support to the important policies and reforms which the President initiates or the First Lady advocates, the Boettigers, who cannot of course join the anti-New Deal press in howling, content themselves with support which is "scarcely perfunctory."

Two great topics agitate the progressive Northwest, electric power and lumber.* It is to the public benefit that power

---

* Miss Ellen McGrath of Seattle has written a long report for me of which the following pages are a part.

remain publicly owned, and that the lumber companies do not destroy all the timber, but if the policies of newspapers are studied, it will be found that they are usually on the side of the privately owned electric light and timber corporations.

The most recent example of timber control of Washington newspapers, outside routine strike news coverage which is not peculiar to Washington, is the position they took in the Olympic National Park question. Conservationists wanted to save the last stand of giant fir and hemlock in the West, but lumbermen looked with avaricious eyes upon those giant trees, some 40 feet in circumference, centuries old when Columbus discovered America.

The newspapers lined up solidly. Including the timber in the park they said editorially, was not for the public welfare. Ickes was misquoted, and when he protested, Boettiger attacked Ickes, but later he incorporated in his own banquet speech some phrases made by the Secretary of the Interior.

The darkest chapters in the history of Washington State, the Centralia and Everett massacres, are properly laid at the door of the timber men's fight against union organization of sawmills and logging camps. Both massacres were whitewashed by the press.

In Centralia vigilantes including members of an American Legion post lynched a member of the Industrial Workers of the World after torturing him for a day and night. The *Business Chronicle,* weekly mouthpiece for the open shoppers, now thought the lid was off. It printed an editorial called: "The Thing. The Cause. The Cure." The editorial read: "Real Americans must rise as one man in righteous wrath. Smash un-American, anti-American organization in the land. PUT TO DEATH THE LEADERS AND IMPRISON FOR LIFE AIDERS AND ABETTORS. DEPORT ALIENS."

This editorial, published by the open-shop weekly, was presented to the *Post-Intelligencer* which prepared to run it on the editorial page without even a "Paid Adv." added.

The printers gasped and called a chapel meeting. They passed a resolution. It read:

"We have been patient under misrepresentation, faithful in the face of slander, long suffering under insult. Little by little, as our patience seemed unbounded, your editorial and business policy encroached upon and further and further overstepped bonds not only of fairness and truth but decency and Americanism itself. But there is a limit to all things."

The printing trades at the *Post-Intelligencer* told the publisher either to "pull" that editorial, call back all the early editions in which it appeared, or there wouldn't be any more newspapers printed for quite a while.

The *Post-Intelligencer* pulled the editorial, called back the early editions and printed an apology.

Edwin Selvin, publisher of the *Business Chronicle,* was arrested by federal agents a few days later for violating Sec. 211 of the penal code for "tending to incite murder and assassination."

It was not until 1935 that lumber workers won their fight for an eight-hour day and union recognition. Governor Martin dispatched state troops with guns and gas to the largest lumber mill in the world, the St. Paul & Tacoma Lumber Co., a Weyerhauser mill at Tacoma.

Toll of the strikers was: 2 dead, 24 beaten, 396 arrested, 100 pickets and 300 bystanders gassed.

Toll of strikebreakers: 9 beaten, windows broken, rotten eggs thrown.

Despite this tabulation, ALL the newspapers gave an impression that violence was committed by the strikers.

A sample of the headlines run by the *Post-Intelligencer* follows:

Protection of Workers Guaranteed by Governor Martin

Guards Rout Tacoma Reds

Troops Called to Halt Mill Strikes

The Times: Rioters Routed with Bayonets After Mobbing 3 Mill Workers

The Star: Workers Rout Union Leaders.

The strikers won, however, union recognition and a minimum wage of 62½ cents an hour. The newspapers have been attempting to get Harold J. Pritchett, youthful president of the International Woodworkers of America, who led the strike, deported to Canada ever since.

The Scripps League of papers—not connected with the Scripps-Howard chain but an outgrowth of another chain formed by E. W. Scripps—made a bid for circulation by championing the "underdog," the underpaid. The *Seattle Star* indulged in this public service so long as the editorial workers writing the stuff did so at $12 and $15 a week. But the Newspaper Guild came along. Better wages were asked. On July 2, 1937, 19 men were fired for refusing to quit the Guild. The NLRB ordered their reinstatement and the *Seattle Star* had to pay about $30,000 in salaries. It now fights the New Deal and defends no underdog.

In the *Congressional Record* for May 2, 1938 Senator Schwellenbach accused the *Star* of perpetrating a newspaper hoax intended to destroy him and Senator Bone politically by quoting them with Senator Nye, Dr. Moulton of Brookings Institute, and others as favoring its plan for the abandonment of Roosevelt's power development program.

"I think that those who are in public life today," said Schwellenbach, "are entitled to some measure of protection against newspapers which without responsibility, apparently without the slightest regard for the truth, and without the slightest regard for the real position of those in public office, ... attempt to put into their mouths words which were never uttered."

The *Star* apologized—and blamed a press association.

The press of the Pacific Northwest is to a large degree the same as elsewhere. The difference is in the Northwest that only one or two newspapers approach the objectivity of such Eastern publications as the *Christian Science Monitor* and the *New York Times.* Another difference is that the papers of the Northwest have virtually lost all their influence. President Roosevelt carried the region about two to one in 1936 with scarcely any newspaper support. The sales tax sponsored by the newspapers has been voted down by margins as high as six to one. A legislative measure to force students to pay a compulsory fee to support the university football team was favored by nearly every paper in Oregon except the *Oregonian,* yet at a referendum at the polls it lost by a margin of better than three to one. Such men in public office as Senator Schwellenbach and Jerry O'Connell, of Montana, never have newspaper support, yet they win consistently. In many parts of the Northwest men running for office boast that certain newspapers are against them. On this basis they assure the people that they must be acting in the public interest else those particular papers would not be against them.

The Pacific Northwest is, according to Secretary Ickes, one of America's progressive spots. He says the East looks to it for liberal guidance. That liberalism exists not because of the region's newspapers but because the people have learned not to believe those newspapers.

CHAPTER 20

Speaker in the House of Lords

FOR several years now the publishers of America have chosen James Geddes Stahlman, of the *Nashville Banner,* as their spokesman and president. Stahlman has been the traveling orator, the vocal upholder of what is known as "freedom of the press" in ownership circles. "The press of this country is not venal," is one of his favorite expressions. At the *Herald Tribune* Forum he told how brave the *New York Times* had been in exposing Boss Tweed—generations ago. And other brave acts in distant cities. He himself is noted for having conducted a crusade against loan sharks. And he would no doubt bravely engage in another against the man-eating, non-advertising Bengal Tiger.

Nor is this sneer unfair. Let us look at two or three items in the record of the man chosen to represent the publishers of America. Does he publish all the news or suppress what he does not like? Do financial interests enter into the conduct of his own newspaper? Is he fair to labor? Is he liberal, pro-gressive, or reactionary? Is he editorially on the side of the public or the public utilities?

In answering some of these questions we may be able to learn something of the relationships of the many parts of a complex system which because of a plethora of names it may be best to label merely the status quo. It is not my object to make out any personal devils in this investigation into the behaviorism of the lords of the press. As a certain Euripides said long ago: "Let the facts speak for themselves."

Very appropriately—journalistically as well as ethically—

the Newspaper Guild investigated the record of the man who was leading the embattled publishers in their fight against the reporters. Since Stahlman, traveling up and down the country, was beating his breast every time he cried "freedom of the press," the Guild went to work on the supposition that he was running a free newspaper back home—free, that is, in the sense that it served the public, not the interests.

The first Guild report—it was followed by numerous others alleging suppression and distortion of news—makes three charges against Stahlman, to wit:

1. Published an article viciously maligning the reputation of the late Mrs. Florence Kelley, one of the leaders in the fight for the Child Labor Amendment, in an attempt to blacken the amendment in the eyes of his readers, and then refused to print an answer and correction from Newton D. Baker.

2. Suppressed all mention of the recent beatings of the C. I. O. organizer in Memphis, Norman Smith, despite the fact that the story was nation-wide news and appeared on many front pages not only in other cities, but in his own rival the *Tennessean;* also despite the fact that his paper has consistently tried to represent the C. I. O. as given to violence.

3. Edited the news of the Chicago Memorial Day Massacre film to distort its revelations about the police and cut the piece down to a two-inch story on the back page.

The attack on Florence Kelley was made with the aid of a committee from the Sentinels of the Republic, "one of America's leading Fascist organizations," which had labeled the famous leader a Communist. The *Banner* used the headline NATIONAL WELFARE ORGANIZATION BRANDS CHILD LABOR PROPOSAL AS WORK OF COMMUNIST LEADERS. Newton Baker protested. He said in his letter that Florence Kelley was "a very great and very noble woman . . . intellectually the greatest woman I have ever known," but the leading apostle of freedom of the press refused the former Secretary of War space for a correction.

Summing up its report, the Guild said of Stahlman that "in his own paper he publishes contemptible distortions, he traduces the memory of great characters when it serves his ends, and when the truth gets in his way he suppresses it." *

Like many sincere men and many hypocrites who proclaim themselves as liberals when in heart and truth they are reactionaries and even worse, James G. Stahlman proclaims himself a friend of labor when all his actions prove him to be the enemy of labor. He resents that classification. In one of his press association orations he called "editorial dishonesty" an editorial in an unnamed paper which said Stahlman is "one of the most rabid open-shoppers in the country." Recently liberal weeklies have published a photostat of a letter in which Stahlman's *Banner* asks that non-union men only be sent for jobs in the typographical department. He cannot deny that his paper broke the union there, refused to employ union men, fought the unions and maintained an anti-union editorial policy, but he gets angry when he is called an "open-shopper."

The Nashville *Banner* locked out its employees in 1929 and imported a gang of strikebreakers. The management refused to hire composing room workers without first checking their pasts for evidence of pro-union tendencies. Union men had no chance. This condition prevailed up to August, 1937, when the Newspaper Guild made an investigation, but in December of that year La Follette's *Progressive* reported that the Newspaper Printing Corporation which prints both the *Banner* and the *Tennessean* did sign a contract with the Printing Pressmen's Union and adds that Stahlman is "violently anti-New Deal and anti-labor."

The Guild goes further and charges the *Banner* with serving "as an informal clearing house for strike-breaking typesetters." Two documents support the charge. First there is

---

* *Guild Reporter*, October 25, 1937.

the *Banner* letter which contains the statement: "Naturally the thing we wish to avoid is the placing of workers with union sympathies, so if (the name of the man seeking the job) has any sympathy for the union that you know of, we would be particularly interested in the most complete information you care to give us." The second is the signed statement of the president of the Nashville Typographical Union, Robert Cuthbert, who describes the "lockout of the composing room of the *Nashville Banner* of which James G. Stahlman, president of the American Newspaper Publishers Association, is publisher." It continues:

"The only alleged reason for that act was that, after the paper's contractual relations extending over a period of forty years or more, Mr. Stahlman posted a notice in the composing room stating that on Monday following the wage paid in the composing room would be at a rate of twelve cents per thousand ems—an arbitrary figure, even at that date wholly inadequate—with no provisions for any method of determining details of such a practice.

"At the moment the notice was posted, Mr. Stahlman had quartered in a local hotel nearby a large number of professional strikebreakers obtained through arrangement with the H. W. Flagg Agency. . . .

"The Typographical Union made every honorable effort to reach an amicable settlement with the *Banner,* but Mr. Stahlman has declared consistently that he never would employ members of the Typographical Union in the composing room of the *Banner.* . . .

"Aside from his own paper's anti-labor attitude, Mr. Stahlman sponsors and foments every effort possible against any organization of labor and every so-called New Deal activity or legislation. . . .

"The *Banner* loses no opportunity to denounce and to issue derogatory statements about the present administration in Washington. It editorializes all news items affecting any labor matters."

This is the record of the man who as president of the publishers' association was chosen by them to fight the Newspaper Guild.

When the A. N. P. A. convened in 1938 Stahlman was re-elected president. He made another oration, this time charging that "labor generally has been extremely obstreperous." He had no criticism of the older labor unions, he said, although his lockout was directed against one of the oldest A. F. of L. unions, but he was opposed to "certain movements which the press of this country considers inimical, not solely to its welfare but contrary to the interests of a free people and to the preservation of free institutions in a democracy." As the C. I. O. Newspaper Guild is the only new labor movement, it was understood that Stahlman was lining up the press against both the C. I. O. and the Guild. He was also opposed to taxes. So in fact were most men who make enough to pay them.

In 1938 the *Nashville Banner* and the *Nashville Tennessean* made a working agreement. It was for their mutual benefit, it was called co-operation—and what economic crimes are committed in that name nowadays!—and publishers everywhere applauded. But the latter newspaper dropped eight men from its editorial department and eight or ten from its business and circulation departments, and the *Banner* also discharged many employees. But that was not news.

Nor was it news for the *Editor & Publisher* and other spokesmen of the owners that the commercial arrangements of the two rival newspapers in an important southern city also put the dominant business interests in control of all the means of journalistic power, as the *Guild Reporter* pointed out. "The coalition," it said, "includes notably men prominent in the power and utilities industries—the TVA fight is hot in Nashville—and in banking, in addition to the newspaper industry itself. If presence on the board of directors of the same bank is evidence of close interests, as it probably is, the circle would take in even such individuals as heads of nationally known patent medicine companies."

The rivalry between the *Banner* and *Tennessean* began to end when Paul M. Davis, president of the American National Bank, bought the *Tennessean* at a Federal receivership sale. Davis is a friend of Stahlman's. He had also been a director of the Tennessee Electric Light Company, and it may be a coincidence that Stahlman has been friendly to this public utility.

It is interesting to note that in an attempt to get the *Tennessean* back, its former owner filed a brief in which it is stated * that "Defendant avers that on account of the position of said Paul M. Davis as responsible head of large financial institutions it has been essential for the said Paul M. Davis to suppress publication of legitimate news items regarding the matters set out hereinabove, and other matters of similar nature. . . ." The conflict between privately owned utilities and the TVA is then mentioned and the brief continues:

The said Paul M. Davis has been active in assisting in hindering, delaying, and obstructing the objects and purposes of the TVA. The defendant is informed and therefore charges that as part of such obstructive tactics, the control of the press is important and essential and for that reason, both the power company, of which the said Paul M. Davis is a director and the said Paul M. Davis want the properties of the defendant to be acquired by the said Paul M. Davis.

After the filing of this brief Davis resigned as utility director.

"Stahlman," said the *Guild Reporter*, "is a close crony of J. P. W. Brown, vice-president of the Tennessee Electric

* Federal Circuit Court of Appeals, Cincinnati; filed by attorney Jordan Stokes, Jr., January 6, 1938.

Power Company. These two and John J. Edgerton, formerly president of the National Association of Manufacturers, and still a power in it, figure together in many local and state activities. Stahlman's paper constantly reflects the close identity of interest with the big power, utility and manufacturing concerns."

There is a large file of evidence. An anti-labor policy of course is usually the giveaway of a big business policy, and the Nashville newspapers, despite their shrill denials, are known by union men as their enemies.

The *Banner* always plays up the pro-private utility news but had no mention of a report by the state utilities commissioner which revealed that the private corporations were paying huge sums to attorneys to fight TVA, charging these dollars to operating costs, which meant high rates and public loss. "Moreover," continues the survey made by the *Guild Reporter*, "the *Banner* uses material by known propagandists for special causes without revealing the source. . . . It ran an article pleading the cause of the private power companies by Dr. Gus W. Dyer, of Vanderbilt University. Dyer is one of the eight professional writers for the Six Star Service, a 'service' paid for by the National Association of Manufacturers and furnished to papers without cost."

The *Tennessean* in many respects represents a more liberal and progressive appearance. It has actually published several stories which criticized the utilities and others with a friendly labor tone. But it was neutral in the 1936 elections.

Stahlman, Banker Brown, and Tycoon Edgerton form a powerful group on the board of trustees of Vanderbilt University where they are charged with reactionary militancy against all attempts at liberalism by the faculty. They have been accused of proposing the dismissals of professors and even the abolition of certain liberal departments.

The ramifications of big business, the press, the utilities, higher learning, and the church were further exposed recently when an attempt was made to start a religious revival in Nashville. The way the two newspapers and big business went about it was so crude that its innate hypocrisy overwhelmed it. The idea was announced by Banker Brown at a Chamber of Commerce meeting; it was proposed to issue a "call to righteousness" in which the leading ministers, the Chamber of Commerce, and the two newspapers would cooperate for the purpose of stilling the labor unrest in the 100 leading industrial plants of the section. The *Banner* and *Tennessean* did not publish this fact, of course, but issued the religious appeal later without mentioning the ulterior motive. But the C. I. O. unions and the *Nashville Labor Advocate* denounced the entire business, and the national weekly, the *Christian Century,* in an editorial which said that "the besetting sin of religion is hypocrisy," added that "this particular reflection is suggested by a recent news report in the *Nashville Tennessean* describing the 'call to righteousness.' . . . Among the half-dozen leaders of the movement one notes the names of J. P. W. Brown, vice-president of the Tennessee Electric Power Company and a vigorous opponent of organized labor over many years; C. C. Gilbert, long time secretary of the Tennessee Manufacturers Association and as hard-boiled an enemy of every effort to ameliorate the lot of the workers and their women and children as could be found; and Leonard Sisk, also with the Tennessee Electric Company and a leader in Red-baiting circles. . . . The thing which lies back of these men's concern for Nashville's righteousness is fear of the growing unrest among Nashville's labor."

The relationship between newspapers and fraudulent medicinal advertisements was recently aired in a dispute between Ewin L. Davis, brother of Norman H. Davis (Mr. Roosevelt's ambassador at large) and of Paul M. Davis, owner of the *Tennessean,* and Paul M. Ward, Washington correspondent. Ward had written in praise of Edward R. Keyes who had used the *Tennessean* as an example of a newspaper publishing advertising making the same fraudulent claims for bad medicine two years after the Federal Trade Commission, of which Ewin L. Davis was chairman, had issued its cease-and-desist orders.

Ewin Davis protested that brother Paul "never owned the *Nashville Tennessean* nor any stock therein, nor had exercised any control whatever of the *Nashville Tennessean,* at the time any of the advertisements in question appeared or either the Keyes or the Ward article was published."*

Correspondent Ward replied: "I have before me an official statement by Jesse H. Jones as chairman of the Reconstruction Finance Corporation, which notes under date of October 31, 1935, that the RFC had some time before that date sold $250,000 worth of the *Nashville Tennessean's* bonds to Mr. Paul Davis as president of the American National Bank of Nashville, and that this brought the bank's total holdings to $460,000 out of the $750,000 in bonds outstanding, the bank having previously owned $210,000 worth. . . . I think that settles the point as to who owns the *Nashville Tennessean.*"

Mr. Ward went farther, offering more copies of the advertisements in question after March, 1937, when Ewin admits Paul officially became the proprietor. Mr. Ward claims the obnoxious advertisements appeared in many newspapers which replied affirmatively to the letters sent out by William P. Jacobs, of Jacobs Religious Lists and the Institute of Medicine Manufacturers, urging pressure on newspapers to defeat the Tugwell Bill.

Having made a thorough study of the *Tennessean* Mr. Ward notes "that among the directors or advisory board members of Mr. Paul Davis' bank are Bolling Warner, J. M. Gray and F. M. Bass. Men of the same names and Tennessee addresses are active figures in the patent medicine industry. One heads the Warner Drug Company, manufacturer of Renfrew Salts for gout and rheumatism. Another is the manufacturer of Gray's Ointment, the erstwhile cancer cure which occupies a prominent position in the Food and Drug

---

* *The Nation,* May 1, 1937, page 519.

Administration's Chamber of Horrors. Attorney Bass has represented the manufacturer of Gray's Ointment in proceedings before federal agencies. . . ." Mr. Ward concludes by asking Mr. Ewin Davis "why FTC control of advertising has been a flop; why the worst frauds in the food and drug racket are fighting to keep advertising control vested in the FTC."

It is hardly necessary, after the presentation of the fore-going facts to draw a moral. If we admit that Stahlman and Davis are representative sincere patriots, fanatical devotees of a free press, the picture of today's journalism is more than clouded, it is actually hopeless. But if we take them for what their actions show them to be, good business men making money out of newspapers in complete disregard of the ethical overtones of the profession, then we have a very fair clue to what is the matter with the press and why the American people have a suspicion that newspapers are biased against labor and in favor of the utilities, why they speak more often for the banks and big business than for the common man, why they frequently suppress the news and more frequently color it; in short why the publishers of America run their newspapers as big business instead of "the palladium of liberty," as they continue to say on their mastheads.

CHAPTER 21

Post-Dispatch, or
Absentee Landlordism

AT THE beginning of the year consumed in the actual writing of this book I had planned as one of the concluding chapters of Part I a short tribute to the *St. Louis Post-Dispatch.* It was intended to be the most optimistic of the few chapters devoted to the brighter chambers in the House of Lords. The defeat of Hearst, the strictures on the present situation by William Allen White, were to be followed by the story of prosperity and absolute freedom in a great newspaper, namely, the *P.-D.*

When the *World* died in 1931 journalists tried to apportion the blame: some said it was due to Ralph Pulitzer because he had not inherited either his father's talents or enthusiasm and because he preferred to play the rôle of absentee landlord, devoting himself to his clubs or his country home; others criticized Herbert Bayard Swope, the executive editor, though the *World's* circulation reached its peak under him, and still others blamed Walter Lippmann, the chief editorial writer, who was becoming a master of straddling and therefore losing for the paper its great reputation of fearlessness, courage, and forthrightness.

The *World* may not have been the great newspaper which we think it today, but it was something to measure the press by, just as the *Manchester Guardian,* which also is not without its faults and weaknesses, is used as a standard for

Europe. In America, when the *World* passed out, there was satisfaction in knowing that the Pulitzer tradition would be carried on in the *Post-Dispatch*. And it was carried on. As late as a year ago the only thing I intended to deplore was the fact that the *Post-Dispatch* was physically in St. Louis, that despite the fact that it was great and fearless and free, it was provincial, that America being what it is geographically, it is impossible for a newspaper, although it may be the greatest in the country, to exercise a great power if its circulation is confined to a Middle-Western state. The *St. Louis Post-Dispatch,* transferred to New York or perhaps Washington, would have been the most important newspaper in America.

I regret to state that considerable doubt, if not considerable disillusion, has entered the situation.

Under Joseph Pulitzer's will his youngest son, Herbert, was given six-tenths of the estate—the great publisher believed in a myth which he thought scientific truth, namely, that the child of late years inherited the greater mental and physical vigor—while Ralph and Joseph Pulitzer got two-tenths and one-tenth respectively, the last tenth being a gift to the executives of the *Post-Dispatch* staff.

Herbert tried his hand at journalism. In 1921, when Russia was open, he went as *World* correspondent and later worked in the *World* office in New York. But it was definitely not his metier. Ralph ran the *World,* and ran it to death. Joseph made a great success of the *Post-Dispatch.* Herbert and Ralph never visited St. Louis. Joseph lived there, but in recent years he spent half his time in his country home at Bar Harbor.

As Maine goes so go the natives of Maine. In October, 1936, within a few days of the great election, Joseph Pulitzer returned to St. Louis to give the *Post-Dispatch* a final Landon spurt. That was the sentiment of Bar Harbor. It was the yacht club sentiment, the absentee landlord sentiment. Some time earlier the *Post-Dispatch* had abandoned the

Democratic party policy, ceased its support of President Roosevelt and the New Deal, but unlike the *Baltimore Sun* it did not straddle the issue of supporting Landon fervently. It also raised the shout that the President was growing dictatorial, it accused him of dangerously centralizing governmental power over the economic life of the country.

"To what extent the absentee owners dictate the policies of the paper," writes Paul Y. Anderson, "has always been a mystery to its employees. There is no doubt however, that all three brothers concurred in the decision to desert the New Deal. Since that time the policy of the paper has steadily become more conservative—more on the side of property rights and the vested interests." In fact the abandonment of liberalism occurred two years earlier, in 1934, Anderson states, when the late Clark McAdams was demoted as editor of the editorial page. McAdams was a liberal and a crusader. He was 100 percent for the New Deal. The Brothers Pulitzer in their yachts, their clubs and their palaces, had begun to waver.

❦

If it is wrong to create personal devils, it may be just as bad to make personal heroes. Newspapers are not only the prolongation of the characters of their owners, but of the forces which are stronger than men, and when they are good, or bad, liberal or conservative, pro-public or pro-public utility, it is due to a combination of many things, material and psychological and what not.

For many decades the *Post-Dispatch* was an ideal newspaper. Whatever mistakes it made were human errors, of which journals as well as men are capable; they were not actions dictated by an owner serving outside interests or, at the very best, his own egotism. Venality never entered the doors of the editorial sanctum.

The best proof that the *Post-Dispatch* was a free news-paper was the angry report of the Missouri head of the propaganda bureau operated by the National Electric Light Association, in which he complained that he had not been able to corrupt this newspaper. He did claim that he had "reached" all the other daily and weekly publications in the state, some 700, and failed only in this one instance. It is probable that there were a few other publications which refused part of the $25,000,000 a year public utility corruption fund, but it is unquestioned that the *Post-Dispatch* angrily threw the propagandists and their money out of the office. (In the case of several Chicago, New York and other great dailies the N. E. L. A. probably did not corrupt by buying advertising space, but their propaganda was used willingly by editors. This is not corruption, this is part of the big business finance system under which we live.)

Refusal to be bribed is negative: the *Post-Dispatch* went after the corrupting elements; it fought them in every field in which they existed, from national politics to petty racketeering.

Take Teapot Dome, for instance. I have given credit to Carl Magee of Albuquerque for unearthing the scandal when he followed his feud with Secretary Fall. Magee unearthed the scandal but it was the *Post-Dispatch* which forced the investigation of the Ohio gang by producing enough evidence to make the attempt by the *New York Times, Washington Post, Philadelphia Public Ledger* and other conservative big business newspapers to squash it look ridiculous.

It was Paul Y. Anderson, Washington correspondent of the *Post-Dispatch*, who gave the Teapot Dome scandal air after the Ohio gang had succeeded in silencing the first reports of vast corruption. It was also Mr. Anderson who in 1927 exposed the State Department for fostering a Red scare in Mexico on behalf of the American oil corporations which wanted an excuse for invasion and inevitable war and annexation. It was also Anderson who exposed the Chicago police as guilty of massacre in the notorious Republic Steel Company Memorial Day rioting which the *Chicago Tribune* had defended.

And it was John Rogers who exposed Lingle, the *Chicago Tribune* reporter, as a racketeer, and it was Rogers who helped get the evidence in many other great exposés.

I could go on for pages telling stories of what reporters of the *Post-Dispatch* have done, all the way from exposing the political corruption such as the Pendergast machine, the Kelly machine, the Hague machine, down to some local kidnaping which involved no political party and no big money. The Ku Klux Klan was exposed by the Pulitzer papers first. Federal Judge George W. English was impeached by the *Post-Dispatch*. And something of a like nature was happening every week in St. Louis.

All this work—it got the *Post-Dispatch* the reputation of being the outstanding "crusading" newspaper in America, but its managing editor denies the predicate-adjective—was done under the direction of Oliver K. Bovard. "Honor where honor is due," Anderson wrote as a valedictory to the most famous managing editor in America; "for most of the distinctions which have come to *Post-Dispatch* men, Bovard is entitled to a large share of the credit. He would show a reporter how to pull off a terrific story—and then insist that the reporter be given a salary increase for pulling it. . . . If there was anything on which he set more store than professional skill—good craftsmanship—it was truth. And when I say 'truth' I also mean precision and exactitude to the limit of human performance. He would fire a man for failing to get a middle initial—or getting it wrong. In the larger aspects of truth he was even more severe."

Bovard made it his business to eliminate the barriers between news and truth. It is news, for example, that a Ku Klux Klan parade took place, or that Kluxers burned a fiery cross, or that they committed a certain crime. That is all surface news. Behind it is the news of who the leaders are, how they organize, what financial interests are involved, what their objectives are, what the social, economic and political significances are. And in Bovard's opinion the news behind the news was the real story, the *true* story. The newspaper that went out attacking corruption was all right, it was a crusading newspaper, it did the public a service. But the newspaper that disregarded all the corrupting forces, notably the big money, and in addition to the surface facts published the hidden facts, the cause of the effect, that was a true newspaper, and not at all a crusading newspaper. That was Bovard's idea, and he made it work for almost forty years.

The more he saw of the pressures which change policies, the more determined he was to keep away from all contact with men and forces which might influence his one policy: to tell the real story. He saw fellow editors joining clubs, flitting about in society, he saw a noted columnist playing polo, he found a noted colleague giving more attention to his Wall Street investments than his editorial page, and it made him more determined than ever to steer clear of entangling alliances. He avoided associations "which might embarrass him in his single-minded determination to get and print all the news." For a quarter of a century Bovard, says Anderson, exercised as much influence on the daily lives of St. Louisans as any individual in the city. He also exercised an influence on the journalism of the nation.

❦

If honor goes to Bovard for the great work for which two of his reporters won Pulitzer prizes and for publishing a really free and uncensored newspaper—uncensored by publishers, advertisers, or the spirit of the times—then in turn there must be honor for the owners of a big property which can permit this freedom. Therefore the three Pulitzer sons, Herbert, Ralph and Joseph, and especially Joseph who is editor and publisher, were deserving of great honor.

But after thirty years of stamping his character and ideals on the *Post-Dispatch*, O. K. Bovard on the first of August, 1938, posted a notice on the bulletin board saying: "To the staff: With regret I have to tell you that I have resigned because of irreconcilable differences of opinion with Mr. Pulitzer as to the general conduct of the paper, and am leaving the office August 13th. I recognize and respect the rights and responsibilities of ownership and make no complaint. I salute you, a splendid body of men and an exceptional newspaper staff. . . ."

On another occasion Bovard had also electrified his staff with one of his bulletin board notices. On election night, 1936, when the electoral vote avalanche spoke for Roosevelt, he wrote this announcement:

The Country 523
The Country Club 8

Can there possibly be any relationship between these two bulletin board notices of 1936 and 1938?

Anderson, who now represents the St. Louis *Star-Times* in Washington, says that "in recent years Bovard has been taking a deep interest in politics and economics, he has studied the great economists not forgetting one named Karl Marx, and he has made several visits to Russia to see how the theory was working out.

"During these years members of the *Post-Dispatch* staff received a distinct impression that Joseph Pulitzer was torn by conflicting emotions—apprehension over the deepening 'radicalism' of his managing editor, and fear that the paper could not survive without him." Mr. Pulitzer referred to "honest differences of opinion" when he accepted Bovard's resignation, which referred to "irreconcilable differences of opinion with Mr. Pulitzer." No other statement was forthcoming. But Mr. Anderson says "the nature of those differences is no secret. They are economic and political." The *Post-Dispatch* has grown more and more concerned with property rights and the vested interests. Naturally honest differences of opinion have become irreconcilable differences, and the most distinguished managing editor in America resigned because he could no longer maintain his policy, which was inimical to the special interests.

The tragedy is all the greater because in all discussions of a free press up to now it was customary to point to the *Post-Dispatch* as the almost unique example of prosperity accompanying a policy of public welfare.

Following Mr. Bovard's resignation the entire staff rushed into the Newspaper Guild. Previously a large number of reporters, owing to some mistaken sense of loyalty, had refrained from joining. To New York Guildsmen Bovard made a statement which had a thundering effect throughout the country. "It's inevitable, why discuss it," he said of the Guild shop. As for the Guild itself, he said it "has proved a good thing for newspapermen. The need for it was obvious. I think it may also prove to be a good thing for newspapers. The ideals of newspapers which the mass of newspapermen hold are high. Because of this I look for the Guild to become in time influential in elevating the tone of the press as a whole; to aid in making it more journalistic and less commercial."

On his way to Europe for his first real holiday in forty years, Bovard was captured by my friend Kyle Crichton and taken to my apartment where we argued freedom of the press until 4 A. M. Mr. Bovard went away still maintaining that it is possible under the present economic system to run a wholly free newspaper which will make money despite all social, economic and other pressures. He said he spoke from practical experience.

CHAPTER 22

William Allen White: Anti-Press Lord

THE most outstanding figure in American journalism is
William Allen White, of Emporia, Kansas.

He is not a press lord. He is a small-town editor and publisher. It is perhaps the most unfortunate thing in our
modern newspaper history that White chose to remain in
Kansas. If he had accepted an editorship in New York, or
Chicago, or St. Louis, and produced a national newspaper as
honest, sincere, liberal and altogether free as his Emporia
Gazette, it would have been the greatest achievement of our
journalistic times.

As it is, William Allen White himself is a national figure,
but his newspaper has no influence outside Kansas. Emporia's gain is America's loss.

What are Mr. White's views on the newspaper problem in
America today? He believes that the press has become too
commercial, he sees that it is losing its influence because it
is not keeping faith with the people, he notes the conflict
of labor and capital, and finds that capitalism has gotten
control of our press. In fact Mr. White at times goes further
in his criticism and strictures on our press and our press
lords, than the present writer, and since he is the president
of the Society of Newspaper Editors and dean of American
publishers, it might pay us to listen to his exact words.

The Curse of Wealth

In a letter to Alfred McK. Lee for his history of American
journalism, Mr. White says the real threat to freedom of the

press lies in the publishers themselves. He continues: "Too often the publisher of an American newspaper has made his money in some other calling than journalism. He is a rich man seeking power and prestige. He has the country club complex. The business manager of this absentee owner quickly is afflicted with the country club point of view. Soon the managing editor's wife puts him in the country club, and then the city editor's wife nags him into it. And they all get the unconscious arrogance of conscious wealth. Therefore it is hard to get a modern American newspaper to go the distance necessary to print all the news about many topics.

". . . On the whole, sooner or later in the long run, the American people do get the truth. But they often get it when it is cold potatoes, and does them no good."

Mr. Lee suggests that "Some would substitute, in the case of employees, the 'conscious arrogance of *expected* wealth' for the 'unconscious arrogance of conscious wealth.' It would be a little more accurate."

This conscious arrogance of expected wealth is particularly noticeable in the Scripps-Howard United Press organization.

Favors the Newspaper Guild

Most of the publishers hate the Newspaper Guild, and fight labor unionization generally. Mr. White takes an opposite stand:

"I believe the union principle is right, and I don't feel the coming of the union, even a vertical union, in the newspaper business, will affect the freedom of the press.

"As a matter of fact, it will be God's unmixed blessing if the newspaper owner who generally buys a newspaper for social or business reasons, can feel at the back of his neck the hot breath of the disapproval of the force when he gets too class-conscious, when he goes too obviously country-clubby, and too strongly pro-clearing-house and chamber of commerce in his proprietary attitude. . . .

"After all, Jesus had the goods on the rich man. . . ."

Of the conflict between the press House of Lords and the Guild, Mr. White says: "It is a typical conflict. It is the conflict between ownership and public interest. It is the gist of all the issues that will come up during your whole life. There is something, indeed there is much, to be said for ownership, but ownership without a considerable consideration of public interest, is probably going to be decided by the American people to be an archaic hangover from feudalism."

Free Press Enemy: Commercialism

Mr. White was the first of the owners to admit that commercialism means the ruin of a free press. When Munsey (who wrecked many great papers which were inimical to big money) died in 1925, White wrote:

"Frank Munsey, the great publisher, is dead.

"Frank Munsey contributed to the journalism of his day the talent of a meat packer, the morals of a money changer and the manners of an undertaker. He and his kind have about succeeded in transforming a once-noble profession into an eight percent security.

"May he rest in trust."

For the past decade Mr. White has spoken more and more bitterly and openly against the money power in journalism. He is almost unique among publishers in admitting that the press is not only commercial, but a part of the ruling capitalist world. In the past thirty years, he says, newspapers "have veered from their traditional position as leaders of public opinion into mere peddlers and purveyors of news . . . the newspapers have become commercial enterprises and hence fall into the current which is merging commercial enterprises along mercantile lines.

"As the newspapers' interest has become a mercantile or

industrial proposition, the dangers of commercial corruption of the press become greater and greater. The power trust of course is buying the newspapers in order to control the old vestige of leadership, the remaining fragment of professional status that still remains in the newspaper business.

"As a commercial enterprise the newspaper is yielding good returns for investment.

"But as a political weapon it is worth to self-seeking service corporations hundreds of dollars in under-cover influence where it is worth dollars in direct returns. If this country turns from a democracy into a Hamiltonian plutocracy, it will be because the moral sense, moral intelligence, and moral courage of the American people are sapped at the roots by insidiously corrupt plutocratic influence undermining the sources of courage and intelligence which have been so ably represented by the American press in other generations.

"Unless democracy is indignant at the encroachments of plutocracy, democracy cannot fight. When plutocracy destroys the sources of information which should make indignation, plutocracy has paralyzed democracy. But it is no sudden thing. It is a part of the tendency of the times. I do not know the answer."

The reader may note a progression of thought in the foregoing quotations from the writings and speeches of the foremost journalistic figure in America. William Allen White is no longer a young man; he has in fact grown gray in the service, and although he has not grown rich, he has at least become comfortably well off, and it would be more natural to find him growing more and more conservative in his views. In 1936, when he supported a fellow Kansan named Alf Landon for the Presidency there were in fact many who saw it as a sign of the old reactionary spirit which comes with comfort and gray hairs.

But all these suppositions are not true. As he has grown older Mr. White has grown more free-minded—his enemies would call it radical, but that really does not matter—on the subject of American journalism. And in 1938, while this book was being written, Mr. White who had just been elected president of the American Society of Newspaper Editors said, in an address to the students of the Wharton School of the University of Pennsylvania, many things about our lords of the press which equal and perhaps surpass in severity all the criticisms made in this book.

The Menace Is Capital

Publishing is a business, he began, a legitimate business, "which in certain of its higher realms may be reasonably called big business." He traced its three distinct periods. The first was pre-Civil War years when a printer or anyone with a few dollars could publish a newspaper. Fifty years ago or so publishing became a "profession," but money was needed to indulge in it, not much, but a little, and the editor belonged to the ruling class; he was a free man, ran a free press, "restricted only by his courage, his honesty, and his intelligence. No outside influence restrained his powers."

The machine age arrived with the turn of the century. Advertising became one of the big influences in America, and "the trade which had become a profession turned into a business, and there it is today." It now requires capital to start and run newspapers, even in small towns. And now Mr. White comes to the crux of the newspaper problem:

"Capital today or tomorrow always has a lively sense of its own advantage. Capital is instinctively, for all the noble intentions of us capitalists, class-conscious. It is that class-consciousness which is discrediting the press of the world today, particularly the press of the English-speaking democracies.

"Any newspaper in any American town represents a considerable lot of capital for the size of the town. The owners of newspaper investments, whether they be bankers, stockholders of a corporation or individuals, feel a rather keen sense of financial responsibility and they pass their anxiety along to newspaper operatives whether these operatives be superintendents known as managing editors, foremen known as city editors, or mere wage earners known as editorial writers, copy desk men, reporters or what not.

"The sense of property goes thrilling down the line. It produces a slant and a bias that in time becomes—unconsciously and probably in all honesty is—a prejudice against any man or anything or any cause that seriously affects the right, title and interest of any other capital, however invested. . . .

"We editors realize that we have lost caste with the American people. We are on the bad books of the public esteem. . . .

"Labor as a class distrusts us. It wouldn't distrust us without reason. The labor press sneers at us—that is to say, those class-conscious newspapers that are circulated entirely in what is known as labor circles. . . . The deficiencies of American journals in treating the news of what we might as well frankly if regretfully call the class struggle in this country are found largely in unconscious political attitudes. It is so easy to 'policy' the news. Indeed, it is hard not to policy the news when the news is affected with a vital bread-and-butter interest to the capitalist who controls a newspaper, great or small. And strangely enough, capital is so fluid that a threat to the safety of any investment seems to be a threat to all investments. Therefore newspapers which represent sizeable investments are tempted to shy off and shiver when in Congress, in the legislature, or in the City Hall a man or a group threatens an investigation in any kind of patent medicine, in any kind of holding company, in any kind of misbranded food, in any kind of railroad security, in any kind of banking affiliate, good or bad.

"It is not longer the advertiser who puts on the pressure. It is not even the boss back of the pay roll who begins to quake. It is the whole middle and upper structure of society. Sooner or later the truth about any social abuse is gladly received by the middle class and by those who own and control newspaper investments. But off the bat, the newspapers representing the innate conservatism of property interests which crystallize middle-class psychology are sometimes unfair in their treatment of men or movements that threaten to disturb property in any form.

"Which is only another way of saying that every new day produces its own peculiar threats to liberty. . . . *The new menace to the freedom of the press, a menace in this country vastly more acute than the menace from government, may come through the pressure not of one group of advertisers, but of a wide sector of newspaper advertisers.* Newspaper advertising is now placed somewhat if not largely, through nationwide advertising agencies. Some of these agencies have lately become advisers of great industrial corporations, which also advertise. These advertising agencies undertake to protect their clients from what the clients and agents may regard as real dangers from inimical social, political, or industrial influences. As advisers the advertising agencies may exercise unbelievably powerful pressure upon newspapers. There is grave danger that in the coming decade, as social, industrial and economic problems become more and more acute, this capacity for organized control of newspaper opinions through the political advisers of national advertisers who in turn are paid to control public opinion may constitute a new threat to the freedom of the press. . . ."

Mr. White interrupts his indictment with references to what he considers another "black mark against editorial judgment," the overplaying of sensational news to please the circulation department, which he considers "as dangerous as the advertising department in menacing the ultimate freedom of the press." The opposite side of this picture is the underplaying of constructive news, such as, for example, the

Scandinavian Neutrality Pact. It is true that it is a desire for circulation, which means more advertising, which means more money, that motivates this handling of news, but in this writer's opinion this is a situation which is easily remediable since it is not forced upon the publisher by outside pressure. It is merely a gesture to the mob. Mr. White concludes:

"The problem of the American newspaper today is to open its channels to new social ideals and to insure fair treatment for any reformer who is obviously honest, reasonably intelligent and backed by any considerable minority of the public. How can this be done? How can the newspapers become open-minded? I don't know. They might try to hire as doorkeepers in the house of the lord on copy desks and in editorial chairs men who are free to make decisions . . . not controlled by an itch to move to the next higher desk by pleasing his High Potency who sits in the mahogany paneled room in front of the front of the front office. If owners would encourage a little chronic arthritis of the knee in the lower realms of reporting and copyreading we might come out from the clouds of suspicion that envelop our noble profession at the moment. . . .

"But I suppose in the end newspapers cannot be free, absolutely free in the highest and best sense, until the whole social and economic structure of American life is open to the free interplay of democratic processes." *

Mr. White here says about the last word. We have no free press, and we cannot have a free press so long as "the sense of property goes thrilling down the line" of capital invest-

---

* Some minutes after making this speech ("A Free Press in a Machine Age") Mr. White discussed politics informally with several students and the result was the *New York Times* heading WM. A. WHITE LIKES THE LA GUARDIA TYPE. The *Times* ran the paragraphs about "the sense of property," but *Time* did not. *Time* ran most of the attack on the advertising agencies; the *Times* had no mention. But neither ran the last paragraph. The *Nation* (June 18, 1938) ran the speech in full.

ment, so long as "capital is so fluid that the threat to the
safety of any investment seems to be a threat to all investment."

The obvious thing is to "change the world." That may
take some time.

But meanwhile, in the third part of this volume, some
more or less practical non-idealistic ways of helping produce
a better, if not a free press, will be mentioned.

PART II

SERVANTS OF THE LORDS

Sirve á señor, y sabrás que es dolor.

CHAPTER 1

Journalistic Noblesse:
Foreign Correspondents

AMONG the servants of the press lords the columnists are the highest paid and rated; they are also the freest, but being syndicated (in most instances) they practically cease being the representatives of a certain paper, or even of a chain, and function as independents. The two highest categories of staff men remain the Washington and the foreign correspondents. These are also well paid, but whereas the Washington correspondent is generally as much a slave of editorial policy as editorial writers at home, the foreign correspondent is without doubt the freest man on any newspaper.

Two reasons for this freedom are (a) the general ignorance of the editor and publisher about affairs European and (b) the don't-give-a-damn policy of newspapers about foreign events.

Of course times are changing in journalism as elsewhere, and one cannot accuse the *New York Times* or the *Chicago Daily News* foreign services of ever maintaining such an attitude. But it was pretty general when foreign services came into being just after the war. Raymond Gram Swing, who was a foreign correspondent before the war, says that the *Chicago Daily News* bureaus in Europe were established chiefly to advertise the paper, to furnish a rest room, reading room and convenient toilet facilities for visiting Chicagoans, and a place to register their names. Swing cabled this list every day. It was his main work. In early 1914 he wrote a series of articles about the war clouds in Europe, practically predicting that war was inevitable before the end of summer, but these stories were cut down until nothing but a sort of tourist guide to interesting capitals remained. When he protested his editor told him that back in Chicago they considered the whole matter preposterous: they had previously heard nothing about the British, German and French rearmament programs, they refused to see militarism in the German order for two army corps—which was the signal of a coming war—and they did not believe in scaring their readers with bolt-from-the-blue type of stories. Thereby Swing's reputation as a major prophet was killed aborning.

A great number of the first members of our foreign services were men who had been in the army. Some were excellent journalists but many were glorified police reporters. On the *Chicago Tribune* a premium was actually paid for ignorance. I remember in the early 1920's when I asked our director why he had chosen Mr. A to succeed me in the capital of X, he replied: "Because A is the only reporter we have who doesn't speak the language. He knows nothing about the country. In fact he is the only man we have who has never visited Europe. So you see he will be unaffected by the propaganda and intrigues of those foreigners. What we want is the real American viewpoint."

In the middle '30's the Mr. A.'s and their colleagues, whose ignorance of Europe served them so well in the formative days of several American foreign news services, supply the intelligent American's guide to international affairs, combining high adventure, derring-do, and romance with philosophic trimmings by Freud and Stekel, William James and Karl Marx. The world is their oyster cocktail and the best seller list their club room.

In recent years we have had Vincent Sheean (once Jimmy to his pals) recounting his personal history, Walter Duranty claiming he writes as he pleases, John Gunther telling the inside story of Europe, and Negley Farson confessing his transgressions, and it was not so long ago that H. R. Knicker-bocker, Dorothy Thompson, Edgar Ansel and Paul Scott Mowrer, William Henry Chamberlin, Louis Fischer, Eugene Lyons, Anna Louise Strong and others uttered historical or sensational remarks on Germany and Russia, while Larry Rue, the first foreign correspondent to fly his own airplane, told of Afghanistan, and Mrs. Marguerite Harrison confessed she was an American secret service operative while mas-querading as representative of the *Baltimore Sun* and Asso-ciated Press.

All these men and women were my colleagues. For fifteen years I worked with them in Europe, and now as I read their best selling books I too am carried away by the excitement, physical or mental, the spirit of adventure, the thrill of history in the making, and at times the tropical romantic pages which have brought such unprecedented popularity to the noblesse of the reportorial profession, the foreign cor-respondents. If these books affect me in this way, how much more fascinating must they appear to the lay reader? And what a heroic portrait they must give of the authors!

Yet, strange as it may sound in realistic days, this knightly stained glass picture is not entirely false. This is the colorful panel begun by Floyd Gibbons in wartime, exhibited on the stage by Sam and Bella Spewack of the old *New York World*, touched up today by Negley Farson, who might have stepped right out of the crossed works of Richard Harding Davis and O. Henry. In other words, this is the picture of the glorified reporter.

Between him and the journalist there is no sharp way of differentiating, inasmuch as most newspapermen on foreign service go through both phases, sometimes revert, frequently remain both. To illustrate, there was the famous Genoa con-ference when the Bolshevik diplomats made their first ap-pearance in western Europe, in mysterious official silence. Well, there were more than 450 journalists at this confer-ence, most of them in spats and canes, and all of them stood around acting respectfully. But there were two New York reporters freshly arrived among them and they did what every reporter and no journalist would ever do: one of them crashed through the third day's diplomatic parade to the convention hall, seized Chicherin by the coat, and extracted the first interview with a Russian, and the other by hook or crook, probably the latter, got a world scoop on the Russian-German treaty. For reporters on European service, manners and ethics, unwritten codes and diplomatic protocol, are of no more importance than they are at home, and they pursue their prey in the manner they made notorious in the Lindbergh honeymoon affair. In fact for them Europe is no more than one glorified police court.

But for most of the time and for the majority of newspaper men abroad all life is not running to a fire, nor even to a revolution. The reporters in time become journalists. The Walter Duranty, catapulted out of Cambridge University and the Paris office of the *Times,* into a life of scoops, the Dorothy Thompson of the King Karl of Hungary adventure, the Jimmy Sheean of the Riffi No Man's Land, inevitably join the non-adventuring Mowrers and Chamberlins and Fischers in serious contemplation of the European scene and the prosaic work which marks the journalist as compared to the adventurer-reporter. At the risk of destroying all illusions, I have summed up under seven headings the main activities of practically all American journalists *in partibus infidelium.*

1. *Ear Biting.* This is not the most important source of news but the recommended first step. It consists of getting oriented by pumping dry your colleagues who live in the capital and know the country well, the term ear biting being the invention I believe of that same Mr. Spewack who broke up the Genoa conference and retired to Broadway and Hollywood. (Incidentally the most famous ear biter in Europe in my time was the journalist Isaac Marcosson who has glorified for American hero-seekers the three leading charlatans of

Europe: Hugo Stinnes, Ivar Kreuger, and our old colleague, B. Mussolini.)

2. *The Press of the Country*. Although some claim only seventy-five percent and others say that ninety-five percent of the foreign news sent to America comes out of the newspapers in countries where correspondents are stationed, it is acknowledged that this press is the source of most of it. In Berlin my assistant and I read forty papers a day, including the leading Hamburg, Frankfurt, Cologne, Munich and Dresden dailies, and got most of our news from them. In London you do not even have to trouble much about translating.

3. *News Services*. Although the Associated Press has tied knots around all the official and semi-official news agencies, most every journalist buys one or more rival services, and also hires a parliamentary reporter, and string men in the provinces—the latter erroneously so called after the American prototype who keep a string of their dispatches and are paid space rates.

4. *Handouts*. Although European governments do not do much handing out of "news," a major Washington activity, the press bureaus furnish considerable usable material, obtain statements which later appear as interviews, and generally supply a fair part of your cable crop.

5. *Scoops*. Bought and paid for. You may remember that Mr. Hearst and one of his reporters named Horan were expelled from France after publishing a world scoop about a Franco-British naval agreement. That document was purchased. You will not remember the world scoop on Admiral Scheer's report on the Battle of Jutland to the Kaiser; that item cost me only $50 in gold. Exclusive interviews with Lloyd George at certain times were part of a contract, and once when I begged Professor Einstein for a statement he agreed, provided the *Tribune* donated $25 to the Palestine fund. Lindbergh and Byrd flew the Atlantic for the *Times;* King Tut's tomb was opened for the *London Times,* the first

Zeppelin trip to America belonged to the Hearst service, and a dozen of the big stories and scoops of recent times, including Queen Marie, were bought and paid for by the North American Newspaper Alliance.

6. *Think Pieces*. Despite forty newspapers, the various news services, the bought scoops and the stuff from the foreign office, the time comes frequently, in fact several days a week, when there is no news or when the situation is in such flux that no definite bulletin news can be made out of it. Whereupon the foreign correspondent sits lightly down and taps two hundred or a thousand words out of his head. These are known as think pieces. The layman can detect them easily by watching for the stock phrases: "I learn on good authority" (a favorite with the British type of journalist); "In official circles it was said"; "A usually reliable source informs your correspondent"; "In diplomatic circles it was the opinion that . . ."; "Persons close to the government believe . . ."; and, when all else fails, an even more anonymous: "It is reported. . . ."

These phrases are not to be confused with "the official spokesman" of the White House, who is usually the President himself. In European dispatches they may sometimes represent that very minor official who is detailed to the North American division of the foreign office, but more likely the qualifying phrases are the self-styled creations of the correspondent himself. And for this very reason they become important.

Take for example the cables from Mr. Duranty. This correspondent has now reached a position when he can put his best pronoun forward and say "I," but it has been an unwritten rule among American newspapermen to hang the news on some one else. "No one gives a damn what *you* think," is the way one of my editors once put it to me. So you write your own think pieces with the phrase "in high circles" and it is immediately regarded with the proper awe by the receiving end. Of course I cannot tell how many of the Duranty cables which contained these qualifying lines were out of high circles and how many out of his mind, but rereading them I find that they were always intelligent, frequently brilliant, and never tendentious.

Consider, on the other hand, the think pieces of Mr. Duranty's colleague in Rome. Last October, for instance, Mussolini was facing a blockade whereupon the Cortesi think piece informed us that "the European situation is considered here to have become critical. . . . It is interpreted as evidence that Britain is ready to go to war. . . . The belief that the present deadlock is inevitably leading toward a European war consequently is gaining ground." Now this is a fair example of tendentious reporting; it is a think piece either originated in the Cortesi head or planted there by the propagandists of the foreign office. Even more tendentious is the July 5, 1935, cable saying that "Official circles scoff the very idea of an economic blockade of Italy" and "other Italian circles are inclined to make light of the British government's reported intention to propose an economic blockade" and again, "It is not believed by these groups that Britain ever would take the initiative on such dangerous ground." Of course what you have here is the typewriter of Cortesi but the voice is that of the Duce. In the view of the *fait accompli* these items sound not only ridiculous but appear reprehensible.

7. *"Original Work"—by Native Assistants.* The foreign correspondent, on taking over a European capital, usually surrounds himself with assistants, American and native. Sometimes the work of the American is signed but usually it is unsigned and frequently it is credited to the head of the bureau. Natives of course get no recognition. But very often when there is a scoop or a fine piece of "original" work produced by one of them it is blazoned and headlined with the illustrious name of the American correspondent who is the head of the bureau. (Having stated orally for a decade that a large number of my masterpieces were the work of my

American assistant, Miss Sigrid Schultz, I now hasten be-
latedly to say so in print.)

These seven headings I believe account for ninety percent
of the time and work of a foreign correspondent. They place
him heavily at a desk in an office, reading newspapers, watching the news ticker or the flimsy brought in from the news
bureau, dickering with some notable over the price of a
scoop, editing the translated pieces, rewriting the stories
supplied by assistants and natives, and writing "situation"
stories which may be intelligent or vicious propaganda, de-
pending upon the many factors which cannot be detailed
here.

At any rate this ninety percent of the journalist's life is
routine work, leaving only ten percent for war, revolution,
coup d'etat, violence, and romantic adventure which occupy
ninety percent of the volumes of personal history, memoirs
and autobiography which in the course of time make their
best-seller appearances. Very naturally their authors are too
good judges of human interest to ask their readers to spend
time on the dull everyday office work when there is so much
to tell about kings and dictators, rebels and charlatans, plots,
the rise and fall of dynasties, the armed march of economic
and social philosophies—the thrilling tithe (*prodnolog* to
you, my Moscow colleagues) of the harvest of the years.

This is what the life of foreign correspondents has been
like ever since the great expansion which occurred during
and as a result of the World War. Up to that time the few
who comprised the corps (outside the news agency men) were
considered a luxury, but in 1919 not only all the New York
morning newspapers but the *Chicago Tribune, Chicago Daily
News, Christian Science Monitor* and *Philadelphia Ledger,*
extended or established services and the *Brooklyn Eagle,
Baltimore Sun, Detroit News, Detroit Free Press, Newark*

News and other important papers sent one or more permanent correspondents to Europe.

While it is true that not many of these men and women who became the nobility of American journalism were chosen originally because of their ignorance and provincialism, as in the case of my successor at X, it is equally true that few of us were especially fitted for the job. Several of us were accidents: we were in the army, or we happened to be in Europe, or we pulled the best strings in the home office because we considered the foreign assignment an adventure or good fun or a chance to see the world on an expense account. There were few Mowrers, Durantys and Chamberlins among the lot, more Gibbonses and Rues and Farsons. The majority, it is safe to say, were reporters, not journalists, and we never had a thought in the world outside the production of news. (I speak of course for only the twenty capitals where I have been stationed.) Some of my colleagues drank themselves to death, several reformed, some made love to each other's wives, one committed suicide, several were married and divorced or psychoanalyzed, most of them shot dice and played poker, one made a fortune in foreign real estate, two wrote poetry, one collected shoes, nearly all tried their hands at plays and novels—in short, they were very much the same group as the American diplomatic, consular, military and commercial groups to be found in all foreign countries.

They were no more cowardly or bold than other workmen who live in economic insecurity, although they gave a swaggering appearance of brave freedom.

Because Europe is *terra incognita,* because the owners of the papers are ignorant about Europe and careless, they rarely instruct the foreign correspondents, as they do the Washington or local men. The journalists therefore do much as they please. For some years one I know glorified Fascism and later his successor attacked Fascism, and it was not until the Roosevelt administration made America cognizant of that word that the publisher noticed this little matter. Up to recently Bolshevism alone among foreign happenings received any attention from the newspaper proprietors; it was recognized early as a threat to possessions and profits and every newspaper worker who could see on which side his bread was buttered 3000 miles away, knew how to handle that subject. If he was so dumb as to think he could treat Bolshevism as fairly as other European phenomena, as one of my colleagues did, he soon found out better. The gentleman in question had been converted after three months at the shrine of Lenin, and reconverted almost instantaneously at the Western Union cable office in Paris at 4 P. M. on a tepid August afternoon.

Generally speaking, the majority of foreign correspondents in my time were men who took no sides, who did "straight" reporting, spent most of their time in their offices, wrote few think pieces, kept themselves neutral in all political storms, never entered entangling alliances (except amorous) in European countries, and maintained pretty well the American provincial attitude of sneering down upon everything foreign. If, in the early days, the correspondents made trips to Rome or Moscow the result might well have been headed: The Richard Harding Davis Boys Discover Fascism or The Richard Harding Davis Boys Inside the Kremlin.

But, reading the numerous important and valuable books of the foreign correspondents, it is apparent that everything is different now. Obviously and almost without exception the men who have been cabling about Bolshevism and Fascism, the collapse of the capitalist system, wars and revolutions, have really been thinking about them. They seem suddenly to have discovered that there are economic forces at work in a world whose adventurous surface they have reported; they not only have found a social conscience loose in Europe, but they seem to have sounded themselves and also found it within. They have apparently advanced from reporters of symptoms to interpreters of cause and effect. At least in their books.

Rather than explain this phenomenon I would just welcome it as another sign of the times, another proof that the first to recognize a sinking social system and move to higher ground is the intelligent minority. But this much I must say: that although from 1917 to just recently the foreign correspondents never appeared to have been shaken by the cataclysmic Karl Marxian thunders, they were never in their lives misled by the false summer lightnings of the shyster professional economists who wrote pieces to the publishers' orders for their daily newspapers at home.

Whereas here in America the left still shouts to the writers "Descend from your ivory towers," in Europe nowadays there is no longer the call to the journalists: "Beat it out of the Adlon Bar!" The journalistic noblesse seems to have come of age since that day when the linguistically crippled, the socially irresponsible, the economically illiterate were thought the best representatives in foreign lands and when Ring Lardner was sent by his Chicago newspaper to write "The comic side of the World War."

CHAPTER 2

The Washington Galley Slaves

LIKE the foreign correspondent, the Washington representative of a newspaper is privileged to write think pieces. He
is in the nation's capital not merely to report actual happenings—the news services will see to that—but to interpret
events for all the people. In other words the Washington
correspondent is really a semi-editorial writer.

And, since no owner would appoint a man to Washington
unless he could rely upon him to continue the home editorial policy, and because correspondents know that they
cannot write contrary to the social, political and economic
prejudices or philosophies of their bosses and get away with
it for long, it had become an accepted supposition in the
trade that the Washington correspondents were servile, contented galley slaves, sycophants, the worst yes-men of all.

But apparently times have changed in Washington just as
they have in the foreign service.

In the 1936 campaign the lay reader might have found
cause for thought in the report, made in a Democratic party
paper of course, that the overwhelming majority of the correspondents traveling with both Landon and Roosevelt, most
of them writing Republican or pro-Landon news, would vote
for the re-election of the President. (In New York at the time
it was reported that almost the entire *Herald Tribune* staff
would vote for the man this paper was attacking.) The reader
might have wondered how it was possible to write one way
and vote another. At the same time liberal leaders and the
liberal weeklies were hinting that Washington correspond-

ents were the most biased of all reporters, and the great publishers were replying that no bias could be found in their papers except in the editorial page.

Newspapermen themselves were not fooled. They knew that most Washington news is cut to fit editorial policy, that despite the fact the capital representative is "reliable" and would not openly or subversively write the truth in defiance of his boss, there are nevertheless numerous instances of distortion and suppression of their telegrams, that news is frequently colored, sometimes faked in the home office, and that a great number of Washington correspondents are cynics who do not themselves believe in much of the buncombe they send and which their publishers use to fool the American people.

The profession has always known that. But there has been no scientific test of this common knowledge, until Leo C. Rosten, emulating the Lynds who wrote their magnificent study of small-town life in "Middletown" and "Middletown in Transition," went to Washington on a two-year grant from the Social Science Research Council and emerged with his book "The Washington Correspondents." *

It is not merely another book about newspaper writers. Nor is it merely a documented study of the situation in journalistic Washington. It is the most illuminating inside story of a newspaper corps ever made. It is partly an indictment of newspapers and publishers. It is partly an exposé of how the nation is fed political dope. It is without a doubt the most illuminating light ever cast upon the human forces which through journalism direct the political thinking of the United States.

This investigation knocks into a cockeyed derby the publishers' claim that editorializing and coloring is confined to

* Published by Harcourt, Brace & Co. Parts of this chapter are from the book review prepared by the writer while editor of *Ken*, and suppressed by that magazine. Thanks for permission to quote is hereby made to Mr. C. McCarthy of the publishing firm.

the editorial page and that the news columns are "free." It supplies the documentary proof that:

1. Either the Washington correspondents themselves distort the news, or 2. That their news is distorted, by order, in the home offices.

The study of the Washington press corps was made largely through a series of questionnaires submitted by Mr. Rosten. Here is a sample question and result. He asked: What is the *most fair* and reliable newspaper in America? Ninety-nine Washington correspondents answered. The great majority did not include the newspaper for which they worked among the fair and reliable ones. The poll showed:

New York Times, 64 first choices, 16 second, 9 third, or 89 mentions, scoring 747 points, and winning by a mile.

Baltimore Sun, 284 points, in "show."

Christian Science Monitor, 90 points, in "place."

Scripps-Howard papers, 85 points.

St. Louis Post-Dispatch, 84 points.

The present writer cannot quite figure out the vote for the *St. Louis Post-Dispatch* which has always been considered one of the most fair and honest papers in America, and which has frequently been given first place in lay and journalistic polls.

But when it comes to the vote on the *least fair and reliable* newspapers in the United States, the vote is startling.

Ninety-three Washington correspondents were willing to go on record on this one, and the vote was:

Hearst newspapers, 59 first choice, 20 second, and 8 third, making 714 points.

Chicago Tribune, 24 first mentions, 37 second, 10 third or 455 points.

Los Angeles Times, 103 points.

Next in order were: Scripps-Howard papers; *Denver Post, New York Herald Tribune;* and *Washington Post.*

The amazing thing was that the entire Hearst press, which consists of twenty-four newspapers throughout the country, should have been so universally condemned as comprising the worst papers in America.

Another outstanding fact is that the Washington correspondents were unanimous in naming the three leading reactionary, Red-baiting papers as the three most unfair and most unreliable. Perhaps this too was a coincidence!

Another sensational disclosure regarding Hearst news in general was the voting on press agencies. Ninety-seven journalists were willing to go on record as to their choice among the Associated Press, United Press (Scripps-Howard), International News Service (Hearst) and Universal Service (Hearst) and this was the result:

	No. of Votes	% of 97
United Press	48	49.4
Associated Press	44	45.3
International News Service	4	4.1
Universal Service	1	1.0

This shows, strangely enough, that the United Press, which is a private business concern and therefore might naturally run its news service to suit its owners, is considered better than the Associated Press, which is the great co-operative of the American newspaper publishers and which is supposed to be more honest than Caesar's wife and a darn sight more virtuous.

This vote was followed by another. Why did the correspondents prefer the stories of one or the other press services? "Because they are better written—more reliable—more liberal—"? The vote was:

	Better Written	More Reliable	More Liberal
United Press	42	19	27
Associated Press	5	43	..
International News	3	4	..
Universal Service	1	..	..

This brings up an amusing conclusion. There was one vote for Hearst's Universal Service in the table on preferences, which may have been that of the Universal correspondent. But when it comes to expressing reliability the lonesome voter who in the table sticks to his own outfit under the heading "better written" can't go the "more reliable" column.

The important fact, however, is the vote on "more liberal." Twenty-seven correspondents vote for the United Press but not one vote is cast for the Associated Press, the supposedly most impartial and objective agency.

The author in a footnote explains that nine A. P. men, seven U. P., five I. N. S. and two Universal Service men were sent his questionnaire, and this adds to the amusing conclusion that Hearst representatives voted pretty consistently against the Hearst outfit in all departments.

What are the politics of the newspaper correspondents of Washington whose writings considerably affect the political thinking of the nation?

Despite the fact the great majority of papers were bitterly anti-Roosevelt the Washington correspondents were for Roosevelt. Of 85 who answered the question, 63.5 percent declared they were voting for the President. In other words a large part if not the majority of the Washington corps was writing pro-Landon news for pro-Landon newspapers and voting pro-Roosevelt.

Only 21.7 percent believed in the old program of rugged individualism.

Eighty percent voted for some form of government control of big business.

Sixty-seven percent "favor higher taxes on the upper income brackets."

Five questions dealing with the press in general were put and the answers constitute an indictment of the publishers by their employees.

1. Does the press devote too much space to trivialities,

scandal, sensations, divorce, etc? Yes, voted more than sixty percent of the 104 who answered. (9.6 percent were undecided.)

2. Is it true that the newspapers fail to give significant accounts of the nation's basic economic conflicts? Here the vote of condemnation was 86.6 percent.

3. "In general, news columns are equally fair to big business and labor." This was the third statement the correspondents were asked to check, and 48.5 percent replied that this statement was false, because the press was generally on the side of big business as against labor, while 43.8 percent thought the press was impartial and 7.6 percent could not make up their minds.

4. The reader may remember the old Blue Eagle, the famous or infamous NRA, the great days of the parades and the codes, and the decision of the Supreme Court which ended that dramatic and colorful episode in our history.

The newspaper code was the one on which the President stumbled. Up to then the going was unimpeded.

The newspapers raised the issue of "Freedom of the Press," claiming that while codes are all right in the chicken business (which proved just the reverse, later) they were not to be thought of in publishing.

Listen then to how the Washington press corps played its part during the code battle. Mr. Rosten says: "Some of the correspondents acted as agents for their publishers in getting information, sounding out opinions, suggesting to Congressmen what the preferences of the publishers were. Many of them were under an obligation to sound the 'Freedom of the Press' alarm. Many believed the code was bad. How did the correspondents themselves feel about the publishers' stand on the issue?"

He put the question to them:

"The publishers' cry of 'Freedom of the Press' in fighting an NRA code was a ruse?"

One hundred and five replied. Sixty-seven journalists or

63.8 percent agreed that their own employers had hurled a dead cat, set up a straw man, pulled a Charlie McCarthy, put over one big bluff on the country. Only 24.7 percent thought no hoax was planted, no skullduggery practiced. (Twelve men were uncertain.)

This is probably the most self-revealing statement of the great political press corps of America and one of the most appalling indictments of the newspaper publishers.

5. Related to the foregoing question was one asking whether the newspaper press of America published fair or distorted stories about the Tugwell Pure Food and Drug Bill. This measure, it may be remembered, was largely an effort to compel manufacturers or processors of food and drugs to advertise them as carefully as they labeled them (under the Harrison Pure Food and Drug Bill of 1906). It is no secret that the newspapers knifed and murdered this bill—and knifed Mr. Tugwell as well.

But while the newspapers universally denounced the measure, their foremost writers, the Washington correspondents, voted 46.2 percent to the effect that their newspapers were unfair and distorted the news about it. Only 21.6 percent thought the Tugwell story honestly handled, and 32 percent were uncertain—the first instance when more than a dozen or so were not sure about the journalistic situation.

Is the news colored?

Sixty percent of the correspondents admitted that they were aware of the definite fixed "policy" of their newspapers. A fraction of a point over sixty percent agreed that "my orders are to be objective, but I know how my paper wants stories played."

This does not mean, Mr. Rosten hastens to add, that "all the correspondents in Washington are the 'tools' of their publishers. . . . Policy is rarely enforced by 'policy orders' from the home office. . . . The policy of a newspaper is maintained through less conscious and more subtle channels: through a choice of personnel, through subjective adjustments on the part of reporters, and through the institutionalization of a scale of values within the organization. . . . As a human being the reporter adjusts himself to the tastes of other human beings who pass judgment upon his work."

Have stories been "played down, cut, or killed, for 'policy' reasons"?

Of seventy-two who replied, forty or 55.5 percent said "Yes." Thirty or 41.6 percent said "No," and only two were uncertain.

Policy means many things. But it does not mean truth.

One correspondent explained he watched how stories were played up and revised his "slant" on the news accordingly.

The statement was made that it was impossible to be objective when one read the editorials in his own paper and sensed its policy. Sixty percent voted this true.

But, worse yet, there were specific instances when correspondents got their orders to color the news. Many are quoted:

1. "Don't forget we are backing 'Al Smith,'" said an editor's telegram sending its Washington correspondent on an "objective" tour of the East.
2. Publishers instructed their Washington men to fight the Pink Slip Law on income taxes.
3. Eight correspondents confessed they wrote "around" the Tugwell story owing to publisher opposition.
4. A correspondent wrote an unbiased story about war bonuses and pensions. It was returned with the comment that the paper was supporting the bonus. He changed it to say veterans demands were "in the American tradition." This story was accepted.
5. A correspondent was asked by telephone if certain facts were true. He replied they were not. The home office kept on insisting and questioning until, he confesses, "I strained the facts" and wrote the story the other way.
6. A correspondent was told "not to crusade" when he wrote a story which had implications the paper did not want.

7. An editor explaining why a story was killed said it was "unwise" to publish it, but did not deny its truth, timeliness, etc.

8. A foreign correspondent's cable from Hungary was rejected because "it does not reflect mid-Western opinion on this point."

9. Three correspondents wrote an honest report on ethyl gasoline. Two newspapers killed it, the third eliminated the name of Standard Oil.

The interested reader will do well to get "The Washington Correspondents" and study it page by page.

It is one of the most revealing documents of our time.

It adds a stream of gasoline to the fire which is burning throughout the country: the fire of doubt about everything that appears in the press.

After all, the Washington press corps is the elite. Its integrity is of the highest. And yet it confesses the fact that the political news of America is colored, distorted, played up, played down, perverted, suppressed, and sometimes completely falsified.

This testimony gives the bum's rush to that famous phrase of the newspaper publishers of America: Freedom of the Press.

It ties the can to the Code of Ethics of the American Society of Newspaper Editors.

It exposes the American Newspaper Publishers Association completely, scientifically, without prejudice, with great objectivity.

CHAPTER 3

The Plutogogues

—Sirve á señor, y sabrás que es dolor.

SERVE a (press) lord and you will know what sorrow is. Serve any other businessman and you sell your hands or feet and perhaps some intelligence, but there are very few of the 49,000,000 jobs in America which involve integrity. Most all the 40,000 newspaper jobs do. The editor, the headline writer, the Washington and foreign correspondent are involved with their conscience every day—provided they have such a thing—and even the lowly wild police reporter at times must struggle with the devil in making his news truthful and honest.

In addition to the regular newspaper staffs there have arrived in prominence lately two new groups whose writings are having a more and more subtle and powerful influence on politically intelligent Americans. One group has been labeled Plutogogues, the other consists of a dozen famed columnists who co-operate in a semi-independent fashion because their vast income is from syndication rather than the lone newspaper which has served as their springboard to fame and wealth.

The plutogogue is not new but the name is. Let the inventor define. Addressing the Institute of Human Relations, Dr. T. V. Smith, professor of philosophy of the University of Chicago, practical politician—he is a member of the Illinois State Senate—and author of many books, including "The Promise of American Politics," said the enemies of our democracy are demagogues, plutogogues and theogogues.

"Demagogue we all know as the personage who mistakes the empty echo of his own cadences for the very heartbeats of humanity. Plutogogue, however, is not so well known nor so easily identified. Plutogogue is the voice of the wealthy when they can no longer speak for themselves, the successor of the plutocrat of other days. He is not Allah, but Allah's public relations counsel.

"You will hear his soft-spoken message in the columns of our sophisticated Walter Lippmanns and our unctuous Glenn Franks. You will see or gently feel his gloved hand in the eulogistic releases of our late Ivy Lees and our ever-present Edward Bernays.

"These men perform wonders in ectoplasmic surgery, lifting fallen faces, enlivening sullen eyes and, in emergencies, grafting entirely new reputations upon financial satyrs who need only to be known in order to be rightfully despised. We who let these elegant lackeys hoodwink us, join them to constitute the plutogoguery of democracy."

In an interview with May Cameron, Doctor Smith enlarged the definition. He said that "we are all more or less in a jitter out of fear of outer enemies . . . but we would not be so afraid if we did not suspect inner enemies who might open the gates to them—the demagogues who promise only what God could perform, the 'plutogogues' who lend their voices to the defense of the wealthy when the wealthy can no longer defend themselves and the 'theogogues' who start by claiming in religion differential access to the Deity and who end by forgetting that they themselves are not God. Democracy needs men who have learned the lesson that the late Justice Holmes said had saved him from many an error namely that he was not God."

The majority of plutogogues—as distinguished from columnists—are not newspapermen. They may be diplomats, college professors, politicians, or persons of neither ability nor intelligence who have become public figures and therefore useful to the special interests. In some instances they are just plain crooks. In other cases they are the hired prostitutes of big business. In all instances they are the voice of the plutocrats, as Doctor Smith has said, and the enemies of the general reader.

The newspapers which employ or publish the work of the extreme plutogogues, that is, the hired agents of such special interests as the Italian government, or the National Electric Light Association, or the National Association of Manufacturers, and do so knowingly, are without question violating every canon in the code of ethical journalism. They are doing exactly what the majority of the French press has always done, except for the bigger profits involved. In France you can buy a favorable review for your play, painting or book, for one thousand francs.

The middle group of plutogogues consists of men who are not bought up for fat sums of money but who are hired by either newspapers or big business because their policies agree. It is of course difficult to differentiate among the college professors who spread the N. E. L. A. propaganda against public ownership of public utilities because they believed in private ownership and those professors who did so for N. E. L. A. money. In either case it was an action against the public interest because it was done for private interests.

But the most important group of plutogogues consists of important and usually wealthy men, including some columnists, who, honest or dishonest in their avowal of liberalism and freedom of the press, become the spokesmen of the plutocrats voluntarily.

No one hires them to do a job of work. No one bribes them to change their views. They are not tempted by the big money which is always on the right, the reactionary or big business plutocratic side, because they themselves are wealthy enough. They have simply become part of the same ruling set-up, giving it their services free while other men doing the same work call their wages the wages of prostitution.

Peace be to the ashes of Richard Washburn Child. But for many years he was the worst of plutogogues, the paid agent of the electric light trust and the Fascist government.* He was also one of the hired hands of the Hearst Red-baiting campaign against college professors and teachers.

Another deceased prostitute-plutogogue was Arthur Brisbane, a renegade Socialist, who made a quarter million dollars a year by serving Hearst, and who had his moments of remorse. But not in his syndicated columns. There he called the income tax and partial inheritance tax plans confiscatory (*Boston American,* July 16, 1935) and uttered reactionary nonsense such as this:

"The United States Chamber of Commerce objects to the income and inheritance tax program, calls it confiscation. The question involved seems simple.

"Does the property of the United States, results of thrift and intelligence, belong to the people that created it, or is it only held in trust by them for public use by those that, for the time being, exercise powers of government?

"The American theory, until recently, was that what a man had acquired without violation of law, usually by working, was his property. . . . This is a rich country, but all the property put together wouldn't satisfy 'the social needs of the masses' if the masses decide not to work."

Readers of the Hearst press for years have been asked to sympathize with the large taxpayers. Whether or not this appeal to public opinion was ordered by Hearst himself I do not know, but Hearst employees as a rule do not need the daily specific order to know what to write. When Hearst opposes taxation every columnist opposes taxation.

Frequently Mr. Arthur Brisbane came forward with daily little paragraphs castigating government for increasing taxa-

---

* Cf. "Freedom of the Press," pages 78, 221-2, 228.

tion. Real estate taxation especially annoyed this columnist. And on one or more occasions he mentioned the needs of the hotel industry especially. Mr. Brisbane, according to a test by *Fortune,* was the foremost columnist in popularity; he appeared regularly in 180 newspapers, and supposedly reached the eye (if not the so-called mind) of 30,000,000 readers. It is a safe bet that less than one percent of them knew that Brisbane and Hearst were large real estate and hotel operators and Brisbane was nothing more than a propagandist and plutogogue when he wrote against taxation of his hotel real estate.

And when it came to labor troubles in real estate, especially in the hotel business, these two hotelkeepers were pulling their hair in fright. Brisbane yelled Red revolution. "You hear a little talk of revolution in the United States and may hear more," he wrote in his column of February 16, 1935, when an elevator strike threatened. "It does not sound quite as silly as it did at first. . . . The present threat of a labor union 'to tie up New York City, its hotels, apartments and office buildings'"—in all of which these two entrepreneurs had big interests—"reminds you that if the United States government refuses to go the whole way in its recognition of organized labor as the real ruling power in the United States, organized labor might well form the nucleus of a revolutionary movement to overthrow existing government. . . ."

Here we have an example of two important situations in present-day journalism: the publisher as real estate (or other business) operator using his paper for private ends, and the plutogogue disguising special pleading as defense of the general welfare.

⚓

Coincident with the secret meetings of the American National Publishers Association have been the meetings of the

National Association of Manufacturers. The publishers discussed ways of fighting the labor movement, and so did the manufacturers. In fact the manufacturers named five pieces of legislation they wanted defeated or emasculated, viz.:

The Wagner Act.

The Wages and Hour Bill.

The chain store tax.

Little TVA.

The Borah-O'Mahoney Industry Licensing Bill.

My authority for the foregoing statement is a Dow-Jones report. There is no authority for stating that exactly the measures which the National Association of Manufacturers wanted passed or killed were supported or attacked by collusion with the publishers, but a survey proves that in these five measures the publishers did what the manufacturers suggested. Perhaps it was a coincidence. Perhaps it has been a coincidence for a quarter of a century that the policies of the N. A. M. have become the policies of the A. N. P. A.

But the La Follette Civil Liberties Committee has questioned that view. It has investigated the N. A. M. and proved to those who read liberal weeklies, and the few who get the free newspapers, that the N. A. M. is the most persistent and powerful lobby against liberal and labor legislation in the country, that in addition to spending millions of dollars for spies and thugs and vigilante and subversive movements —as Senator La Follette and his chief investigator Captain Robert Wohlforth proved with documentary evidence—it is also the worst propaganda agency in the country at present. In the 1920's the National Electric Light Association spent about $25,000,000 bribing the press; in the 1930's the N. A. M. is spending millions to "influence" the newspapers. Senator La Follette proved that since the passage of the Wagner-Connery Labor Relations Act in 1935, until sometime in 1937 when Captain Wohlforth made his investigation, the manufacturers' propaganda department spent

$1,350,000 waging war on that bill. Walter B. Weisenburger, executive vice-president of the N. A. M., admitted at the hearing that 5,900 newspapers today are using what he calls "news" and features which his propaganda agency is furnishing them free.

Weisenburger objected to Captain Wohlforth's introduction of evidence he had seized in N. A. M. files showing that although the organization consists of 4,000 members (who employ 4,000,000 workingmen) it is actually a dictatorship of 207 industrialists, notably the Du Ponts, Chrysler, Weir, Rand, Sloan and a few other "leaders." Sixty percent of all the poison gas purchased by all industrial firms in the United States for labor warfare between 1933 and October, 1937, was bought by these 207 industrialists who run the N. A. M., Wohlforth discovered by going through the gas company records, and he testified further that the books of the industrial detective agencies he had seized or subpoenaed show the same men are the largest employers of labor spies, fifty-five of the big men of the N. A. M. alone spending $2,500,-000 for stool pigeons in four years.

These same 207 leaders of American industry were proven to be the subsidizers of vigilante and reactionary and pre-or-pro-Fascist organizations. Testimony was given that the supposedly spontaneous Johnstown Citizens Committee was financed by the industrialists. Other organizations named were the Liberty League, the Crusaders, the Sentinels of America, National Economy League and the so-called Farmers Independence Council. The largest contributors to the propaganda fund are the big business monopolies and the anti-labor industrialists, notably E. I. Du Pont de Nemours & Co., General Motors, Standard Oil, Chrysler, Swift & Co., Weirton Steel, Bethlehem Steel, Republic Steel, Westinghouse, Remington Rand, and the American Smelting and Refining Company.

In 1934 the N. A. M. spent $26,500 for publicity, but the

annual fund grew until it reached $793,043 in 1937. Ernest
T. Weir, of National Steel, was the chief collector. The
money was spent for propaganda via the following channels:

Industrial Press Service, clipsheet, sent to 5,500 newspapers.
"Uncle Abner Sez," given to 300 daily newspapers.
Harmony Campaign, furnished 367 newspapers.
You and Your Nation's Affairs, 250 daily newspapers.
"Let's Go America," shown in 2,812 movie houses.
The American Family Robinson, heard over 268 radio stations.
George Sokolsky program, over 246 stations.
"Industrial Facts," a bulletin of industrial propaganda,
sophistries, doctored figures, supplied workingmen at plants.

"You and Your Nation's Affairs" is also known as "Six
Star Service"; it consists of the writings of eight professors,
mostly economists whose knowledge of national affairs and
economics is so magnificent that it fits exactly into the manufacturers' pattern. One paper in each city and town was
given the right to publish free of charge daily the stuff produced by these men. The noted authors * are:

Prof. Gus Dyer, of Vanderbilt University.
Prof. Clarence W. Fackler, of New York University.
Prof. Eliot Jones, of Stanford.
Professor Lutz, of Princeton.
Prof. Walter E. Spahr, of New York University.
President James S. Thomas, of Clarkson College of Tech-
nology.
President Ernest Patterson, of the Academy of Political
and Social Science.

These articles appeared in newspapers without any statement as to their hidden origin. The Senate lobbying committee immediately took notice. It found that one of the
writers, President Thomas, of Clarkson, had figured in the

---

* The weekly *Labor* adds two names, Prof. E. McK. Eriksson, of University
of Southern California, and Dean J. E. Le Rossignol, of the University of
Nebraska.

Federal Trade Commission investigation of utility company propaganda, the old N. E. L. A. $25,000,000 a year slush fund. The committee reported to the Senate that Thomas, while in charge of extension work for the University of Alabama, received $10,500 from the Alabama Utilities Information Bureau, Birmingham Electric, and Alabama Power Company.

"America's biggest propaganda network" was shown by the La Follette committee to be spending an annual average of $500,000. Most of the opium for the people was dispensed in palatable doses via the newspapers. One of the documents was a letter from a Missouri editor who wrote: "Because of the known prejudices of our people we have not credited Washington Snap Shots to your news service as we have believed, under the circumstances, that it would carry more weight without being so credited." (A nice case of prostitution, my lords, but "the American press is not venal.")*

If the reader finds the greater part of the foregoing story of the N. A. M. propaganda machine and its machinations in the newspapers of America new, he will himself confirm the charge by members of the La Follette committee that the newspapers generally either suppressed the hearings or buried the news in exactly the same way four-fifths of the American press did with the utilities exposure of 1929.

The press suppressed and buried this story alive because it is the most up-to-the-minute indictment of itself. The investigation proved that journalistically things have not changed from the days of the N. E. L. A. corruption fund. It makes impossible the usual editorial explanation that all the charges deal with past history, that the evil condition has been long cured. When the N. A. M. held its 1938 convention in New York the press presented it with the front page, and all the inside space it could use for its reactionary programs and speeches. It printed the hymns of hate of

---

* Actually very few newspapers using propaganda material disclose its sources.

industry against the New Deal. It reported President George Cutten, of Colgate, saying "God is a reactionary. What would happen if God started a new deal every day?" and his philosophy about the "proletariat, the lowest class" being in the world only for the purpose of reproducing itself and carrying on the heavy work. The press of the land lionized the N. A. M. and tried to make a monkey out of the Senate investigation of the same organization.

The honest plutogogue, the out-in-the-open plutogogue, the agent for big business who is not a hypocrite or a sinister underhand propagandist, is generally known as a public relations counsel, and the most noted or notorious of them was the late Ivy Lee who before his death was completely exposed as adviser to Hitler in America.

The McCormack-Dickstein Committee also exposed the firm of Carl Byoir & Associates as Hitler propagandists. Byoir previously had played the same game for the brutal tyrant Machado of Cuba.* In 1938 Byoir was press agent for Republican China. I mention the fact to show that the plutogogue is merely the hired mouth of an individual, a corporation, or a state, which speaks its piece regardless of right or wrong, good or evil. The same plutogogue who spread the propaganda for tyrants and murderous big business in Cuba and Germany will for a fee help the distressed people of China in their war against the Japanese tyrants.

The plutogogue of plutogogues is Edward L. Bernays who usually hires himself for the better causes, the democratic nations. But he is also the best defender of our business civilization. For example he has sent out wholesale his piece entitled "Presenting American Business" with the sub-title: "Present-day business sails little-known waters studded with

---

* Documentation in "Freedom of the Press," pages 132 to 137.

the bars and shoals of adverse public opinion. Small wonder
that the captains of industry need advice from a pilot—the
public relations counsel." In the light of the N. E. L. A. and
the N. A. M. investigations the obvious reply is that business
has by bribery and advertising and other pressures and the
employment of plutogogues galore been caught influencing
the public against the public welfare and what business
needs is not more public relations counsel but a new relationship with the public. (A new relationship must affect business profits, and history teaches us that business has engaged
in wars and organized Fascist regimes rather than share
profits with employees, so it is natural to expect new propaganda campaigns rather than a new philosophy.)

Business has listened to the plutogogue rather than to the
man of good will. But "business men are just as subject to
being led astray by plutogogues as farmers and laboring men
are to being led astray by demagogues," said Secretary of
Agriculture Wallace recently. "They have been led by their
plutogogues to believe that government rules of the game
should be loaded in their favor. . . ." And John T. Flynn
feels that the collection of apologies for rackets on the stock
exchange "which have been fabricated for it by third and
fourth-rate college professors at so much per fabrication,"
constitutes a distressing phenomenon.

The press of the nation of course is open to all men so long
as they write on the side of money. Writing for the side of
money naturally means writing against labor, and the liberal
and progressive movements.

For example, the *New York Times* gives three columns
(August 8, 1937) to the views of President Samuel Harden
Church, of Carnegie Institute, which are summed up in the
heading:

LABOR MAY BLOCK ENTRANCE TO PERIOD
OF PROSPERITY

In order to prevent this, it is held, just demands must be

met, radical leaders ousted, and former spirit of loyalty renewed by mutual fair play.

Here the plutogogue is his smiling sinister best. He speaks of the coming era of the greatest prosperity in American history "if only her labor population can be restored to their former spirit of loyalty by satisfaction and contentment through a cordial concession to their just and humane demands." He denounces "the ugly and vociferous demands of ambitious and mercenary labor leaders . . . one big union and the closed shop." He favors "loyalty as the first essential to tranquillity in industry"; he mourns the passing of the day when American workmen referred "with pride and trust to 'our company' as if it really belonged to them" and the "contented and happy co-operation in a system which seemed to be steadily advancing toward a higher standard of living." In other words the plutogogue deplores the awakening of labor which has been doped by the opium of the plutogogues. He refuses to see or cannot see the difference between loyalty and industrial serfdom. Furthermore he calls the new type of labor leaders who is divorcing union labor from racketeering and building an enlightened socially conscious organization which intends to use the political as well as the economic weapon for the betterment of the vast majority of the people, "ambitious and mercenary."

I know Samuel Harden Church very well. Pittsburgh reporters all know him. His utterances are "must"; they may be nonsense but they are nonsense which fights for the employers and the rich lords he serves. Here is the head of an educational institution who in the social field would obstruct the spread of education and liberty and thought. A typical volunteer plutogogue.

We have now had examples of the three classes, the prostitute-plutogogue, the hired man, the volunteer. The National Association of Manufacturers also sends out propaganda which consists of the writings of noted men and women which agree with the ideology of American reactionary big business. For example there is the pamphlet entitled "What's Going on in America" which the N. A. M. disseminated in midsummer 1937. The oracles contained therein are General Hugh S. Johnson, Frank R. Kent, David Lawrence, Walter Lippmann, Westbrook Pegler and Dorothy Thompson. All six are daily columnists.

CHAPTER 4

The Wages of Reaction

Tell him too much money has killed men
and left them dead years before burial:
and quest of lucre beyond a few easy needs
has twisted good enough men
sometimes into dry thwarted worms.
—"The People, Yes," by Carl Sandburg.

THE majority of columnists are conservative at best, re-actionary at worst, wealthy, successful, members of polo clubs, friends of the money bags, members of the ruling class. Morally many of them were left dead on the shores of jour-nalism many years ago; materially they have gained the highest places in the country; and their power is great and growing.

I have known about a dozen of the leading columnists of America and I have watched more than one, who had taken the vows of journalistic poverty, chastity and humility, go whoring after the big money and the bitch-goddess Suc-cess. I have known one who is now syndicated in about 150 newspapers and read by perhaps 5,000,000 who was intensely for Karl Marx only a few years ago and today would prefer the triumph of Mussolini's ideology in America. And for what reason? "Because a reactionary victory would not dis-turb my estate, whereas a radical movement, which I still believe in, and which I hope will triumph say fifty years from now, would destroy what I have built up for my family."

Some of our best known columnists, who once got their ideas from Marx, Veblen, Henry George, Mill, Adam Smith, Thomas Paine, Walt Whitman, Jefferson and Voltaire, now run to Thomas Lamont, Wendell Willkie, Albert Lasker, Alex Sachs, Benjamin Anderson and the "economists" of the Chase National Bank for their enlightenment. And not one of them believes he has "changed" or sold out; he has merely grown up and become more intelligent and more realistic. They never question their own integrity or their own ethics. They see themselves as leaders of men, giving profound and useful philosophical advice to a confused people, providing intelligence for the masses and helping to preserve the nation from experiments and from sudden change in the status quo.

William Allen White has pointed out the corruption of social relations upon editors who want to publish a free newspaper, but this pressure is even stronger upon a man or woman who begins to syndicate a column of views and is suddenly made the pet of every mercenary organization in the country, showered with orders for lectures, articles, testimonials, with invitations to dine, speak, join, discuss, debate, participate, and lead.

The columnists of the liberal and left wings have to fight for their existence, the columnists for the big money have nothing to do but write their apologies—and wrestle with the devil occasionally. Rare indeed is the person who grows old without growing conservative and suffering from a disintegration of the mind. But the most tragic figures of all are those columnists who stalwartly proclaim they are still the bold bright radical minds of their college days, that they alone march along the straight path to a nobler life, while all their old friends have either fallen into the gutter on the right, or down the radical precipices of the left. There are many such renegades.

But so far as is generally known there is only one case of a columnist who while plying his trade in a cheap reactionary way was also taking the money of the special interests whom he was always defending. This action may be legal on his part, but what about the ethics of the publisher who hires him and continues to publish him even after he has been exposed?

Let me quote from the Nye-Vandenberg Senatorial investigation of the munitions industry. One of the "merchants of death" was being interrogated about sales to China and Japan:

Senator Clark: (reading letter from munitions maker) Along further in that letter, in the second paragraph on the second page, you say:

"So you would know what we are doing, we gave you in confidence the name of George Sokolsky, who is now in New York, and, according to our information, although he does not say so himself, *Mr. Sokolsky represents the Soong interests.* You know Mr. T. V. Soong is the Chinese finance minister, and his sister is the wife of President Chiang Kai-shek. At our request Mr. Sokolsky about two weeks ago sent a cable in his private code to Mr. T. V. Soong, asking if he was interested in obtaining supplies of 7.9 cartridges, but so far no response has come in."

So you identify Mr. Sokolsky, whom you had send cables over to China for you.

Mr. Monaghan: I do not recall how I met Mr. Sokolsky. I did meet him in New York at that time.

Senator Clark: During that time he was a foreign correspondent for the *New York Times,* wasn't he?

Mr. Monaghan: I recall reading articles of his in the *New York Times* that impressed me greatly.

Senator Clark: That was his ostensible business, was it not, being correspondent for the *New York Times?*

Mr. Monaghan: I do not know.

Senator Clark: Mr. Sokolsky, so I am informed, is now touring the United States lecturing in the interests of the necessity for heavy armaments.

Several years ago Agnes Smedley, writing on China's corrupt press, described the various English-language publications in the Far East which are subsidized by the Chinese and Japanese governments. She mentioned "the *Far Eastern Review*, an American-owned and registered engineering monthly which is openly financed by the Japanese. The owner and editor is George Bronson Rea. . . . When Mr. Rea was away from China on his sacred mission of aiding Japanese imperialism his position on the *Review* was taken for a time by another American, George Sokolsky. Mr. Sokolsky, however, seemed a bit more broadminded than Mr. Rea, for he traveled back and forth between the *Review* office and the office of the Ministry of Finance of the Nanking government, with occasional side trips to the British consulate."

Sokolsky, however, not only survived the Nye exposure, but apparently used it as a stepping-stone to a bigger job.

If we had a free press in America the biggest scandal of recent years would have been the exposure by the La Follette investigating committee of the National Association of Manufacturers and the part this same Sokolsky played. But because we do not have a free press we got practically no news about the La Follette hearings in January to April, 1938, and only a column story on Sokolsky in July.

Sokolsky is one of the columnists of the right. It is true he is the extreme right. He is right next door to Fascism. He is playing exactly the same rôle which several other Fascist Jewish columnists played as agents for the Ruhr industrialists in Germany before 1933. There are probably no other well known columnists who are secretly in the pay of advertising and publicity bureaus, steel institutes, manufacturers' associations and chambers of commerce, but there is little difference between the writings of George E. Sokolsky and a dozen of his right-wing colleagues.

Sokolsky is not a journalistic prostitute. In journalism as in real life, a line must be drawn between the inmates of houses of prostitution, known years ago as "white slaves," miserable victims of violence and terror for whom there was no escape, and women of a higher level of society who enjoy the association of wealthy men, serve them well, and cannot refuse the regular wage. Sokolsky merely worked for the manufacturers while appearing in the columns of the *New York Herald Tribune* and several other newspapers as an impartial journalist.

When Sokolsky returned from China penniless, he became a free-lance writer: he wrote an article "America Drifts Towards Fascism," in which he heard "rumbling sympathetic reactions to the Fascism in the New Deal" and in which he exposed the Silver Shirts, also "a Fascist organization called the Vigilantes . . . managed by Harry Augustus Jung . . . one of many anti-Communist propaganda groups . . . tending toward Fascism." After naming a dozen organizations, but not stating what Liberty Leaguers, manufacturers, and other moneyed interests are behind them, Sokolsky warns against dismissing them and their Hitlers and Mussolinis as ridiculous, and concludes that the soil in America is ready for Fascism, "and the New Deal is in a very real sense the father of all these Fascistic tendencies."

In another article, a noble defense of American Jews, he attacked the numerous myths, forgeries and propaganda against the race and paid homage to those members who preferred the cultivation of talent to that of wealth. He lauds Einstein, Michelson, Elman, Epstein, Walter Lippmann, Professor Seligman, Justices Brandeis and Cardozo.

But when next heard from, Sokolsky had written a book ("Labor's Fight for Power") against labor. It did not have much of a sale but in dinner conversations Sokolsky hinted he was making good money. The *Nation* said at that time that "If Mr. Sokolsky's book has not been subsidized by the National Association of Manufacturers, it should have been." The *Nation* reviewer either had inside information or a prophetic soul.

In 1936 we find Sokolsky running a column on the *Herald Tribune* and syndicating it to twenty-five other papers. On April 20, 1936, he calls his colleague Dorothy Thompson to task for getting excited about thugs who break strikes and the 200 detective agencies which intimidate laborers from joining unions. "Who hired these agencies? Why not give the names of the agencies?" he asks bravely. The answer is that the members of the N. A. M. employ both him and the thugs, as was revealed in due time. A week later he attacks Heber Blankenhorn, La Follette committee expert, for daring to say that industry employs detectives, spies and strike-breakers. Sokolsky calls this statement a publicity trick, a circus trick. The statement should not be allowed to stand. Sokolsky calls on Blankenhorn to prove it or shut up. Well, it was proved 100 percent. And in the course of the La Follette proving, came the exposure of Sokolsky.

In August, 1936, this agent for the steel institute and the manufacturers began writing for the *Atlantic Monthly* (then under the editorship of a man named Ellery Sedgwick who ended a long literary life by becoming the chief defender of the child-murderer Franco in Spain). "I speak as a conservative," wrote Sokolsky. "In my youth I ran the gamut of revolutionary movements. Anarchist, pacifist, I. W. W. sympathizer, I have sought a better, a more commodious life, not only for myself, but for all men. . . . Let no man think of me as a tory . . . a heartless marauder in a predatory world. For I have nothing to defend. I have nothing of the goods of this world but what I earn and consume today." This was about the time Sokolsky told me he had arrived penniless from China and had now salted away more than $15,000 in the bank. In all his magazine articles Sokolsky masquerades as a penniless liberal, the true American who believes in freedom for all, and while he seems to attack Fascism with the equal vigor he belabors Communism, he is actually using both merely as foils to show the benefit of the American big business system.

But he has now become a prominent figure in our journalism. He is worth the attention of the liberal press. And he gets it. An editorial in the *New York Post* recalls that during the Manchurian crisis Sokolsky "seemed anxious for the world to understand Japan's 'civilizing' mission in China," and now he has become a labor expert whose articles are "reprinted by the manufacturers' associations and Hawaiian pineapple interests and distributed broadcast to fill editors' wastebaskets." But when Sokolsky attacks John L. Lewis and the C. I. O. and speaks about a Communist, Socialist, C. I. O. plot to elect Lewis President in 1940, the *Post* brings up contrary proof from the *Wall Street Journal,* which also laughs at Sokolsky, and concludes with the advice that "Mr. Sokolsky had better peddle his red herrings elsewhere. Even the Wall Street market insists on fresh fish these days."

Much stronger advice is given the lesser of Sokolsky's employers, the *Herald Tribune,* by the *Nation* (October 24, 1936). If the *Herald Tribune* had taken it it would not now be standing naked to its enemies. The *Nation* said: "The *New York Herald Tribune* is a conservative newspaper, dignified, well edited, and lively. The liberal reader may feel that Walter Lippmann has gone over to the enemy with altogether too much gusto, or that Dorothy Thompson's sympathies lie too far to the right to be consistent with her experience in Hitler's Germany. As for Mark Sullivan, he is almost an appealing figure as he stands roundly in the ranks of Red-baiters much more vicious than himself, still striking out at Tugwell with his trusty cutlass. Even a 'Red' would scarcely accuse these writers of being worse than conservative or reactionary. There is, however, one burned-out star in the *Herald Tribune's* galaxy which should be replaced before it short-circuits the whole string. We refer to George E. Sokolsky. On October 19th Mr. Sokolsky wrote an article on the American Labor Party. Maintaining his old pretense of being an 'expert' on labor and radicalism (some of his best friends are radicals!), he cooked up a mess of misrepresentation, labor-, Jew-, and alien-baiting which Sokolsky himself has seldom surpassed. We feel that the *Herald Tribune,* aside from soiling its pages, is keeping apart two minds that run as one. Isn't it possible that Mr. Sokolsky could be auctioned off to William Randolph Hearst? He long ago reached the stage of journalistic ripeness which usually precedes that fall."

But the *Herald Tribune* continued to peddle the red herrings for which Sokolsky is getting paid double or more by the manufacturers' associations. The propagandist continued to attack labor and the New Deal and to charge it and Lewis, "spearhead of the revolutionary movement in labor," with plotting the overthrow of the government.

When the Newspaper Guild went from the A. F. of L.— "that body of death"—to the C. I. O., the *Herald Tribune* permitted Sokolsky to publish one of his wildest, most nonsensical and vicious propaganda pieces. It is also, incidentally, a public plea by Sokolsky for honest, unbiased journalism— a free press talk by a man secretly being paid by a private organization of industrialists while practicing the open profession of journalism.

Sokolsky says: "A government can only be as democratic as its press is free." This has been said before. "And now the Guild has switched from the A. F. of L. to the C. I. O. That is altogether different. Here is not just a union of mutual protection. Here is the agency of revolution." The Guild passed the lie to Sokolsky.

The plutogogue then declares he has noticed certain things happening in the press and asks, "Are these slips honest errors of judgment or does a Guild member poison the paper for which he works?" He then predicts that if Lewis succeeds in getting the C. I. O. established among news writers, "he will go after the press," and "then this will happen: The C. I. O. will issue orders that no newspaper can be published which does not advocate its policies or its candidates for office.

"Perhaps Heywood Broun, as president of the Guild, will become the American Goebbels. . . .

"The American people would do well to grasp now exactly what is happening to them and to their sacred institutions. There is no use minimizing the effects of the revolution. A process is at work to take over the government, to abolish democratic institutions, to put an end to human rights. . . ."

And to think that all the emotion, this apparent forthrightness, this seeming rectitude was, as we now know, being displayed by a man who was at that very moment being investigated by the La Follette committee as a plutogogue, a hired spokesman for special money interests!

An amusing episode occurred at this time. Benjamin Stolberg—who later sold to Roy Howard the series of articles in which the Moscow herring was dragged all through the C. I. O.—was still writing for the *Nation*. He had written: "Another reactionary free-lance writer is George Sokolsky . . . a rather tragic-comic figure, for with his Eastern European Jewish background he ought to know better than to incite the vigilante spirit. Big business enterprises distribute numerous reprints of his articles." Sokolsky replied, "The fact that I prefer E. T. Weir and Tom Girdler to Earl Browder and Heywood Broun is a matter of taste, and I rather revel in the fact that my taste is different from Ben Stolberg's because I started where he is. . . .

"Also I am more than pleased that business associations like my writings and have reprints made because I believe in the American capitalist system; I advocate its continuance; I believe in organization for its perpetuation and I am the enemy of every man who is seeking to destroy it. . . .

"When I see a figure like John Lewis looming on the horizon I am conscious of his similarity to Hitler. . . ."

Commenting on these statements by this paid public relations agent of big business, Ernest L. Meyer of the *Post* quotes the following paragraph from Clinch Calkins' "Spy Overhead": "Strike breakers may cease to look and smell like finks; they may look and smell like public relations men instead," and suggests that Sokolsky read and reread it.

But Sokolsky went on with his propaganda. In November, 1937, he ridiculed the work of the Institute for Propaganda Analysis and sought to liken himself to some of the greatest men of America and the best known columnists. He wrote "I personally am a confirmed propagandist.... Uncle Charley (Prof. Charles A. Beard) is a mighty propagandist. . . . And another on that list is James T. Shotwell. . . . Among current propagandists the four I like best are Walter Lippmann, Dorothy Thompson, Westbrook Pegler and Boake Carter. . . ." One may well wonder whether the four colleagues like Mr. Sokolsky.

In December the La Follette committee investigating corrupt practices and anti-labor activities on the part of corporations announced it would probe the National· Association of Manufacturers. The *Peoples Press* hinted that Sokolsky and several others who had just addressed the N. A. M. convention, "the Congress of American Industry," in New York, would be called. At that congress Sokolsky had spoken. The press paid no attention to him—with the exception of that "voice of business," the *Sun,* which had a double column headline:

SEES MONSTERS IN WAGNER ACT
Sokolsky Says It Created Discontent and Fear
—Calls Wage-Hour Bill Paralyzing

The word was getting around in journalistic circles that the La Follette committee had the goods on Sokolsky. It would show that while he appeared as a columnist along with Lippmann, Dorothy Thompson, Mark Sullivan and other in the *Herald Tribune,* he was actually on the payroll of the steel corporations and the manufacturers. So what did Sokolsky do? He made a sort of semi-confession for the purpose of spiking the guns of the announced exposé. On December 20, 1937, he wrote in his usual place in the *Herald Tribune* (and syndicated papers):

"Well, it was not long before I became a sort of consultant for the National Association of Manufacturers. What they wanted of me was my point of view, and then they seemed to go their own middle course. I never minded that. I know my own weakness for pushing too far and too hard, and I could not expect those who had something to risk to go along with me.

"Subsequently I came into the same relationship with the American Iron and Steel Institute, and there I found some congenial spirits, but others who regarded me as a queer duck. I never really worried about those who did not like me because they had their problems, and their problems were not mine. They were seeking to save their companies, while I was interested in preserving the kind of capitalism which I liked in this country. . . .

"We clashed . . . we parted company. . . . Still that did not stop business men from consulting me about things. . . . There is tremendous value in this relationship—particularly since I have been writing these (columnar) pieces. Journalism is supposed to be objective, but objectivity has the defect of always seeing things altogether from the outside. This relationship has given me an opportunity to see things from the inside. . . . It has been fascinating and serious work.

"But through it all there has been this magnificent possibility, that I might be doing something of value for a country which I happen to love, because I was hammering on a fundamental philosophy of life. . . . And my conservatism made me a Republican. . . ."

Mr. Sokolsky concludes with a stirring prose-poem, a national anthem, a credo, with three cheers for the United States, democracy, and "the kind of capitalism which I like in this country." The N. A. M. certainly got more in the way of enthusiasm than their weekly checks warranted. As for the *Herald Tribune,* it continued to publish the

Sokolsky anti-labor, anti-union, Red-baiting, reactionary propaganda despite the fact its writer had confessed being "a sort of consultant" of the N. A. M. and having a "relationship" with the American Iron and Steel Institute. This too is known as freedom of the press—for tory publishers.

In January, 1938, Sokolsky shook hands and forgave Ben Stolberg for his last year's criticism. "Ben regarded me, and I suppose he still does, as a writing slave of the independent steel companies," wrote Sokolsky, giving the impression that such things could never be. He continues: "Now Ben Stolberg has written a dozen articles for the Scripps-Howard papers in which he literally spills the beans . . . his description of Communist activities within the C. I. O. is sufficient to convince Tom Girdler that he was right. . . .

"Ben Stolberg is in good company. . . .

"Those of us who have been opposed to the C. I. O. have taken our stand on an earlier recognition of the Red poison. . . ."

The fear of impending exposure continued to put Sokolsky on the defensive. He was probably aware by now that the La Follette committee had among books and records it had seized the receipts Sokolsky had signed for the advertising agency handling the N. A. M. propaganda. He knew he would be exposed as secretly in the pay of the worst enemies of liberalism and labor. So he sought to drag in his fellow writers. In the *Independent Journal* of Columbia University (April 1, 1938) he wrote an article sneering at the liberal columnists and praising the tories. He continued:

"I am the youngest and the poorest of columnists. . . . I am what you call conservative. . . .

"Many columnists are not exclusively newspaper men. Walter Lippmann writes books related to foreign relations. Hugh Johnson is a business man. Heywood Broun is an officer of the Newspaper Guild and the C. I. O., which is a business that sometimes can be a profitable one. I am associated with the National Association of Manufacturers and

am often consulted by large business organizations as to
what their policies should be on public questions and labor
problems. Such relations give us more experience and better
relate us to the events of the moment and make it possible
for us to be closer to the actual current of events. The public
should be told, however, what a man's relationships are.

". . . Many reporters develop into public relations counsels
—a profession which is going to develop in this country. . . .
No large business, no labor union, no charitable organization will be able to conduct its affairs without adequate
public relations.

". . . In this field (column writing) there are no prejudices,
or antagonisms. . . ."

No, none whatever.

Sokolsky invents an alter ego he calls "Sam," who expresses
a nice Fascist viewpoint: "Politics is just a lot of guys selling
us marijuana cigarets. . . ." "So far as I'm concerned the
Old Deal and the New Deal and the Raw Deal and all the
stuff the politicians feed us is just plain cow feed. . . ." "It
isn't only in Washington that the politicians is lousy. Go to
any state capitol. . . ."

Then he has his fling at the Communists, in this manner:
"I met a female Communist the other day. You can spot
them easy. They wear cotton stockings and look like hell.
So I didn't want to pick her up. . . ." This was at a time the
silk boycott was growing—in fact it had become so serious
that Dow-Jones were reporting it as affecting Japanese
economics. Sokolsky was still writing pro-Japanese pieces.
It so happened that many of our most beauteous film stars
were displaying cotton stockings to help the boycott. Still
claiming "no prejudices, or antagonisms," Sokolsky, on March
7th, wrote a vicious Jew-baiting column, in which he said
"A communist parade looks Jewish." If he had been in the
pay of Hitler rather than Girdler he could not have done
better.

On July 21, 1938, Sokolsky was exposed by the La Follette committee. The *Post* and *World-Telegram* gave the news the front page, featuring Sokolsky's name. Even the propagandist's other employer, the *Herald Tribune*, used the name in the second part of the heading, but the *Times* left Sokolsky out of the head and used a minimum of the news, even less than the *Herald Tribune* did. It was shown that Hill & Knowlton, steel corporation press agents, paid Sokolsky $28,599 from June, 1936, to February, 1938, chiefly for service to the American Iron and Steel Institute. The propagandists also contracted with the N. A. M. for $1,000 a month for the Sokolsky services and paid him the entire sum. They also sent out bulletins describing Sokolsky as "a Communist and a radical. . . . He has now reformed and has a real message to deliver to those of us who are interested in the welfare of industry. He calls a spade a spade." But not a check a check.

After this exposure it was expected by all persons who knew anything about the code of ethics and the canons of journalism that at least an apology would be forthcoming. But this came forth instead, an editorial in the *Herald Tribune*, "What is Pressure?"

"What is pressure, anyway? It is exercised on a newspaper in a thousand ways, some of them trivial and laughable, a few of them serious and even dangerous, but for the most part not at all sinister. A publisher runs into an old college chum at his club; the chum buttonholes the publisher and argues with much eloquence and logic that the publisher's paper has been paying much too little attention to some pressing problems—any pressing problem, from grade-crossing removal to whether men should remove their hats for ladies in elevators. That is pressure. . . ." And so on, to more serious pressures, such as the K. K. K., but not a word about the Sokolsky case. And Sok himself continued on his Monday way with an anti-liberal article, concluding, "Dr. Wirt's prophecy will come true: Roosevelt will be the Kerensky of the American revolution. His New Deal is a prelude to Fascism." Up to now it had been Communism.

If the La Follette committee had discovered that Sokolsky or any other columnist on any big paper had been secretly (or semi-secretly) in the pay of any radical or liberal organization, the scandal would have rocked the journalistic foundations of the nation. If it were proven that a columnist was getting Moscow gold, there would have been hell to pay. But when it is found that Sokolsky was merely getting anti-Moscow gold, not a word was said in any tory newspaper in the country, and the agent of the special interests brazenly resumed his department in the newspaper which annually holds a forum at which not only freedom of the press but the ethics of that freedom are lauded to the skies by Mr. Sokolsky's columnar colleagues.

The House of Press Lords has called no special meeting to discuss l'affaire Sokolsky.*

---

* Replying to a protest from the Steel City Industrial Union Council, Paul Block wrote August 19, 1938: "I think we will cut him out of the *Pittsburgh Post-Gazette.*"

CHAPTER 5

1936 and the Columnists

NINETEEN THIRTY-SIX is one of the great dates in our political history because it is also a social and economic date. Its significance will undoubtedly grow. Journalistically, it marked the most important repudiation of the press by the public. How important that repudiation was only time can tell, but it was certainly the first time in our history that a large number of people became aware of the newspaper as a political force—a fact which even the humble European peasant has known for at least a century.

Nineteen thirty-six also showed up the place of that new power in American journalism, the columnist.

The Washington correspondents, those several hundred men who write the politics of the nation, were overwhelmingly on the side of Roosevelt and Reform, although overwhelmingly their papers were opposed. Most of the columnists, however, had no compromise to face, no conscience to trouble them: they as well as big business, the millionaire oil man of Kansas, Hearst, the manufacturers' association, the Liberty League, were all on the same side.

The Washington correspondents voted nineteen to one for Roosevelt. In the *Chicago Tribune, New York Herald Tribune,* and other towers of Landonism, the vote among the working reporters was about the same ratio.

When politics cooled, in 1937, the editorial board of the *New Republic* prepared a study of "The Press and the Public," which said that among the debris scattered across forty-eight states on the morning of November 5, 1936, "were

331

the microphone of Father Coughlin, the silk hats of the Liberty League, the high stiff collar of Dr. Townsend and, like the accumulation of wreckage left by the recession of every flood, 'the power of the press.' . . . Some of the country's foremost columnists were included in the repudiation of the press."

The General Press Repudiation

The circulation figures, the number of newspapers, and other statistical tests of the repudiation of 1936 do not tell the whole story. *Editor & Publisher,* for example, tries to make out a case for its friends, the membership of the A. N. P. A., from the fact that 1935 circulation figures were used by the liberal journals in estimating the readership of 1936. I do not think it necessary to quibble. The fact is that if the press was not nine to one against Roosevelt, it was seven to three, or six to four against him, and that in 1938 this percentage increased still more, and the reason, as Captain Patterson of the *New York Daily News* so bluntly said, had more to do with pocketbooks than principles.

The fair, impartial *Christian Century,* without using statistics, said that thousands, probably millions of the ballots cast in the 1936 elections were not merely for Roosevelt but votes against the newspapers in general. "Election Day, 1936, was judgment day for America's daily press."

Unfair, partial apologists for the publishers have listed the papers in the solid South, with their millions of readers, without explaining that no opposition press existed there, and no contest. On the other hand, the anti-press case could be made much worse by testing the specific gravity of the papers officially listed as pro-Roosevelt.

In New York City, for instance, the *Post,* the *World-Telegram,* the *Times* and the *News,* with more than two and a half million circulation, are listed as supporting Roosevelt, against two and a quarter million for Landon in the Hearst press, the *Herald Tribune* and the *Sun*. A rather fair set-up. But one must not rest on figures, one must attempt to measure emotions.

The passion which Hearst put into his pro-Landon campaign was a combination of all the yellowness which has made him notorious for half a century and earned him the boycott of most decent and intelligent people in America at long last. As Doctor Beard recently pointed out, there was no cesspool which Mr. Hearst has not searched, no art of character assassination which he has not practiced. And so stories were invented, headlines were colored, news was puffed up or suppressed, and everything possible done to smear and destroy the reformer in the White House.

The *Sun* refrained from yellowness: it ran no gargantuan headlines, invented no pure fakes, kept out of cesspools, but it showed that in a nice, gentlemanly, well-bred upper class and aristocratic manner it was able to join hands with Hearst in coloring and distorting and smearing. If the Hearst journalism reeked of the sewer, the *Sun's* smelled of a royal charnel house.

The *Herald Tribune* gave its usual biased Republican news.

All in all, the pro-Landon press was strong in its support and extremely active in propagandizing the electorate. The 2,296,050 circulation of the four papers was thoroughly exploited by partisan news and editorials, with little attempt made at objectivity except in the *Herald Tribune*.

But the same cannot be said for the pro-Roosevelt press. The *Times* published one editorial announcing itself for the President and then continued its policy of presenting the news impartially as between Roosevelt and Landon. Its editorials were never alarming or decisive. Its editorial policy did not affect the news. The *World-Telegram* supported Roosevelt, but it was not with any magnificent enthusiasm.

Its support was not very strong. It did not color the news, suppress or distort, or indulge in the usual tricks of the rival pro-Landon press.

The *News* was strongly pro-Roosevelt. This support was important. But the *News* was broadminded enough to inaugurate a "battle page" in which the Republican and Democratic parties would tell their stories, deride the claims of rivals, put over the worst sort of propaganda. The Republicans made great use of this page in the Democratic *News*.

The *Post* was 100 percent for Roosevelt.

If, therefore, an attempt is made to gauge the quality as well as the quantity of circulation, it will be found that the Landon support was actually much more intense than the cold figures indicate, and that a considerable proportion of the Roosevelt figures cannot be rightly placed in his column. In other words, the seventy-one percent pro-Landon circulation in what the *New Republic* called the fifteen competitive areas, where both candidates had a chance of winning, is actually opposed by less than the twenty-nine percent pro-Roosevelt circulation of the statistics.

Curiously enough in four large cities where the President had not one newspaper on his side he won by about two to one. In Chicago, where the circulation was almost ten to one for Landon and that "favorite" son, Knox, the voting was just under two to one for the "outside agitator."

Apologists for the press are still interpreting the 1936 figures in an attempt to restore prestige out of debris. But even they admit that the majority of the papers, the circulation, the editorials and the bias were on Landon's side and that Landon was defeated by just about an inverse ratio.

Columns of Strength

The President himself has made the distinction between the Washington correspondents and the Washington columnists.

"I consider it an interesting fact," wrote Franklin D. Roosevelt in the introduction to his state papers, "that in spite of this array of editorial opposition, which apparently has been unable to exercise adequate influence upon public opinion in the United States, the majority of newspaper correspondents who cover the White House are personally friendly to the administration, and in general approve its objectives, most of its methods, and the legislation adopted to accomplish its goal. I know that a number of the newspaper correspondents who write so-called 'unfriendly' articles are not personally opposed to the things they write about. I think that the first part of this anomaly can be explained by the fact that many hostile newspaper owners require their Washington correspondents to give their news dispatches a critical or unfriendly touch. . . .

"The writers of news stories . . . are in a different class from columnists and writers of business news letters. In recent years the writers of these latter groups have found a ready market. In most cases their columns are based either on the pure imagination and invention of the writer or untrue gossip which, of course, can be obtained almost for the asking to fit any objective. . . . These pseudo-news services do little real harm however . . . and are generally appraised as having little value, so far as really affecting public opinion is concerned. With this general estimate, bona fide newspaper reporters and correspondents agree."

I wish I could.

The Gallup poll, *Fortune*, Margaret Marshall in the *Nation*, the *Christian Science Monitor* and other tests of the popularity and power of the columnists have, it is true, shown that their circulation, which runs from half a million to twelve million, is not a real test of their readership and their influence, nevertheless it is generally agreed that their power increases at a time the editorial page influence decreases, and that people have more faith in columnists than in most molders of public opinion. They are still gaining followers, whereas the newspapers themselves are more and more forsaken as leaders.

The two columnists with the largest following, respectively, Arthur Brisbane and O. O. McIntyre, have died since most of the tests of influence and popularity have been taken. The first was a renegade liberal weakling who parroted Mr. Hearst's stupidities in a stupid way for many years, and did not have much political influence, while the second was merely a small-town boy agape in a big world about which he knew nothing of any significance.

The third ranking popular columnist is Walter Winchell who for years grew wealthy and famous by reporting the gossip of the great and faux-great, and who lately has joined with many others who are forsaking their glass houses and ivory towers. To the spectacle of the majority of columnists growing more fog-bound daily, we have the heartening sight of the Prince of Trivialities becoming the chronicler of significant trends. Walter Winchell suddenly has become a ray of hope in the artificial fogs so many of his fellow columnists themselves create.

Fourth is Westbrook Pegler. He is a wayward youth, lost in No Man's Land between the entrenched interests and the general welfare, playing with matches and occasionally touching off great big bombs. When the bombs fall in the enemy camp, as the one in which he preferred to see General Franco in hell rather than in church, he is magnificent, but you cannot tell whether or not the next grenade will fall at your own feet and lacerate one of your own convictions.

Fifth in *Fortune's* popularity ranking was Dorothy Dix, a woman's page writer, and sixth was Lippmann.

One of the excellent results of the Roosevelt-Landon campaign was the self-withdrawal of Walter Lippmann from the field of liberal and progressive journalism. He had already been expelled from the minds of all liberal and progressive intelligent persons, but still maintained a considerable following among the unintelligent who believed themselves liberal and progressive. Mr. Lippmann's declaration for Landon, followed by many weeks of his usual brilliant but meaningless production of hundreds of thousands of words straddling the issue, was a complete betrayal of a man using words to camouflage a compromising mind.

The prophet of the Harvard Liberal Club had become the profit of the Union League Club.

Friends who know David Lawrence intimately describe in detail his years of wrestling with the devil, all during which time he was able to keep an eye on the source of butter for his bread. Employees of the *United States News* the time Mr. Lawrence ran it as a daily, vouch for the publisher's sincere liberalism. More recently Mr. Lawrence has become another of the majority of columnists who are merely plutogogues.

Mr. Lawrence, moreover, has been able to combine plutogracy with nonsense. Thus during the 1936 campaign he was able to predict that the tide had turned against the New Deal on September 8th, when he interpreted a reduced majority for the President, and two days later he found a counter-revolution going on. The very next day he had a blast against Federal spending and one day later he discovered that the New Deal machine, which he called a "political racket," had grown to such amazing proportions that he found it "hard to believe, unless one examines the situation first hand." It went on like that until November, 1936, and it still goes on like that.

In the 1936 campaign Heywood Broun, with forty-two papers, a large number of them Scripps-Howard, and Jay Franklin with forty-seven, were the leading supporters of the President. Their combined circulation was small compared to the columnists who wrote anti-Roosevelt stuff. The five Landon stars were Mark Sullivan, Lippmann, Lawrence, Alice Longworth and Frank Kent. Three who were generally critical of Roosevelt although not going the whole Landon hog were Brisbane, Paul Mallon and Miss Dorothy Thomp-

son. Broun himself is not a Roosevelt man, it being a lesser-
of-two-evils choice for him, and this leaves exactly one Roosevelt man among the most popular columnists whose favored
candidate was so thoroughly defeated by the newspaper
readers of the nation.

The Washington Merry-Go-Round was not included in the
survey because it is primarily a news, not an editorial column
taking political sides. In many respects, however, Drew Pearson and Robert Allen are the fairest and most important
political writers. They have not hesitated to give names,
dates and places even when it meant endangering their
sources of information and violating the taboos of religious
and secular pressure organizations. Allen and Pearson exposed the pro-Fascists in our State Department and their
intrigue to keep the embargo on munitions for the Spanish
republic. They named our Fascists and they told of the
Catholic Church lobby in Washington. They have been as
free and honest in telling of big business lobbies and pressures and have never written either pro-Republican or pro-
Democratic propaganda, something which cannot be said for
the majority of columnists. They are the iconoclasts of
Washington.

During the 1936 campaign a slip by the Republican
publicity director, Theodore A. Huntley, put four pro-
Republican columnists on the spot. Huntley had written to
Republican editors offering assorted Republican propaganda,
adding:

"We have thought of a daily or weekly political letter out
of Washington and could arrange for this if there were a
sufficient demand for it.

"Most of you, however, undoubtedly will prefer to run
the letters of Mark Sullivan, Dave Lawrence, Frank Kent,
Paul Mallon or other syndicate writers available to you
through the regular services."

Charles Michelson, Democratic party publicity director,
and former Washington political expert for the *New York*

World, saw this letter and blew up righteously. He answered with a broadside.

"The Republican National Committee has formally taken over the Three Musketeers of anti-Administration, Frank Kent, Mark Sullivan and David Lawrence," Michelson thundered. (Mr. Mallon's name was not included.)

"Now, I don't know that the Republican organization had the permission of these eminent and talented gentlemen in presenting them as the authors of campaign material.

"In fact, I have received intimations that they considered the Democratic organization was being unfair in listing them as Republican propagandists.

"The recent announcement, however, directed 'To All Editors,' makes it perfectly plain that the G. O. P. strategists consider them as valiant and unalienable allies, for the minority party would hardly suggest to the G. O. P. press that they should publish articles that voiced anything other than G. O. P. views.

"There may be an ethical question involved, for either the Republican organization has justification for its listing these writers as elements of their publicity campaign—in which case, of course, it is hardly ingenuous for the writers to continue to pose as non-partisan observers merely conveying information to the public—or it had no license to so list them and, consequently did them a considerable disservice in conveying to editors that their work was Republican propaganda."

But lest the reader think the three have not been aiding the Republican party while posing as non-partisans, Michelson piles on extracts of Sullivan and Kent columns to prove his contentions.

Post-1936 Columnists

After 1936 publishers and columnists, with the exception of Mr. Hearst who immediately after his private debacle likened Roosevelt to Jackson and changed his antagonistic tune, attacked the President and all his deeds. It is now generally accepted that the fight against the Reorganization Bill, a measure first proposed in Republican times, was not a fight on a principle, but a fight against a personality. Everyone knows the reform is needed and will come in time.

A survey of the press made by the *Christian Science Monitor* in 1937 proves that while the Gallup and other polls show that the President is still about holding his popularity, there is a decided swing in the press against him. Of that small percentage left which did not previously oppose him the majority now does. The *Monitor* survey shows:

1. More than two-thirds of the responding newspapers which supported the President for re-election do not support him on the Supreme Court issue.

2. More than half of the newspapers that have deserted the President on this issue are openly and vigorously opposed to the plan. Others are critical to the plan, seeking a better method for enlarging Federal powers.

3. Of the seventy-five newspapers included in the survey, nineteen support the Supreme Court proposal, fifty-two are opposed either to the whole project or to the method, and four remain non-committal for the present.

4. The pro-administration papers supporting the President on this issue have a total circulation, according to Ayer's Directory, of 3,136,198. The pro-administration papers opposing the plan have a total circulation of 13,191,693.

In the view of La Follette's *Progressive* the columnists are largely to blame for the continuation of the fight on Roosevelt reforms. Declaring that in 1936 editors of eighty-five percent of the northern newspapers "forgot ethics, logic, sanity and even good taste" in their "frothings" at the New Deal and liberalism, Editor Evjue writes that "today another wrecking crew of journalists has crowded into the spotlight to outdo the reactionary editors for the national title of champion beraters. They are the syndicated columnists on the side of the tories, most of them owing their present prosperity to their tie-up with some big reactionary paper like the New York *Herald Tribune.*

"Of the top-flight columnists assailing Mr. Roosevelt and virtually everything progressive and forward looking in his administration, almost all are being presented to the public as being 'liberals.'

"But the type of daily columns these writers grind out long ago destroyed any claims to liberalism they may have had. All are now tub thumping in the same beat as the most rabid editorial spokesmen for our financial and industrial Mr. Bigs.

"What better proof of this could be offered than a pamphlet which has just been issued by the National Association of Manufacturers and distributed far and wide throughout the country. The pamphlet is a collection of columns written by Miss Thompson and Messrs. Hugh Johnson, Frank Kent, David Lawrence, Walter Lippmann, and Westbrook Pegler.

"The label of the National Association of Manufacturers on a collection of columns by these writers ought to be enough to convince most people of the utter hypocrisy of any claims of liberalism that are made for them by their sponsors.

"If they had been kissed en masse by the Liberty League (as they have frequently been kissed individually and privately) their sham and pretense of being liberal could not have been more thoroughly exposed."

All one has to do is pick out any measure or idea which any liberal editor, organization, or individual approves and it will most certainly be attacked by the corps of ex-liberal columnists—the most noted of whom are the subject of the succeeding chapter. There was a time when liberals spoke for public ownership of the railroads and the public utilities, but today the utilities republish the friendly views of the columnists. Messrs. Lippmann and Sullivan and Miss

Thompson united in demanding that the President make peace with the utilities—peace at almost any price. Of course a soap-box orator in Union Square (and I am not attacking him because I have heard sounder economic wisdom expounded there than in the drawing rooms of some of our columnists and their bank-director-economist friends) might shout that the columnists are merely upholding the ubiquitous capitalist system because their papers were involved with the utilities (which of course is most true), or that the writers were holders of interests in the utilities (about which neither he nor I can know anything, although a suspicion at least is warranted) or finally that it is merely the expression of persons who are part and parcel of the same ruling class in America, whose interests are identical.

The third indictment of course is the most valid. It is the one the columnists will most violently deny, because none feels nor believes that such a thing is possible, and that in his or her intelligent and rational mind all these views—which the rest of the intelligent and rational world calls reactionary—are the epitome of reason, intelligence, liberalism, and forthright wisdom.

Mr. Lippmann and Miss Thompson offer a good laboratory case.

CHAPTER 6

Two Leading Liberals

Walter Lippmann

WALTER LIPPMANN rarely criticizes his fellow columnists and
rarely if ever answers his critics. Like great newspapers
themselves and the Pope only on the occasion when he is
speaking *ex cathedra* on matters of doctrine—and that only
since about 1870—Mr. Lippmann maintains the pose of in-
fallibility. But because he began life as a Socialist, a wealthy
playboy Socialist perhaps, but nevertheless active enough to
go into politics for a while, and because today he uses his
enormous talents—he is supposed to be the most lucid writer
in America—in favor of just those very objectives which the
Socialist system would destroy, his enemies generally speak
of him as a renegade.

Perhaps the most brutal words ever written against Walter
Lippmann was his biography in the pro-big business weekly
Time: "From Socialism to G. O. P., from *New Republic* to
Herald Tribune . . . transitions which the contemners of
Walter Lippmann today cannot forgive and will not allow
to be forgotten. Although his sincerity is above cavil . . .
they question whether the lucidity of his writing . . . is more
than a meretricious semblance hiding a confused mind.

"Sharpest dig at Walter Lippmann was made by Mabel
Dodge Luhan, whose Manhattan salon Lippmann frequented
as a young man: 'Walter is never, never going to lose an eye
in a fight.' . . .

"Whatever Walter Lippmann may have lost, it is a fact
343

that he has gained a great deal of this world's goods, has a more than comfortable income ($54,329), three houses—in Manhattan, Florida, and Wading River, Long Island. . . . Even by the standards of U. S. success, Walter Lippmann does not lead an underprivileged life . . . . Afternoons he rides, fishes, plays golf (fairly), tennis (better) or referees a polo game for his Long Island friends. In the private matter of personal friends, he is more apt to be on intimate terms with Morgan partners than with union leaders. . . . All these things provide grounds for those who question whether he has any title to be called 'liberal.' "

The liberal criticism is well represented by the *Nation's* editor, Margaret Marshall, who writes that Lippmann (a man "born fifty years too late in the wrong country") "has moved steadily to the right; his prestige and prosperity have increased concomitantly. There is a temptation to dismiss him, in an old phrase, as a man who began with a wealth of thought and ended with the thought of wealth. But the Lippmann processes suggest a multiple and more subtle diagnosis. It is a truism that the effective apologist, like the cruder type of demagogue, must be himself at least half-deceived." Lippmann, she adds, "removes himself from the battlefield and yet maintains his claim to liberalism. In the writing itself there is a lack of tension, and a pompous, measured elegance that match the profound irrelevance of his much-advertised point of view. He recently called Anthony Eden the knight with the wooden sword. It's a perfect description of Lippmann as social thinker. His rôle as an apologist for the status quo is another matter." Lippmann's column, headed "Today and Tomorrow," Miss Marshall concludes, offers his readers "the triple appeal of snobbism, escape and justification of things as they are. . . . His claim of liberalism, especially since it is his most valuable asset, should deceive no one, least of all himself."

On an earlier occasion the same magazine said that although Lippmann "may write, as a colleague remarked in the *Herald Tribune*, 'like a revolving door,' he thinks like a bird-dog."

In Heywood Broun's column he once said that Lippmann "espouses the comforting idea that we are safe in the arms of Morgan." Broun ridicules Lippmann's views on the free press. "Does Mr. Lippmann really think," he asks, "that when he bobs up at breakfast in the daily press from Maine to California that his own fresh-minted views are wholly surrounded by other nuggets? Where was he during the general strike in California, the campaign of Upton Sinclair and the textile strike along the seaboard? Is it not possible that here and there items which he mistakes, in his survey for pure gold, may turn to be brass checks on closer scrutiny?"

In reviewing the latest Lippmann politico-philosophic book, "The Good Society," Prof. John Dewey wrote, "He does his thinking in something like a vacuum."

On Mr. Lippmann's becoming a Republican—and John T. Flynn insists that *that* fact, and not Lippmann's becoming a Landonite, should be recognized—Flynn wrote * the *requiescat in pace* for his ex-liberal colleague. He told how Lippmann, "a radical leader in Harvard," began "that long march to the right which has carried him over nearly all the continents of the mind . . . until he finds himself marching along lustily, his face toward the setting sun, with Colonel Knox, Senator Hastings, Senator Dickinson, Ogden Mills, the Liberty League, behind the banner of the little oil man from Kansas. . . .

"As Mr. Lippmann marched from left to right, from camp to camp, he neglected to change the flag he carried. He employed the vocabulary of liberalism to support the doctrine of the mortgage noteholders. . . .

"When business men were hailing it (the NRA) as a new charter of freedom, he was all for it. He began losing his faith in it about the same time that our great business leaders

* *New Republic*, September 23, 1936.

did. When the poor banker and broker hath cried, Lippmann hath wept. . . . He was profoundly distressed at the munitions investigation, he was particularly upset at the grave injustices done Mr. Morgan. He was as much against the war-profits bill as Charlie Schwab and as much against the neutrality act as the Du Ponts. He was against the Utility Holding Company Act, against government interference in business, and has revealed as tender a sensitiveness to the terrible doctrine of soaking the rich as Andy Mellon or Albert Wiggin. . . . Time has made him into as good a Republican as Ogden Mills. After all his wanderings he is home at last."

Finally here are a few hard words from the left. Lippmann had contributed to the old *Masses*. Writes A. B. Magil in the *New Masses:* "Lippmann once sneered at John Reed. Reed is dead and Lippmann is alive; but in this case all the life is on the side of the dead. The words of Jack Reed will be meat and drink for the hearts and minds of free men in generations to come when the name of Walter Lippmann is not even a whisper in the wind." (Unless "Liberty and the News" is remembered.) And Corliss Lamont writes in the same weekly: "Walter Lippmann constitutes an American tragedy, . . . Starting out as a radical and a socialist . . . Lippmann ended up by giving over his exceptional gifts to the service of reaction smirkingly posing as liberalism. And by some strange coincidence he at the same time attained an eminent position in New York and Long Island society. . . . (This cannot be charged to sour-grapes snobbism, coming from the son of Thomas Lamont.) We should not be surprised when young radicals become old or middle-aged tories, but it is legitimate to feel disappointed."

But Walter Lippmann is not without new friends. Here, for example, is the accolade given him by the *Brooklyn Tablet,* the leading pro-Franco publication in this country. "As Walter Lippmann grows older," it writes editorially, "his viewpoint becomes wider and he sees through the half-baked 'liberals.' . . . His articles . . . unmask the shoddy thinking, and hypocritical practices, of the advanced thinkers of the left. . . . The *Tablet,* as one of his old critics, is glad to salute him today as a teacher who is performing fine service in ranks where true liberalism seldom gets a hearing."

The heading over this paragraph in this official organ of the Catholic Church in Brooklyn is: LIPPMANN IS AWAKE.

Dorothy Thompson

Mr. Lamont deplores the fact that men "turn tail and seek consolation on the bosom of Mother Capitalism." This is most noticeable among writers who cannot very well deny their past. But they can rationalize the "treasons" of their youth.

Walter Lippmann deplores the conduct of all his old friends: they have either become too reactionary or they have gone too radical while he alone, he believes, has maintained the liberal road. Nothing pains him more than the charge from the colleagues of his youth that he has sold liberalism down the river in just the same manner Chamberlain sold out Czechoslovakia. The most interesting analysis of the Lippmann case is Prof. Max Lerner's. "I do not subscribe to the theory, held by some of my contemporaries," says Lerner, "that Walter Lippmann has 'sold out' . . . Lippmann has not had to sell out. . . . The compass of his thinking has swung round under the pressure of events from the liberalism of the left to the liberalism of the right; the catchwords have remained the same, but the content is the opposite of what it was. Mr. Lippmann is a rich man; his friends are the possessors of the earth; he is their prophet. . . ."

This analysis could very well cover Mark Sullivan, Frank Kent, Dorothy Thompson, and all the other writers who start on the Left and in the process of growing powerful and wealthy arrive at the Right, still denying that they have changed sides. These are the columnists who land on the Right bank alongside George Sokolsky, Arthur Brisbane and many Hearst writers by drifting there rather than openly chasing the $1,000 weekly check from the manufacturers' associations.

Miss Thompson, however, by denying she was ever among the Leftists, thereby claims immunity from criticism of old friends and liberal publications. These former friends still applaud Dorothy when she brilliantly attacks, exposes and destroys the reactionary pretensions of Nazis, Fascists and Francoists but deplore her failure to use her column and position—she is considered the outstanding woman in America by those who challenge Eleanor Roosevelt's right to that place—to detect and destroy Fascist ideas in America.

That she is aware of this movement is apparent from occasional paragraphs. "The wage-worker who has no control whatsoever over his job, that is, over his life, who can be dismissed at will, from one day to the next—is he a free man?" she wrote in one of her earliest columns (May 30, 1936). "Ask the employee of United States Steel whether he is a free man and he will laugh at you. These are facts in American life." But recently she wrote that the Wagner Act was an atrocious piece of legislation, atrociously administered. It is true that when Carl Randau of the Newspaper Guild challenged her to debate the statement she changed it to "bad" act, "badly" administered, and when rebuttal time came, she was willing to admit it was better than no act at all. But in all her attack on the NLRB and the Wagner law she shares the position of the National Association of Manufacturers, the Chamber of Commerce, the Liberty Leaguers and Union Leaguers and all the Fascistic elements in America. Her motive may be better but the end is the same. And this is typical of the columnists who fight faraway Fascism and somehow find themselves by its side at home.

One of the bravest pieces of writing in America since 1917, when a few intellectuals defied the war mania, was Dorothy's defense of Loyalist Spain and defiance of the Catholic hierarchy, which supports the bloodiest movement in the name of Christ the modern world has seen.

Miss Thompson denounced the murderous Fascist aviators who destroyed Guernica and who killed ten thousand civilians in Barcelona and other Loyalist cities. She paid no attention to the Catholic hierarchy's answers on Guernica, as other columnists did, and she was right because the slaughter at Barcelona, which even bishops and cardinals find hard to defend, was an even worse atrocity.

Braver yet is criticism of the Catholic hierarchy at home. We find Miss Thompson, who time and time again has attacked the miserable mayor of Jersey City, taunting the Catholic Church with condoning corrupt political machines which its members operate in many cities. She wrote (January 10, 1938):

I remember also that a number of important Catholics rightly opposed the Supreme Court reorganization scheme because they realized that the Bill of Rights, embodied in the Constitution, is the greatest bulwark that a minority like the Catholics has against possible persecution. But we don't hear the Catholic hierarchy protesting vigorously against what is happening in Jersey City. On the contrary, the Catholic hierarchy in Jersey City itself is collaborating very closely with Mayor Hague.

Or I might find some little community forum in Jersey City whose leader would have the courage to get together a few people, in a church perhaps, and let me come and speak.

But then whoever sponsored me would probably have to go through the inquisition and blackmail which confronted the chairman of the meeting that invited Signor de Los Rios to come and speak on Spain. Senor de Los Rios is the Ambassador of a friendly power in the United States, but the chairman of a meeting that invited him to speak was visited by the Monseigneur of Jersey City, who backs up Mayor Hague, and queried as to whether he was a Communist. And it was made very clear to him that if he backed up the meeting his business would suffer.

I don't think that this is very bright of the Monseigneur. He should take a look at Germany, where exactly the same thing is happening to priests of the church that is happening to C. I. O. organizers in Jersey City, and against which this column has repeatedly protested.

Perhaps it is a personal prejudice, but I happen to dislike intensely "liberal" Fascists, reactionary Fascists, labor Fascists, industrial Fascists, Jewish Fascists, Catholic Fascists and personal Fascists. When it comes to choosing the particular brand of Fascism, I'm not taking any.

You don't have to choose between them—you can always die first.

Miss Thompson is willing to die in the fight against Fascism —abroad, but is either unwilling to see the same phenomenon here or incapable of doing so. Although Miss Thompson today denies that the preponderant majority of her old friends were of the Left, she cannot deny that among those with whom she now associates are many who belong to the Reactionary Right.

In December, 1937, the Liberties Union celebrated its seventeenth anniversary and Secretary of the Interior Harold L. Ickes, himself a seasoned journalist, spoke on "Nations in Nightshirts." The most important paragraphs of this magnificent oration are the following:

And just as certain nations, uttering the excuse that they are stamping out communism, commit crimes at which savages would blush, so in our own land those who would undermine our democratic institutions do it under the same hollow pretense. Every candidate for office in America who lacks a real issue proceeds to shout "Communism." Any male or female hysteric, gluttonous for notoriety and unscrupulous about achieving it, can always uncover a "Red network."

Employers who deny to their workers the right to associate together in a labor union for the common good of all frequently declare that they do so because of "Communistic" influences which are at large in their factories. It does not require much intelligence to see that such Communism may become a wooden horse within the bowels of which ruthless Fascism may enter the shrine of liberty.

As a matter of fact, it is the Fascist-minded men of America who are the real enemies of our institutions. They have solidarity, a common interest in seizing more power and greater riches for themselves and ability and willingness to turn the concentrated wealth of America against the welfare of America. It is these men who, pretending that they would save us from dreadful Communism, would superimpose upon America an equally dreadful Fascism. . . .

Supposedly liberal writers who have droned on quietly for years while the Tom Girdlers, the Jimmy Rands and other corporate czars dictated the labor policies of the nation, suddenly become alarmed for human liberty when it is proposed that the state protect the worker who cannot protect himself.

We see a Walter Lippmann with the obsequious dignity of a butler, shoving intellectual fodder into the rack for the Fascists whom he once despised.*

Our ancestors fought to prevent a state censorship of news and ideas. Our ancestors did not fight for the right of a few LORDS OF THE PRESS to have almost exclusive control of and censorship over the dissemination of news and ideas. Yet, under the stress of economic forces, our press and news agencies are coming more and more under the domination of a handful of corporate publishers who may print such news as they wish to print and omit such news as they do not wish to print. They may even color the news. †

Mr. Ickes' whole speech was reasoned and temperate; there were suggestions that Mayor Hague, the Chicago interests responsible for the Memorial Day massacre, concentrated wealth and special interests, are the Fascist-minded men of America.

---

* This paragraph was suppressed in the *New York Times* and *New York Sun*.

† This paragraph was partly published in the *Sun*, suppressed in the *Times*, published in full in the *Daily Worker*.

The Fascist-minded men of America are the real enemies. Unfortunately they are also the friends of most of our columnists.

On March 31, 1938, Jay Franklin, leading Democratic columnist, called Miss Thompson "the syndicated spokeswoman of the stiff-shirt Fascisti." Previously he had written that "she is the only self-labeled anti-Fascist, anti-Communist who can dismiss Democracy whenever it runs counter to her wishes." On another occasion he used an entire column to assert that Miss Thompson is "for economic servitude and political impotence." He referred to his rival as "the Florence Nightingale of the wounded Tory intellect and Clara Barton of the plutocrat in pain." In still another column which Franklin devoted to his controversy with Miss Thompson, he quotes this letter from one of his readers:

"I note with satisfaction that Dorothy Thompson devotes her column to annihilating you and your ideas. . . . It takes a lot to make her come down out of that foggy stratosphere, haunted by pale, screaming ghosts of Hitler and Stalin, wherein most of her thought processes are conducted. . . . Dorothy Thompson is Lady Macbeth in pink tights, alternately babbling of industrial democracy and screaming with rage at every actual attempt to attain it."

On the same subject a writer in *The Nation* says "It is high time someone called Miss Thompson on her bitter anti-labor bias. While she has a perfect right to be as anti-labor as she likes she has no right to be anti-labor under the cloak of extreme liberalism."

Another of Miss Thompson's colleagues and most bitter critics is Heywood Broun, who once wrote an article appraising all columnists. He said that "poor Miss Thompson . . . is the victim of galloping nascence. . . . If all the speeches she has made in the past 12 months were laid end to end they would constitute a bridge of platitudes sufficient to reach from the *Herald Tribune's* editorial rooms to the cold caverns of the moon. . . . Never since its inception has the

Union League Club permitted a woman to enter its portals, much less address its members, and then one evening suddenly there was Dorothy Thompson stampeding the old gentlemen into riotous enthusiasm with the ringing declaration that she purposed to support the capitalist system."

Do They Sell Out?

It is not a question of bread and butter that makes men sell out, argues Robert Forsythe, columnist of the *New Masses*. He cannot explain the case of Newton D. Baker, great reformer and liberal who became a Morgan lawyer and died in the odor of dividends. Sinclair Lewis also is a wealthy man. "What is it," asks Forsythe, "that causes a Sinclair Lewis to collapse while a Henri Barbusse fights to his dying breath for humanity? What is to account for the frantic desire of Lewis to break with his past? Can money and the influence that comes with position really do that to a man? What satisfaction can he possibly get out of the acclaim of the stupid and the reactionary he formerly professed to despise?

"The disease seems to be endemic among liberals. Without attempting an analysis of liberalism, I should say that the typical liberal is at heart a utopian. He wants a better world but he wants it done up in ribbon. Almost anything is enough to discourage him. When he discovers that the individuals working with him in a liberal cause are human beings rather than angels, he is unable to go on. The blow shatters him, robs him of his faith in human nature, prompts him to doubt the good of any reform. The curious thing, however, is that he rarely stops at that. Instead, he becomes aggressively reactionary and repudiates with virulence the very ideas he has lately been upholding. In some mystic way this seems to constitute amends for his waverings. It is a form of propitiation of the gods, an abasement which will put him again in their good graces. . . .

"If what a man craves is attention and fame, of what use
is transitory fame to him? John Reed and Walter Lippmann
were classmates at Harvard. Is there anybody who doubts
their respective place in history? John Spargo and Lincoln
Steffens were contemporaries, but Steffens was alert and
open to ideas to his death. He was a great man and a great
influence, and his fame will be lasting. Spargo is now confined to writing Red-baiting letters to the *Times*. Many of
you won't recognize his name, but he was an important
figure in the American labor movement before the War. If
he achieves a footnote in history, he will be fortunate.

"In writing this I am not advocating martyrdom, but
simple common sense. Renegades are vicious, but tired
liberals are merely disgusting. They bore me. They have
large notions and no stamina. They wilt. They whine. They
sell out even before the offer is made. What under the sun
would prompt a man of Newton D. Baker's intelligence to
defeat himself? From a common sense viewpoint, what
actually did he gain by surrender? . . . What do the puny
people get out of their money and their passing fame that
can recompense them for the failure of their lives?"

CHAPTER 7

"Treason" on the *Times*

EVERYWHERE but in America newspapers themselves are news. Publishers are news. Our own journals almost daily report that "Rothermere Supports Hitler," "Beaverbrook Warns Parliament," "Gayda Threatens Loyalist Spain," or "Italian Press for War" and "German Press Defiant," but with the rare exceptions of a Greeley, a Harding or a Knox running for office, our great press lords prefer to remain anonymous in their power.

That there is a tremendous curiosity about what the American press itself is up to is either overlooked or intentionally ignored by our publishers. (That they suppress or bury all items about their own affairs is an old story.) Many laymen find the press sections in *Time* and *Newsweek* the most interesting departments, many mourn the infrequence of Guy Fawkes' "The Wayward Press" in the *New Yorker* which once took the metropolitan papers for a hebdomadal ride, and thousands of leading citizens buy the liberal week-lies largely for their inside stories of what the great newspapers are doing or misdoing.

Among the rare and usually ephemeral publications produced by newspapermen themselves and devoted entirely to criticizing or exposing our press there have been *The Hearst Worker*, the Scripps-Howard *Beacon*, *The Brooklyn Eagle* "*Eagle Eye*," and the most sensational success of all, the monthly secretly started as *Better Times* and now published as *The New Times*. Although the objective of every attack is the *New York Times* itself I select this publication for that very reason, because in my opinion the *New York Times* is now more so than ever the most important paper in the country, and criticism of it constitutes a criticism of present-day journalism. It also shows what the extreme left thinks of our foremost journal.

Volume 1, No. 1, of *Better Times* appeared in November, 1937. It had two mottoes, "All the News" and "Free the Press." It was frankly "published by the Communist Party Units of the *New York Times*." That fact itself was sensational and disarming. No one could drag a red herring across its trail: it admitted it was itself the red herring. But my investigation shows that about three-quarters of every issue is contributed by non-Communists. The sheet was dedicated to the several thousand employees of the paper. In a later issue a four-point program was given, No. 3 being to "expose false and misleading news in the *Times*. We believe that the press cannot be free as long as it is privately owned, but despite this we shall try to point out to the *Times* workers the fact that the *Times* is far from the impartial medium that it pretends to be. We demand the removal of the Fascists Carney and Cortesi."

Three methods are used in the attack: first, the time-honored deadly parallels with *Herald Tribune* and other tory headlines compared to the disadvantage of the *Times;* second, comparison of *Times* headlines and news items in the light of later developments which disprove them; and third, the exposure of really secret intramural news. From the first several issues it would appear that the conservative or tory press was fairer to the C. I. O. in Michigan troubles than the supposedly liberal pro-New Deal *Times.* There is also much ado about the family demanding an advance copy of Felix Warburg's obituary, its displeasure, its editing, its demand for a favorable editorial, and its censorships.

With the second issue the note of bitterness enters, the lie direct is passed, and a gossip column appears permitting considerable personal stabbing. The first item, headlined "Red-

Baiting *Times* Story Proven Lie," says of a report that "Reds in Union Urge New Type General Motors War," that "this story is a complete fabrication and is just one more instance of *Times* policy of coloring news when it affects a large advertiser." The first item in the gossip column, "Topics in the *Times*," mildly relates the fact that night managing editor McCaw wrote managing editor James that the office boys had not been paid their promised extra for election night; "it's things like this that make them join the (Newspaper) Guild."

Innocuous as this story appears it exploded tremendously in the *Times* editorial office. How could a note, from a night to a day editor, handwritten, sealed, personal, become public? The stench of treason rose from the explosion. The *Times*, from its owners to its office boys, became aware of *Better Times*.

The miniature Winchell of *Better Times* may not be as brilliant and brittle, but he is more bitter. Every item is destined to hurt. There is no picturesque, Winchellesque contribution to the American language, but thrusts such as these:

What prominent member of the classified advertising department is greatly interested in the German-American Bund, the Nazi organization?

When Colonel Adler is in uniform his chauffeur must give him the regular army salute. . . .

What semi-executive had better stop making passes at the girls in his department if he doesn't want to be reported or arrested? . . . The only reason he hasn't been turned in, is because of his wife and baby. . . .

Joe Shaplen now calls Oliver Holden "Fink." And Holden calls Shaplen "Trotskyite." . . .

Despite the *Times* editorials favoring a boycott of Japan, the ornaments on the *Times* Xmas trees were marked "Made in Japan."

Speaking of Carney, his cable to Sulzberger to the effect that the other correspondents would not accept him socially because he didn't wear riding boots arouses our sympathy.

When —— was fired for Guild activity his job was given to——, spy for the fourteenth floor in the advertising department.

Alexander Kerensky's tour of the United States . . . was sponsored by Simeon Strunsky. . . .

Harold Denny will soon be withdrawing from Moscow. . . .

Times reporter John Hinkle put himself on record for Franco and Fascism in a letter signed by 64 U. S. reactionaries.

Arthur Hays Sulzberger told George Seldes not long ago that he would like to fire William Carney, General Franco's press agent on the *Times* payroll, but couldn't do so now for fear of losing face.

Investigation shows the majority of these items true, but I object to the last item. Mr. Sulzberger did not tell me he would like to fire Carney and couldn't for fear of losing face. It is simply a gossip column rumor, a distortion. And it brings up the whole question of the reliability of *Better Times,* because in many respects it is an important publication, since it is the one critic of a great institution which hitherto has held itself above criticism.

The cheap and easy trick is to say, as Romans did, *falsum in unum, falsum in omnium,* and dismiss the magazine entirely. But that, in fact, is the very method the great *Times* recently employed when it condemned the La Follette Civil Liberties reports because in the 2,500 cases of industry employing spies and thugs there were eight cases questioned and one proven an error. On this error the *Times* condemned the fourteen volumes of documentary evidence and 2492 unchallenged cases. A much better way would have been to investigate before editorializing.

I have made a fairly thorough investigation of the entire file of *Better Times* and *The New Times*. I find to its credit that it had a notable scoop on Henry Luce's offer to buy the paper and Mr. Sulzberger's rejection. As for the price, *Better Times* reported $15,000,000 and the fact is that $40,000,000 was offered. On the other hand the story that the *Times* has invited F. D. Roosevelt to its editorship after 1940 is generally denied. It is true there is such talk in the air, but no action has been taken.

To the credit of *Better Times* must go the exposure of the war correspondence from Spain, both the publication of false news from Carney and the continual badgering of Matthews. *Better Times* may hold the publisher responsible for the situation, but it so happens that the present writer, having been in Spain when the telegrams of censure were sent Matthews and having placed the evidence before Mr. Sulzberger himself, is convinced that the publisher is in no way guilty. But a serious and reprehensible act has been committed and its exposure is in my opinion the most praiseworthy thing *Better Times* has done.

The facts in the case should be of general interest. It is now well known that reactionary Catholics (as distinguished from liberal Catholics who are either for the Loyalist government or neutral) have used their tremendous pressure, plus threats of boycott, and the withdrawal of advertising money, to change the opinion of American newspapers regarding the war in Spain.

At the end of this chapter I will tell the story of the *Times* Madrid correspondent, William P. Carney, as I learned it in Spain. It is an excellent illustration of many things journalistic. But at the moment the subject is the action *Better Times* has taken in the Carney case.

At the time of the capture of Teruel by the Loyalists Carney reported a week later the recapture by Franco. It is possible that this was an error due to false information, but whereas others merely cabled the falsehood, Carney gave a description of marches within the recaptured city, rejoicings, and celebration. This story cannot be condoned; it is a falsehood. And in addition Carney, with the Fascists, continually reports events within the Loyalist lines about which he can know nothing, and almost every day injects propaganda into his dispatches. On July 11th, he put into the mouths of American prisoners a statement that the American Friends of Spanish Democracy were a propaganda outfit "connected somehow with United States Communists." Both the Rev. Dr. Reissig and Bishop Paddock protested this falsehood which has been disproven in the *Times* itself months ago, but the *Times* permitted Carney to repeat it and without investigation wrote an editorial upholding Carney. The exposure of such practices by *Better Times* and *The New Times* therefore deserves a medal for journalistic service. Not since the famous *New Republic* exposure of the falsity of the Russian news from 1917 to 1920 has there been such a valid criticism of the *Times*.

As for Matthews, he was decorated by Mussolini for his war correspondence in Ethiopia. He then said and still believes that the Italian troops were excellent there and the invasion probably for the best. He was friendly to Italy when he came to Spain. He has of course realized the rightness and nobility of the Loyalist side. But from the very beginning he has been held in check by the *Times* editors whereas Carney has had a free hand.

Better Times tells the story of how the cable and managing editors have insulted and intimidated Matthews. When I asked Mr. Sulzberger about it he told me he has never heard of such actions, and I believe him. But I know that *Better Times* is absolutely right in its charge. And I have not had the facts from Matthews. The mystery is easily explained: when the telegrams from New York saying "Stop sending propaganda" and "Why do you say there were Italians at Guadalajara when Carney denies it?" and similar cables arrived in Madrid, Ilse Kulczar, the censor, showed them around.

Better Times states (January, 1938, page 3, column 1), that "the Fascist phalanx in the bull pen" is pro-Franco, anti-Matthews, pro-Carney. One of this group is responsible for the change between the first and city editions of the headline on Father Duffee's address, PRIEST DEFENDS FASCIST NATIONS to PRIEST SEES SOVIET REAL FOE OF U. S. This is a typical case of slanting *Times* headlines until they become Hearstian in their Red-baiting. Night Managing Editor Raymond McCaw is accused by *Better Times* of being responsible for the order to substitute "insurgent troops" wherever Matthews wrote "Italian troops." This also parallels Hearst's order to change the Associated Press and United Press cables, using "Reds" for "Loyalists," proof of which I have in letters from these agencies.

"In vain," continues *Better Times,* "the copy reader protested the whole point of the story was Matthews' proofs of military intervention by Mussolini. So, he carried out his orders with malicious glee when he came to a line declaring 'these troops were Italians and nothing but Italians.' " Does the reader perhaps remember his confusion over the Matthews story which concluded, "These troops were insurgents and nothing but insurgents"?

Better Times further charges the assistant editors with sending a pro-Fascist to head the copy desk for a while, describes his discomfiture and transfer and also sees a plot in the orders which prevented Matthews' vacation coinciding with Sulzberger's trip to Europe. But its full bitterness was apparent in its February issue when *Better Times,* reporting the publisher's speech at Chapel Hill, added:

"Mr. Sulzberger is quoted as saying of the Spanish War, 'I confess to a vast sense of relief that I do not have to take sides either with Loyalist or Rebel.' He is glad he is not compelled to choose between right and wrong."

Such an editorial opinion is hard to understand. If the Communist unit knows what is really happening at the *Times*, and it gives factual evidence it knows a lot, it should also understand that Arthur Hays Sulzberger is a convinced neutral-liberal, that his intentions are honest, and that he is woefully ignorant of the Carney situation and of many things that happen in his office. It is true that if the sabotage, intimidation, distortion, coloration and suppression that happens on the *Times* was directed to advance any progressive or leftist cause, instead of a reactionary, pro-Franco or generally rightist cause, the editors, sub-editors, reporters and others engaged in it would immediately find themselves out of a job. But being reactionaries they are not only in, but going up. I think this is the most important factor about the *Times* at present. Mr. Sulzberger says he is a liberal. There is no reason to doubt that he himself believes his liberalism a fact. And Mr. Sulzberger's idea of liberalism is to permit men of all opinions to occupy his editorial jobs, even when a majority of them are not only non-liberals but anti-liberals, and ultimately enemies of liberalism. He seems incapable of spotting reactionary sabotage, but smells "radical disloyalty" far away.

In the March-April issue *The New Times* (as it was now called) under the headline, "Civil Liberties Probe Sabotaged as News," said that "The *Times* sabotaged news of the La Follette Civil Liberties Committee's investigation of the National Association of Manufacturers in the first part of March so completely that it ought to get paid with more advertising for publishing only what the manufacturers think is fit to print." I was shocked by this statement because I thought it false. I took the statement to one of the chiefs of the La Follette committee, one of my best friends. His reply was general: Practically the entire American press sabotaged or suppressed the hearings of the manufacturers' association.

So long as the La Follette committee dealt with strikes, and strike breakers, its hearings were reported, but when the House of Lords of Big Business was investigated, the press, including the *Times,* purposely threw the story down. On several occasions the labor-hating *Sun* gave more N. A. M. investigation news than the supposedly impartial *Times.*

In the May-June issue the *Times* is accused of changing to an anti-New Deal policy and proofs are advanced. A large part of the issue is taken up with an editorial, "Lenin and Jefferson." There is the usual mixture of fact with bitterness and propaganda. But this issue, as all the rest, is intensely interesting.

On publication day the *Times* office loses its Olympian dignity. Laughter, shouts and a deep curse from the "Fascist phalanx" mark the appearance of *The New Times.* Everyone marvels at the disclosures. Managing editor James sends a boy into the street to get two copies. He frequently accuses a reporter of being one of the "disloyal" who produce the sheet. To one who proved his innocence he remarked "Why, those —— —— Reds are even in Sulzberger's office." (*Better Times,* January.) The secret sheet accuses the *Times* of sending detectives to its printing shop, intimidating its "newsboys," and trying to put it out of business.

So far as I can tell there is nothing illegal and nothing libelous in *The New Times.* There are propaganda editorials which do not interest me. There are a few mistakes. There is also evidence of intense enmity against Sulzberger and the *Times* itself, and while this is interesting as a social phenomenon in a world where employers still wave the old falsehood about the interests of capital and labor being identical, it is not the one significant fact.

The significant fact, which is implicit, although *The New Times* might give monthly emphasis to it, is that the newspaper, admittedly the most important in America and popularly believed the best among metropolitan publications, is far from being a free newspaper. Its claims to liberalism cannot be mentioned in real liberal circles. Its motto "All the News That's Fit to Print" has been challenged too often. The evidence is provided in every issue of *The New Times* that the great Canons of Journalism—Independence, Truthfulness, Impartiality, Fair Play—do not always thunder on the American Thunderer; in fact some of them barely whisper and at times all are silent.

The little *Times* tries to make a personal devil out of the publisher. I do not think this is quite fair. But I do think that Mr. Sulzberger must realize that no matter how much he prefers to remain in the neutral background, his paper continues to push into the front line of active social-political forces. The *Times* itself is news. It might therefore be better policy for Mr. Sulzberger to make a living force out of his announced liberalism than to let that credo become a football for some elevated police reporters who have become editorial powers and who speak of Sulzberger liberalism as "the bunk."

Mr. Sulzberger should not forget that his paper is so powerful that hundreds of others take their tips from it. The *Times* not only influences its million readers but many more millions through newspapers which follow its policies. The *New York Times* today is approaching the *London Times* as a national institution.

The truer this statement becomes the more pessimistic must be our judgment of American journalism, because *The New Times* proves every month that in the greatest of our papers there is also a slanting of news, an exaggeration of headlines, bias in politics, worse than bias in labor reporting, burial alive of "bad news," subservience to big business if not to individual advertisers, and the usual bowing down in the House of Rimmon where the ancient golden calf has become the sacred cow of American journalism.

What this little Communist gadfly of a paper has proven is that even our most important and best respected newspaper is far from being free. How deplorable then must be that journalism of the majority of the press which has not a fraction of the integrity and freedom from venality which the *Times* rightly claims. Journalistically the voice of *The New Times* is but a whisper, but figuratively it is a national hook-up roaring out an indictment of the whole press of America. And the unanswerable point of the indictment is that our whole press, the greatest power in shaping public opinion, is not playing a fair game with the American people.

The Case of "General" Carney

The case of William P. Carney, of the *New York Times,* deserves special attention because it illustrates the power a reporter can have if his views are backed by a pressure group such as the Legion, any church, the N. A. M., or other seekers of special privilege.

When General Franco marched on Madrid in November, 1936, his associate, the drunken buffoon, General Queipo de Llano, speaking over the Seville radio, betrayed one of the many Fascist conspiracies. He announced that Franco was marching with four columns and was relying on "the Fifth Column," the secret Fascist conspirators living in Madrid and pretending to be loyal, to stab the Republic in the back.

This announcement resulted in the government taking appropriate action. The prisons of Madrid and Valencia are full of traitors—at least all the known ones except the thousands who were able to buy their way into South American pro-Fascist embassies and the headquarters of European ministers favorable to the reactionaries and the mines and money they controlled.

But no announcement has been made from General Franco in Burgos on the support his treasonable cause has had from his sixth column: the column commanded by "General" Carney in the *New York Times.*

This support of Fascism did not begin in July, 1936, when Franco, after conspiring with Italian Fascist and German Nazi authorities and arranging for the guns and airplanes now in use, openly began the land owners' and mine owners' rebellion. This support from William P. Carney, the *New York Times* correspondent in Madrid, began in the early days of the Spanish Republic. It was intensified in 1936. It became fanatical when the Fascist columns were stopped.

Carney was the friend of Robles and Lerroux who formed the Clerico-Fascist government of 1933 and which in 1934 imported Moors and the *Tercio* to massacre the Asturian miners. Carney throughout this period wrote in support of this pre-Fascist movement. The *Times* refused to listen to protests from all liberals, including a lengthy one from Madariaga.

When Franco rebelled and the government put on a censorship, Carney, according to government officials, attempted on all occasions to write into his cables to America items to aid and comfort Fascism and to betray government positions and army plans to Franco. The censors in Madrid make the statement that from almost every cable which Carney sent to the *Times* they had to delete military information which he injected despite daily warnings.

In public cafés and in gatherings of journalists and others, Carney throughout the months of July to December, 1936, continued to express his allegiance to the Fascist cause; he openly supported Franco; he cursed the liberal-republican government and he called them "Reds."

On leaving Spain in December, 1936, Carney wrote a very long cable in which he pretended to tell the uncensored truth. The Paris office of the *Times* informs me that the entire staff would have nothing to do with this cable, because although it did not know what was the truth, it realized that Carney's was not, because his lies and prejudices were too apparent. Also, and this is most important, one American of the *Times* Paris staff did realize that Carney's cable contained a list of the artillery batteries of Madrid and their disposition. However, the *Times* bureau informs me, it was not able to cancel the cablegram of another *Times* man; it merely washed its hands of the matter, and Carney therefore filed the ten thousand words himself.

In the government press bureaus in Madrid and Valencia the truth of a large part of the Carney cable is denied. From my own experience in Spain I can say that parts of it are evidently ridiculous and all of it prejudiced.

One of the most vicious of all of "General" Carney's statements is also contained in this dispatch. "Madrid cannot be considered an open city," says "General" Carney. "Madrid is an open city," states General Franco. When, where and how did Franco come to make this statement? You will find it in the *New York Times* of March 16, 1937. In a dispatch signed by Carney. In other words Franco is more honest than Carney. Carney, apologizing for Fascism, attempted to defend the murder of innocent people in Madrid by telling the *Times* readers that *he* did not consider Madrid an open city, whereas the man who ordered the murdering calmly admits that Madrid is an open city.

Carney, professional Red-baiter, then repeats the biggest myth of the Spanish war. He cabled: "There were foreign volunteers—the International Column as they were termed—comprising the tenth, eleventh and twelfth battalions. They were mostly Russians. . . ."

This statement is a lie. (Why call it a misstatement, or a falsehood, when the word lie is the right one?)

All the correspondents in Spain then and now know that there never were and are not now any Russians in the International Brigade. They know there are no Russian troops in Spain. They know that there are or were once some Russians in the Spanish aviation and tanks corps, Russian engineers and experts. Some estimate the number at five hundred, others at seven hundred. But no Russian troops have ever been sent to Spain and to call the tenth, eleventh and twelfth battalions of the International Brigade "mostly Russians" is to utter a lie.

But the most vicious part of the cable is the description of the defenses of Madrid. Carney tells of machine guns and anti-aircraft guns "mounted on the tops of all the ministries and tall buildings in the center of the city such as the Fine Arts structure, Calle Alcala, Madrid's main street, and the Palace of the Press in the Gran Via or Broadway. Batteries of six-inch guns have been placed in the Callao Square, directly in front of the park; near the Prado museum, the observatory and the Ministry of Public Works. The Atocha or Andalusian railway station where more batteries were placed. . . . Observation posts for the government's artillery are stationed in the towers of the taller buildings in the center of the city. . . ."

As a war correspondent I know that if I had sent such a dispatch from the American Expeditionary Force, I would have been taken out and shot.

Moreover, there was in Spain at the time a United States government officer—I cannot identify him further because pressure might be brought against him by the pro-Fascists in America—who said to me: "The man who sent that list of gun emplacements should be shot. If he were on Franco's side and sent such a cable, he should be shot. I make this statement without any emotion and without any prejudices. In any war, and no matter what side you are on, a war correspondent sending out a list of gun emplacements is committing an act of espionage, and shooting is too good for him. Professional spies do such things and take the risk of being shot. But the correspondent of a big and powerful newspaper is not only committing an act of espionage, he is hiding behind the power of his newspaper."

Carney also defended the slaughter of the women and children of Madrid. "It cannot be helped that women and

children and aged persons have taken refuge in the base-
ments of these structures, say the insurgents," he cabled, not
only trying to excuse the murders but actually reporting
from Madrid what the Fascists on the other side were saying,
an unheard-of feat in journalism but an old trick of propaganda.

"Despatches submitted for censorship had to be accompanied by Spanish translations," continues Mr. Carney.

"This is an absolute lie," says Ilse Kulczar, the censor to
whom Mr. Carney submitted his dispatches.

After Carney's vacation in Paris in December, 1936, he
was sent to the Fascist side, and this seems to me one of the
most reprehensible actions in modern journalism.

To the dismay of the entire Anglo-American press corps
in Valencia and Madrid, including the numerous *New York
Times* representatives, a new series of Carney dispatches,
dated Gibraltar, began appearing in the *Times*. Carney had
joined Franco's side. On February 25th he began quoting the
exaggerations and murderous boasts of Queipo de Llano.
From Franco's side he was also able to tell what the government side was doing. He reported from Motril that "retreating government troops are reported to have burned the few
remaining churches and to have executed 200 persons, including four priests who were burned alive after a gasoline
bath. . . ." The authenticated reports from this front, confirmed by other reporters with Franco, is that the government did not even harm the Fascists in the prisons. The
Carney report is another of the thousands of hearsay atrocities.

I can state on the authority of six *New York Times* correspondents in Europe that each one is disgusted with the sort
of journalism which Carney has produced. Without exception these reputable journalists declare Carney should have
remained with Hearst.

CHAPTER 8

Freedom for Newspapermen

THE elite in newspaperdom is made up of publishers, editors, foreign correspondents, Washington correspondents, columnists, etc., but the rank and file consists of reporters. Quite recently the term "working" newspapermen was invented to distinguish them from all sorts of near and pseudo-newspapermen, "trained seals," certain columnists, and others who compose the fringes of journalism.

The reporter throughout our history has been the lowliest of animals. Believing himself too good to join in any organization or movement, he has found himself exploited by everyone, and he has been so blinded by his egotism that he has refused to look out for his own material interests.

Being a rugged individualist he was usually also the hired stooge of the owners. Lacking any sort of security, he was always in fear of being fired, and this fear quickly drained all the high ideals and great courage with which he usually came into journalism as a cub reporter.

The old phrase "journalistic prostitute" was popular for generations. It had its justification. But it ceased being appropriate the day Garland Ashcraft, of the *Cleveland Press*, began the formation of a union of editorial workers. Today there is one big union, one small one, several company unions, some independent unions, but generally speaking it must be admitted that the American Newspaper Guild, of which Heywood Broun is president, has led the American newspaper workers out of the red-light district of journalism and into the green pastures of human dignity.

The Guild, and the other unimportant organizations which have arisen as a result of Guild activity, have again made journalism a profession, and one no longer akin to the oldest—and worst paid. Unfortunately there is still a percentage of newspaper workers about as dumb as a corresponding percentage in other businesses, which does not realize there is a world war going on at present between progress and reaction; unfortunately there are still journalistic street walkers, some in the higher brackets, some in little bordellos known as company unions, and some individuals who parade their subserviency, if not prostitution, in lonely grandeur. There are still some who think the brass check a medal of honor. But it may be said that the Guild under the leadership of Broun, Jonathan Eddy, Carl Randau, Morris Watson, Victor Pasche, Milton Kaufman and Clyde Beals, who edits its weekly journal, means to eliminate all suspicion of harlotry from the profession, and give America the example of a union which is allied with all the powerful, enlightened and progressive forces.

In the Autumn of 1938 the Guild listed 15,000 members of whom 12,000 were working newspapermen. The total journalistic population of the nation is less that 40,000, of whom 10,000 or more are one-or-two-man shows which do not enter the Guild field. There are no more than 20,000 urban editorial workers and more than fifty percent have joined the Guild in less than four years.

In some cities the Guild operates in every newspaper office, in others it has no foothold whatever, but whether it is in control or merely attempting to enter, it furnishes the absolute proof that the majority of publishers and the most important percentage of their employees are enemies. This enmity was created by the publishers. After generations of merely frowning upon the idea of organization—during which time they paid organized typographical employees higher wages than writers—many publishers began threatening them after laws made unionization possible, and many violated the laws by firing men for joining the Guild. Espionage, intimidation, coercion, and other methods usually associated with big business of the steel corporation and auto industry type have been found by the La Follette Civil Liberties investigators existing in newspaper offices. And as a result hatred of writers for the big lords of the press has spread throughout America. It is a new phenomenon.

Falsehood and trickery have also been used by many publishers in attacking the Guild. The Guild has been called a closed shop, which is untrue; it has been accused of attempting to dictate the coloration of the news—a right heretofore exercised only by the owners—and it has frequently been reported schismatic and decadent. And of course that old lie about Communism was also dragged out despite the fact that *Editor & Publisher,* mouthpiece of the A. N. P. A., declared unqualifiedly that "charges that the American Newspaper Guild is unduly friendly with the Communist Party have come to us recently, part, no doubt, of the current anti-Red hysteria. Brief investigation discloses no basis for them. . . ." There is of course a unit on the Communist *Daily Worker*— just as there is on the Fascist *Il Progresso.*

In the famous June, 1937, special convention of the publishers the notable attendants were Arthur Hays Sulzberger, of the *New York Times;* Norman Chandler, of the *Los Angeles Times;* Harry Bitner, of the Hearst press; John Cowles, of the *Des Moines Register & Tribune;* Frank Gannett, chain lord, and Colonel McCormick, of the *Chicago Tribune.* A. N. P. A. president Stahlman said: "A closed editorial shop means a closed editorial mind." That was the keynote. Sulzberger was the chief backer of a resolution which after intense debate over the use of the word "determination" or "refusal," finally was passed as a "determination not to enter into any agreement" with the Guild on a "closed Guild shop or any other form of closed shop" basis. *Editor & Publisher* headlines are typical:

FIRM STAND AGAINST GUILD CLOSED SHOP
VOTED BY ELEVEN NEWSPAPER GROUPS

Editorial Union Demand Viewed as Menace to Press Freedom

The facts of course are these: The Guild contract, which most publishers reject, permits the publisher to hire anyone in the world he likes; it provides, however, for recognition of the Guild and the adhesion to this organization of the new employee within thirty days.

Therefore the use of the words "closed shop" is a case of smearing, just as the *Herald Tribune* invention of "youth control" for freedom from child labor was, and when Hearst changed "tax the rich" to "soak the rich."

President Broun of the Guild replied that the A. N. P. A. was "holding to the philosophy of Tom Girdler" in union matters.

The publishers then and now insist that the unionization of press employees will mean a labor bias in the news. Thus Wilbur Forrest, assistant executive editor of the *New York Herald Tribune*, told the Williamstown Institute of Public Relations that "for the Guild to inject the closed shop means that perhaps unknowingly you will inject into newspaper writing unconsciously and between the lines, a pro-labor view."

(This would result in the most heinous crime against freedom of the press, of course, because it would replace the present anti-labor slant of some ninety percent of the newspapers.)

Walter Lippmann, America's best known ex-liberal, refused to continue to pay his dues "as long as the American Newspaper Guild stands committed to the political opinion adopted at the St. Louis convention or any other political opinions." New York executive secretary Milton Kaufman replied that "individual members of the Guild are no more

committed to resolutions . . . than are editorial employees of
the *Herald Tribune* committed to the editorial policy of the
Herald Tribune," a thrust which probably hurt the conservative catechumen.

All anti-labor forces have attacked the Guild on the same
basis. Thus Merwin K. Hart, of the New York State Economic Council, an organization which would go Hitler one
better by disfranchising men out of jobs, accused the Guild
of attempting to gain control of the nation's press by strikes
and intimidation.

To all these attacks the Guild has replied that there is not
a single instance of proof. It is not the Guild intention to
seize the newspapers or change their editorial policy or in
any way to interfere with the editors and publishers.

An investigation by the *New Republic* led to the conclusion that "there is not the slightest evidence that the
Newspaper Guild has tried or ever will try to dictate the
editorial policies of the newspapers where its members are
employed."

Another investigation by the *American Press,* a publisher's
organ, which asked every paper which had a Guild contract
to report on it, led to the conclusion that "all editors who
responded agree that so far there has been no attempt to
color stories or dictate news treatment and without exception
the men were willing to work as long as necessity demanded.
. . . All admitted there had been slight payroll increases."
Lewis B. Seltzer, editor of the *Cleveland Press,* replied: "By
and large our morale, the general attitude of everyone on the
paper, the enthusiasm and happiness—individually and as a
group—is higher than in fifteen years."

What really happens when a newspaper office is made into
a Guild preferential shop is that the reporters, assured for the
first time in their lives of economic security so long as they
are efficient, begin telling the real facts, the truth behind the
news, and stop slanting the news—consciously or unconsciously—to please the First National or the Peoples Light, or

the other pecuniary forces with which the owner is allied in some way.

Of course the publishers, who openly admit their enmity for the Guild, have replied by charging it with being dictatorial, and with being pro-labor and altogether too liberal.

The Guild claims there is not a case on record where Guild reporters failed to cover a labor dispute honestly or where Guildsmen influenced either the handling of the news or the editorials on any labor dispute. Says the *Guild Reporter:* "The hypocrisy of all the pious bleating about 'the danger of pro-labor bias' becomes apparent in a moment's reflection on the present handling of labor news. Editorially and in their news columns most publishers conduct a ceaseless campaign against labor unions. The *New York Times,* like most of the others, plays up such organizations as the Flint Alliance (strike breakers) and 'back to work movements' (later found to be paid for), trumped up for strike-breaking purposes; it plays up statements laying responsibility on unions, plays up anything suggesting the defeat of a strike, and buries in stories any details showing the gains won in the innumerable victorious strikes. . . ."

Of course everyone in the profession (outside the usual number of knownothingists) understands what is really going on behind the parade of words. Everyone knows that the Guild is not a union in the old A. F. of L. sense, and is even miles ahead of the C. I. O. The Guild has realized that labor unions whose whole objective is better working conditions and better money for its membership, are only a small step forward in American progress. Its own members are aware of the social issues.

And it is just because the newspaper publishers of America are either unaware of the social issues, or, worse yet, insistent that the public be kept in ignorance of the social issues, that they have united all their forces and venom to fight the intelligent leadership of the socially conscious Newspaper Guild.

From the very beginning all the smug and the wealthy and the supercilious critics have had their fun about the Guild "going out of its way" to endorse a pardon for Tom Mooney for example, or to uphold the civil liberties of a man or a movement where some atrocious denial of justice has taken place. The Guild has been told to stick to its trade and concentrate on better wages and hours. But it has consistently branched out into all social and economic problems which affect its membership and the whole people, and when the test came of this policy it was upheld by its membership.

It is most interesting to note that whereas some ninety percent of the publishers have gone on record for or against certain public measures, the employees of these publishers have usually gone on record by the same percentage, but on the opposite side. The Guild has supported the C. I. O., it has denounced the Chicago policemen for the murders of Memorial Day, it has supported the Roosevelt Supreme Court Plan, it has approved WPA appropriations, and generally denounced the American brand of Fascism which masquerades as patriotism. It has always passed resolutions in the belief they were for the general welfare of the American people, not the special welfare of a small group. Its most important action has been its declaration in favor of a press free for the reader instead of freedom of the press for the publisher at the expense of all the rest of the world. Being therefore always on the side of the general welfare as against the special interests it has naturally been opposed to the publishers' program in almost all cases.

At various times during strikes and other conflicts with the publishers the Guild has obtained proof that the employers are no better or worse than members of the National Association of Manufacturers or the U. S. Chamber of Commerce. In other words, it has been an open fight between capital and labor, with the publishers using the police, the injunction, and many other weapons—except bullets and infrequently tear gas—to defeat the newspapermen. Moreover, having almost complete control of the channels of communications, the publishers have distorted the facts and in some instances lied about the issues. Guildsmen at various times have published little sheets giving their side of the case and making the foregoing charges against the newspaper owners. The publishers, reported the president of the Guild at the Atlantic City meeting in 1937, "used their own news columns without restraint for a campaign of distortion and misrepresentation of the Guild and its acts, seeking to injure its position with the public."

The Guild has found out that there is no free press. The Guild knows that the press is not fair to labor. The Guild knows that the publishers are anti-labor; in fact, that they are anti-social. I cannot for the life of me see how Arthur Robb,* editor of *Editor & Publisher*, can write editorially that ninety-five percent of the press is honest, fair and accurate and only five percent guilty of sins of omission and commission, when there are more than ten thousand organized and enlightened writers for this press who testify that the figures are just about the other way around. The Guild has the complete proof that about five percent of the press is honest, accurate and fair, and that ninety-five percent is not honest, accurate or fair. In other words we have no free press in America. We have a few free newspapers. Too darn few.

The Guild today represents American journalism. There is also the American Press Society, of which George E. Sokolsky is the chairman of the entertainment committee.

There is an independent organization on the *New York Sun*. A large number of its members are for Franco.

In several towns, notably in Nashville, the employers have

---

* To whom I owe many thanks for assistance in obtaining documentation.

obtained oaths of fealty from their workers. These gentlemen have refused to join either the Guild or other unions. None of these organizations is important.

The important thing is the organization of working newspapermen into a socially conscious, intelligent and progressive movement. The newspapermen unfortunately have no say in the making of newspapers, but the fact they have come alive is the best single event in modern journalism.

PART III
BATTLES OF THE LORDS

CHAPTER 1

Let Newspapermen Run the Newspapers

IT IS the custom, in this day and age, to ask of any critic that he make constructive suggestions. Practical suggestions, if possible. It is of course quite easy to make idealistic suggestions, such as "change the world" or "introduce a new system," but even the smallest tinge of idealism is looked upon with suspicion, and a strong attempt at reform arouses almost violent opposition, as any public official can easily find out for himself.

In this section of five small chapters I would like to make five practical—or near-practical—suggestions for producing a better press than the press lords have given us.

First of all I think the time has come to recognize the fact that the newspaper business is a business, a big investment, "no longer a mere million-dollar affair; it calls for tens of millions," as Lewis Gannett has said. Well, big business has generally recognized the unionization of its employees. The publishers and the Typographical Union have gotten along splendidly. They should recognize the Guild or any other newspaper union as a union.

Once this were done, I suggest that the next step should be to invite the newspapermen to run the newspapers. After all, doctors run hospitals and lawyers run the courts, and it would not be strange if newspapermen, who know all there is to know, were actually in complete charge of their business. There is no other in the world where the employees can take over so easily without the help of bosses and owners.

Several years ago I wrote that "what the Guild really wants

is a say in newspaper making in America. It is entitled to that. The day of the irresponsible employers is over . . ." but apparently I made a terrible blunder there. The Guild attacked me angrily. Its executive secretary, Jonathan Eddy, wrote: "I hope Mr. Seldes is right when he pictures the Guild as the cleanest and most progressive force in American journalism today, yet he is very wrong (perhaps out of a personal 'wish-fulfillment') when he seems to imply that the Guild aims to exert editorial control over newspapers. But since he does believe that our organization is a great and healthy force in American life, it is difficult to understand how he can take seriously the pretensions of bitter and unscrupulous enemies of the Guild."

It was not unscrupulous enemies of the Guild that gave me the idea, nor was it wish-fulfillment. It was pure logic. And I am sorry to know that the Guild is not interested in editorial control of newspapers, or in editing and publishing them. So long as the papers remain private property there is of course no chance for workingmen to make such demands from the owners, but it seems to me obvious that the Guild, which includes all the men capable of running the industry, and which has proven that it means freedom of the press and not freedom of the lords, and which has a program which puts it in the forefront of liberal and progressive organizations in America, should at least have a say in the business. They ought to ask for it. It ought to be given them without asking.

Newspapermen can challenge the publishers. They can say: Prove you mean freedom of the press by letting the editorial staff run the newspaper. Here we have men of many different political, economic and perhaps religious viewpoints, but all of them know just what a free newspaper should be. If you put them on the editorial board—as some great newspapers have done in the past—you will produce a free newspaper against which no honest man can raise a word of protest.

At present most newspapers run under a sort of dictatorship. Not Fascist, but still dictatorial. When Hearst sends an order to run Marion Davies' picture every day for a month, it hurts no one, but when he sends an order to smear a certain liberal Congressman, that is journalistic dictatorship. Nor is Hearst unique.

I regret that I have to retract my statement that the Guild wants a say in newspaper making. I know that the Guild has never tried to run the press, and says it will never try to dictate editorial policies on any paper. And I repeat: newspapermen should demand a voice in newspaper making. It would be one of the few real practical ways of establishing a free press.

CHAPTER 2

Subsidy: Weapon for a Free Press

IN THE days of the frontier, when Utah had a population of 11,000 and Minnesota 6,000, and all of the State of New York half what the city now boasts, the wise fathers in Washington thought up a law for the purpose of spreading education, enlightenment and eventually culture throughout the land, giving the wild and partly unexplored West the same privilege as the East, bringing the means of culture up to the very doorstep of every inhabitant.

In 1887 the original law of 1851 which permitted newspaper and periodical publishers to send their products everywhere at a fraction of cost, was amended, and since then the second-class mail matter clauses have undergone minor changes, but they still provide a subsidy to publishers. The American government is willing to take an enormous loss provided education, enlightenment and culture flourish. It is supposed that printed matter provides all of them.

Westbrook Pegler is the only journalist who has ever questioned the size of the subsidy, but he has not forgotten that it exists. He claims that the loss through free newspapers carried in the county of publication is only $8,000,000 a year, and that the postmaster general should not compute first-class rates on it, since newspapers do not get first-class treatment.

The *New York Daily News* is the only paper in America which, although its beneficiary, has consistently criticized the subsidy. Its editorial writer, Reuben Maury, commented (on January 6, 1938) that the "benefits are admittedly substantial, for all the papers. As just revealed by Postmaster

General Farley, it cost the post office $38,000,000 to deliver daily newspapers last year, but the newspapers paid only $9,000,000 to be delivered.* To the extent that *The News* mails papers, it participates in this subsidy—a subsidy which smells louder as time goes on."

The outstanding fact about the whole matter is that in the past ten years the government has presented publishers with $1,000,000,000, as Mr. Farley claims, and that the chief beneficiaries, the newspapers, have kept the fact hidden in their closets. Certainly every time they attack some other subsidy and keep their own silent they are giving that old skeleton another push into the darkness.

Now, no one in America, not even Colonel McCormick of the free press committee of the publishers' association, is a greater advocate of a free press than the present writer, and I would not for a moment suggest any check or barrier, blinder or halter, shackle or manacle on our free press. All I would suggest is going back to fundamentals. The press should recognize the subsidy.

Real recognition would mean including education and enlightenment in its columns—and banishing their opposites: prejudice, bias, and distortion.

---

* Fiscal year ending June 30, 1937.

	Post Office handling cost	Payments by publications	Loss to Post Office
Daily Newspapers	$38,001,739	$8,999,158	$29,002,581
All other Newspapers	14,293,411	2,999,241	11,294,170
Magazines	33,583,007	9,246,108	24,336,899
Philanthropic, Fraternal papers, etc.	18,512,038	1,903,590	16,608,448
Papers free in county	7,906,711	none	7,906,711
Total Government Loss			$89,148,809

CHAPTER 3

Ten Tests for a Free Press

"WE MUST never tire of protesting," wrote Romain Rolland recently in his protest against one of the many myths which circulate throughout the world and work against its welfare.

The newspaper is a very sensitive organ. Its success or failure depends on the public; only rarely is there such a situation as in Chicago where many persons who have to buy either the *Tribune* or the *Herald-Examiner* have been heard to express their lack of confidence in both. In most cities people believe in the printed word, even when the type is the largest and the word far removed from the truth.

The failure of a free press in most countries is usually blamed on the readers. Every nation gets the government— and the press—it deserves. This is too facile a remark. The people deserve better in most governments and press.

Readers, in millions of cases, have no way of finding out whether their newspapers are fair or not, honest or distorted, truthful or colored. Intelligent readers frequently ask for means of testing the press.

The easiest way is to buy copies of newspapers for a week or so, study them carefully, and compare news and headlines. If the reader does this with a news item about a strike in which he is a participant, or a mass meeting where he was a speaker or listener, or some event where bias and perversion for special motives may enter, he will be able within one hour to find out which is the honest, which the dishonest newspaper. (Let him not be guided by his own bias—if possible.)

Beware of the newspaper which calls itself independent. Of the (say) ninety percent of the press which howled down the President in 1937 and 1938 a goodly portion called itself independent, or that hypocritical paradox, "independent Republican" and "independent Democratic." There are less than a dozen independent newspapers in the whole country, and even that small number is dependent on advertisers and other things, and all these other things which revolve around money and profit make real independence impossible. No newspaper which is supporting one class of society is independent. And while William Allen White, who heads our editors, insists that our publishers are unconsciously class-conscious, he admits they are class-conscious. Class-conscious newspapers cannot be free newspapers.

If we accept the statement that this feeling is still "unconscious," then we can proceed with tests of the freedom of these papers. Here are a few simple tests for the publishers which every reader can insist on:

1. Give equal space to the political parties.
2. Give some space to minority parties, at least space relative to their strength. (These two tests will put the majority of our press, which styles itself independent, on the spot.)
3. Publish the Federal Trade Commission reports. (These reports are not enough, but they do expose many of our greatest manufacturers of food, drink, clothing, tobacco, milk, etc., as fraudulent.)
4. Tell the truth about cigarettes and automobiles, the two largest advertisers.
5. Give the consumer a square deal. (Publish the same reports on consumers' goods which only the liberal and left weeklies publish nowadays.
6. Reject organized pressure. (Inform the American Legion, the Catholic Church organizations, the business and advertising organizations, and all the other sacred cows, bulls and elephants of journalism, they will no longer influence the news. If all publishers in any one town agree on this, no losses can follow.)

7. Publish the labor news. Give labor a square deal. (Everyone admits that the press has fallen down worse in the labor field than elsewhere.)

8. Throw Mr. Hearst out. (The Associated Press accused Hearst of theft of the news. It won its case. But it did not throw him out. Neither did the A. N. P. A. No press organization can make any ethical claims so long as it has a Hearst around.)

9. Stop defending child labor because of the few dollars you save on newsboys.

10. Print both sides of a controversy. (The *New York Daily News* published both a "Presidential battle page" in the Roosevelt-Landon campaign and an "economic battle page" on labor. It offered them free, but only a few papers took them. No paper can claim to be free if it refuses to publish both sides.)

These are ten simple tests which come to me on the spur of the moment. Other newspapermen will think of better ones, no doubt.* But all of them look fair to me. If a paper announces itself as a Republican sheet and wants to publish nothing but Republican party news, that is fair and honest, but few newspapers so announce themselves. Not only the self-styled independent paper but any paper which claims it is a newspaper, must publish the news, and that is all that one can ask.

But if it claims it is a free paper it must give equal space to both sides.

I know that no newspaper in America will publish anything like Consumers Union's *Reports* on foods, automobiles, cigarettes, but it is reprehensible of them to refuse the

---

* The following tests for a free press have been suggested by newspapermen, editors, and school of journalism professors who have read this manuscript:

1. Defend public welfare instead of public utilities.
2. Publish the facts about radicals, "Reds," etc., without Red-baiting.
3. Discover the co-operative movement in America.
4. Run the advertisements of Consumers Union.
5. Stop publishing letters which agree with editorial policy only.

advertisements of the Union itself. This co-operative, non-profit-seeking organization tests all consumers' goods; its scientific reports are frequently at variance with the advertisements, and no one can challenge their truthfulness. The newspapers show their prostitution to advertisers every time they refuse a Consumers Union advertisement. The advertisements merely solicit membership in the organization. They do not distinguish between good and bad products. But the monthly report of the Union does list good and bad products thereby serving its members well, but offending the manufacturers of bad products who are also large advertisers.

If I were to be asked for one specific proof that the old-fashioned venality still persists in the press, and that the advertiser still dominates the newspaper business, I would offer the experiences of the foregoing organization in dealing with the business managers of newspapers and magazines.

The element of hypocrisy also enters the situation: in numerous cases the Union has requested the publications to place their refusal to carry its advertisements in writing. But the publications have refused to give the organization documentary proof of their dirty work.

The excuses given by some of the great newspapers are strange and varied. One says it does not accept the "type" of advertisement, and another declares the ad is "controversial." The Union advertisement is not an advertisement offering anything for sale: it is simply a notice that a non-profit making public service society seeks members, and these members are promised a scientifically truthful service about consumers' goods.

Among the advertising managers who said by telephone they would not take the Union's announcements and who refused to send written confirmation, the Union informs me, are the *New York News* and the *Philadelphia Record*. On the other hand the Union has a frank (although oral) admission from a salesman from the magazine *Esquire* that

that magazine "had received complaints from some of the big liquor firms because *Esquire* had run a C. U. ad describing our liquor report. They threatened to withdraw their advertising if *Esquire* ran any more C. U. ads." I recall that at the time I was associate editor of *Ken,* published by the *Esquire* company, I proposed to the advertising department that it solicit C. U. for a page advertisement, which it did. The Union offered to pay the usual price of $900 for a page. But the ad did not appear because the salesman who rejoiced one day that he had landed the order, found out the next day that it would offend all the other advertisers.

The Union ran full page advertisements in the *New York Times* in 1936 and the result was a tremendous growth in membership. But in February, 1937, the *Times* management held up an advertisement and questioned the competency of the Union's laboratories. At a conference the non-profit making organization submitted its evidence, whereupon the *Times* representatives, although seemingly satisfied, suggested that an investigation be made by the Better Business Bureau. This bureau is an organization which is run by big business and advertisers and some of its officials make drugs, foods and commodities which have been criticized by Consumers Union. The proposition was ridiculous. It would be equivalent to have the ethical doctors of America investigated by the patent medicine makers. Finally the *Times* suggested it might run the advertising if prominent men would endorse the work. Senators, Representatives, college professors, writers, and others did so. But the *Times* still continues to play the game of straddling and evading.

Among the sixty publications which through sheer fear of losing money from other advertisers have refused the Union advertising (in addition to those mentioned) are the *New York Herald Tribune,* the *New York Post,* the *Christian Science Monitor,* and dozens of magazines.

The *Post* has been "considering" an ad for two years; on

May 3, 1937, it wrote it was "not in a position to determine the accuracy of the Consumers' Union reports" and would communicate when it had done so, and there the matter rests.

The *Christian Science Monitor,* which has a great record for throwing fake advertising for the very drugs, foods and commodities, which the Union also exposes, out of its columns, could not, however, bring its integrity to the point of accepting the advertising for an organization which has a social and progressive policy and a social conscience. "It is not possible for us to give the reason for this decision," it wrote.

A letter mailed in a Scripps-Howard envelope informed the Union that John Sorrells, executive editor, had sent instructions to all Scripps-Howard editors to kill C. U. press material. The Union complained to Roy Howard. It received a reply from Mr. Sorrells saying: "We have not instructed Scripps-Howard editors 'not to use C. U. press material' . . . but we have from time to time cautioned our editors with regards to the use of handouts material from *any* of the various consumer bureaus. . . ." In other words the Scripps-Howard press uses thousands of columns of handouts from the automobile and other industries which advertise, but cautions its editors not to use press material which would benefit the consumers—perhaps at the expense of the advertisers.

Time after time Consumers Union has protested this boycott by the press in its own monthly reports. Frequently many among its 65,000 members have written to publishers and received no satisfaction. The *New York Times,* however, has adopted a form letter to deal with such protests. It reads:

The *New York Times* accepted the advertising of the firm you mention for many months. We suspended it when some of our executives raised the point that an important part of this company's service comprised attacks on the products or services of other companies or industries. This the *Times* does not permit. So far no satisfactory basis has been found for renewing the advertising.

C. McD. Puckette.

This is the nearest to a confession that it is advertising agency pressure which is directing the policy of the newspapers. A better confession of this sinister business can be found in *Editor & Publisher* (August 6, 1938) where Edward Davenport, a merchandising expert, writes a tremendous attack on all consumers' organizations. Since he cannot possibly say anything just or rational against them, he calls them names and "enemies of the American industrial system and social order."

In a way this is true. Consumers' organizations favor their members, the public, and expose such things as excessive utility rates, fake advertising, shoddy goods, false bargains, poisonous patent medicines, and many useless and fraudulent companies and products which help put big publishers in the upper income tax brackets, and therefore maintain their social order.

I challenge any newspaper in America to publish the findings of Johns Hopkins University on the effect of cigarette smoking in shortening life and generally weakening the system.

I challenge all publishers to run a department on consumers' goods written from the viewpoint of benefit for the readers instead of the advertiser.

I challenge any newspaper to omit all advertisements for drugs which the medical profession believes harmful.

As one way toward a better, if not a free press, I suggest that every newspaper reader demand that his publisher make the ten tests listed above.

The greatest cause for optimism in America is the result of the boycott of the Hearst press, from New York to California. Stop buying Red-baiting papers. Stop patronizing colored, biased, perverted papers. And write to the editors. Never grow weary of protesting. In this sensitive business of dealing with the public which depends on faith and good will, protest is a most effective weapon. Therefore protest. And if that fails, boycott the corrupt newspaper. Support the honest newspaper just as strongly.

CHAPTER 4

Investigate the Press Lords

THE radio has proven its worth as a means of communication with the public when the press unites against a leader or a policy.

"You must realize," said Senator Sherman Minton, in a radio address in March, 1938, "that it is chiefly by means of the radio that the point of view of the administration in Washington on anything it is doing or proposes to do, is brought to you, since ninety-eight percent of the metropolitan newspapers are opposed to the administration and do not hesitate to misrepresent it. You found that out in the last election. If you want to know the truth about things going on in Washington you won't find it in the metropolitan newspapers. . . ."

Senator Minton proposed an investigation of the press.

Before I report on the fantastic national editorial jitters that followed I would like to quote from a letter from Senator Minton. He writes me as follows: "When you have had time to read my speech criticizing the press, copy of which I am enclosing, you will find I was not attacking the free press. I was defending free speech that was being attacked by the so-called free press. You will also discover that this speech was misrepresented in the press, as everything else is that they don't like.

"The bill I introduced has at least been successful in exposing the hypocrisy and impudence of the so-called free press in their efforts to curb free speech."

The Senator had named names, he had spoken of "the unspeakable *Chicago Tribune*," and the *Philadelphia Inquirer*, the *Washington Post* and *New York Herald Tribune* among the ninety percent of the press which deliberately distorted the news in trying to destroy the New Deal. He read the misleading headlines and falsifications of many newspapers into the *Congressional Record*.

The aggrieved parties went hysterical. The *Herald Tribune* published a piece under the quotation "What is Truth? said jesting Pilate"; the *Times* came out for a free press; Landon said the Minton bill would end liberty; Boake Carter wrote three of his most smeary columns against Minton and Colonel Frank Knox himself wrote an editorial advising editors to "tell Minton to go to hell."

But the President of the United States said at a press conference that if a law were passed jailing editors who deliberately published falsehoods the Federal government could not handle all the prisoners such a statute would land in jail.

The prison bill, as Senator Minton writes, had its effect: it exposed a lot of hypocrisy. But months passed and there was no answer to Senator Minton's proposal that the press of the country be investigated.

Quite naturally the publishers met the proposal with silence or ridicule. But this united front was rudely broken by Patterson's *Daily News* which on the occasion of a terrific attack on James Roosevelt by Alva Johnston in the *Saturday Evening Post*, suddenly leaped forward with a big editorial demand that the Minton "press probe" should be made. "We think the time for such an investigation has now arrived," said the *News*. "It should be conducted by an impartial commission, composed of equal numbers of pro-New Dealers and anti-New Dealers to avoid whitewashing or mud-plastering.

"This newspaper, much as it dislikes the idea of having its private life investigated, offers itself as the first specimen to be probed. There are several things about this newspaper

which a lot of people would like to have investigated. O. K.
. . .

"Let's have the facts. There is the charge that advertisers influence the policies of *The News,* as of other newspapers and magazines. Let that be probed.

"There is the talk about the relationship between the New Deal *News* and the old deal *Chicago Tribune.* Cynics snicker that this organization's plan is to work both sides of the street, so that in any event it will have a friend in the White House. Let's have that gone into.

"The *News* having been thus investigated by a commission of, say three anti-New Dealers and three pro-New Dealers, we think the *Saturday Evening Post* might be investigated next.

"Does it, directly or indirectly, employ child labor; and if so, how much? Does it benefit by the fact, stated often in these columns on information and belief, that the post office department carries newspapers and magazines at about $100,000,000 a year below cost; and if so, how much? What is its financial setup and dividend policy? And so on.

"We think the investigation should also include Mr. J. David Stern, pro-New Deal publisher of *The New York Post;* Mr. S. E. Thomason, pro-New Deal publisher of *The Chicago Times,* and other pro-New Deal publishers.

"Then the anti-New Deal Scripps-Howard chain might have its turn in the wringer, its feature writer, Westbrook Pegler, being an enthusiastic attacker of the President's family.

"After that, the Hearst chain's financial setup, and backing should be looked into, and the findings published. Likewise, *The New York Times* and *The New York Herald Tribune.* And so on down the line.

"We don't say all this out of anger. We say it for this reason:

"We believe the great majority of anti-New Deal newspapers and magazines are trying to build up a fanatical hatred of President Roosevelt.

"We do not believe they can succeed in entirety, judging from the election returns to date.

"We believe that if they do succeed even partially, they will stir up class divisions and class hatred which will have consequences the most disastrous, not only for the newspapers but for the entire country."

Senator Minton took his fight to the metropolis when (on August 13, 1938, before the American Press Society) he charged a section of the American press with being in control of wealthy men who "in my opinion would not scruple to throw this country into Fascism rather than surrender their privileges." This is of course the ultimate in indictments and the Senator who proposed an investigation must be prepared to produce proof of this charge. Mr. Minton accused the news services of "monopolistic practices": "Often we find their stories are edited in the making or made in the editing to conform to the policy of the moment." As for freedom of the press, he declared that the Bill of Rights did not preserve it "for corporation publishers to make six percent on their investment" but "that all men might know the truth." The warning issued by the American Newspaper Publishers Association that the Federal government might encroach upon American democracy through the use of the radio Senator Minton termed "an impudent, hypocritical proposal."

If the investigation of the press is made, Senator Minton continues, "I believe it will disclose that there is no longer a free press . . . that facts no longer are given to the people in full and cannot be, under the monster we have created and permitted to control the press."

Subsidized sources are responsible for much that appear in the press. "Behind all of this we find control by great banks and financial institutions. The power of the advertiser representing big business . . . control of thought in this country by . . . command of money."

It is interesting to note that the *New York Times* published only about a fourth of what the *Sunday Worker* published of this speech.

By all means, let's investigate.

Let's put all the cards on the table. Let's find out if there is a joker in the journalistic deck. Let's call all bluffs. Let's find out all about the money in the pot—whose it is, who plays with it, who wins, who pays.

If the press is the greatest force for democracy in America and if that force can be used for other purposes, for purposes all the way from falsifying the social issues to "throwing the country into Fascism," we can best know how to continue the fight for democracy by discovering the armed strength and the armed finances of this power. Let's investigate.

CHAPTER 5

Labor Must Fight the Press Lords

OLYMPIAN critics have always defended the big press by alleging that there are also prejudice, bias, distortion, favoritism, coloration, and all the usual evils present in the antipodal press, the left or liberal press, the non-commercial press backed by labor, progressive or Socialist and Communist parties, or certain trades, or even a church. For example, there is more bias, coloration, distortion in the *Brooklyn Tablet,* the diocesan organ of the Catholic Church, than in any other publication in New York State outside the Nazi German sheets.

I do not believe that the charge made against the non-commercial press will hold. I will admit that usually the news coverage in this press is inadequate—but this is due to lack of funds—and that as a rule there is more mingling of editorial and news in the news columns, but I insist that it is the liberal left which realizes the fact that truth itself is the greatest weapon in the world. By that truth I do not mean necessarily that two and two make four—although that truth is denied almost every day in the great press and notably by the reactionary columnists—but the facts and the causes of the facts as Bovard published them when he ran the *Post-Dispatch* without interference from the Pulitzers.

My ideal newspaper would publish nothing but the facts as far as it is humanly possible to get them. But it would have a staff of men who would be out every day looking for the facts and who would never be content with the surface news. With such a newspaper it would not be necessary to have an editorial page, because the facts would write their own editorial.

But until such time as such an ideal newspaper is founded, it is necessary that we have a press which will publish the considerable body of news which the commercial press suppresses or buries, or distorts; and a press which will have an editorial policy counteracting the poisons which flow from the editorial pages of the great majority of party and corporation newspapers.

Outside of the commercial press I have mentioned the *Christian Science Monitor* and the *Jewish Forward,* two powerful daily newspapers, which are not motivated by profits and which have a great influence. But, as I have also pointed out, they are parochial in their views.

The Communist Party supports the New York *Daily Worker* and its Chicago and San Francisco colleagues. These newspapers are marked Communist. There is no pretense about them, no dishonesty about ownerships as with the dailies which proclaim themselves the public defender but really represent the utilities, banks and other interests.

The La Follette movement has a few liberal supporters which state their ownership and interests honestly.

But the great mass-majority of the American people, organized and unorganized labor, has no daily press of its own, and has not yet awakened to the fact—as French and British and other workingmen have done—that the commercial press only pretends that the interests of labor are its first interest also.

There is not one labor newspaper in America to equal the London *Herald.* (That paper, alas, has been turned over to a commercial printer by the British Labor Party and has lost a great deal of its power.) There are 570 labor publications in the United States, with 8,778,000 circulation, and there are several independent weeklies which are decidedly friendly to labor.

The *Peoples Press,* founded a few years ago, has attained

a circulation of a quarter million copies. It is a weekly. It is supported by unions and devoted to their cause, but it is actually a general newspaper. It publishes special editions for various sections of the country and for special events, such as big strikes. One of its greatest achievements was the scoop on the death of 476 workers in a West Virginia tunnel enterprise: the cause of death was silicosis. At that time the *New York Times* wrote an editorial exonerating the corporation and joking at the whole idea of silicosis, but a Congressional investigation substantiated the *Peoples Press*. This weekly also does its readers many services, one of which is a consumers' department exposing fraudulent food and drugs. A few hundred thousand dollars subscribed for this weekly would make it an important force in the country.

Another weekly, *Labor,* founded two decades ago, now has a circulation of 500,000. Its editor, Edward Keating, tried to induce Samuel Gompers, late president of the American Federation of Labor, to back a chain of labor newspapers throughout the country, but Gompers, although impressed, found he had no time for the idea.

Recently there were rumors that John L. Lewis would found at least one, and possibly three big newspapers which would help the C. I. O. movement, but nothing has come of them.

For its own interests, if not for the interests of a better press, labor should have its own newspapers. It can publish either a string of journals devoted to general information, or it can publish purely journals which editorially would counteract the news propaganda of its enemies. To get millions of readers the labor press will have to supply the comic strips, the stories dealing with sex, money and crime, which have made many tabloids successful, the baseball scores, all the stuff the general public wants and now gets in the non-labor or anti-labor press.

If the labor newspaper existed it would act as a purge for the general press. No editor and publisher would continue to distort and discolor the news if he was certain that his rival, a labor newspaper, would detect him in this work and expose him every day. The existence of labor newspapers would raise the standards of all newspapers. A labor newspaper would be for journalism what the TVA yardstick is for electricity.

⚡

Labor must challenge the press lords. It takes a million to start a newspaper nowadays, and organized labor can raise that million.

Newspapermen should ask for a share in newspaper making.

The reader should challenge the bona fides of his home town newspapers under the code of ethics and the canons of journalism which the editors and publishers proclaim.

Congress should go ahead with the proposed investigation of our lords of the press.

More so today than in the time of the World War and in generations and centuries ago, the press of the world has become the most important weapon of dictators and commercial powers. In no dictator country do the people have anything to say to their rulers, political or journalistic. Only in democratic countries is there the beginning of a suspicion that the old axioms about the press being the bulwark of liberty is something that affects the daily life of the people—that it is a living warning rather than an ancient wisecrack. A people that wants to be free must arm itself with a free press.

Index